PEPPER

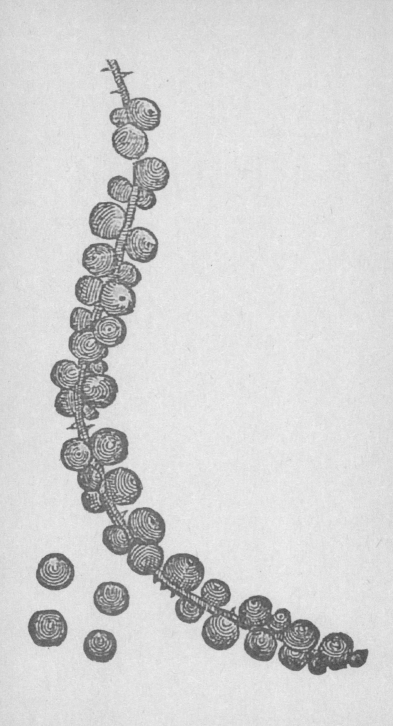

PEPPER

A History of the
World's Most Influential Spice

Marjorie Shaffer

THOMAS DUNNE BOOKS
St. Martin's Press New York

THOMAS DUNNE BOOKS.

An imprint of St. Martin's Press.

PEPPER. Copyright © 2013 by Marjorie Shaffer. All rights reserved.
Printed in the United States of America. For information, address St. Martin's Press,
175 Fifth Avenue, New York, N.Y. 10010.

www.thomasdunnebooks.com

www.stmartins.com

Maps by Alison Muñzoz

ISBN 978-0-312-56989-1 (hardcover)

ISBN 978-1-250-02100-7 (e-book)

Thomas Dunne books may be purchased for educational, business, or promotional use. For
information on bulk purchases, please contact Macmillan Corporate and Premium Sales
Department at 1-800-221-7945 extension 5442 or write specialmarkets@macmillan.com.

First Edition: April 2013

10 9 8 7 6 5 4 3 2 1

*To my mother
and the memory of
my father*

CONTENTS

PREFACE

A seasoning used in countless meals for thousands of years, pepper reaches our consciousness with a sharp zing, like a good kick to our taste buds. The spice bursts in the mouth and tickles the back of the throat, announcing itself with a triumphant, unmistakable sharpness. Inhaling the rich aroma of newly ground black pepper can be as intoxicating as sniffing a glass of robust red wine, and today we can savor black pepper from various regions of the world, each carrying its own distinctive flavor.

It is hard to imagine a spice rack without black pepper. The *Zelig* of the culinary world, the spice insinuates itself into an endless medley of food, creating hot or earthy sensations, depending on where the pepper is grown. Few recipes can resist the spice. Today, you can walk into any food store and usually find an assortment of tins containing ground pepper or jars of brightly multicolored peppercorns to grind at home. Pepper shakers grace the tables of restaurants all over the world.

Although it is a nearly universal spice, many people in the West don't know where pepper comes from and mistakenly believe that it grows on trees. However, if you were raised in Kerala, on the southwest coast of India, you would have no problem identifying a pepper plant. It would be as familiar as dandelions crowding a suburban lawn on a summer day in the eastern United States. Black pepper, a vine, thrives naturally only in tropical soils, and its stubborn inability to grow elsewhere is one of the reasons it has had such an impact on world history.

I first saw a pepper plant in the greenhouses of the University of Connecticut in Storrs, where I wandered around admiring a rich array of strangely ornamental tropical plants. A week earlier, a corpse plant, a giant that grows in Indonesia and shoots up like a spaceship (and in Latin is aptly named *Amorphophallus titanum)*, had blossomed in one of the greenhouses. Luckily, I wasn't there for the actual flowering, which sends out a horrible stench, hence the name "corpse" plant. By comparison, the pepper plant was diminutive and rather drab. But when I considered how the modern age of trade and trade's pernicious twined branches, colonialism and imperialism, evolved from this rather prosaic organic substance, a simple condiment, a seasoning that everybody uses, I thought its modest appearance was deceiving.

I originally had wanted to write about the Jesuits who served in the court of Chinese emperors as repairers of elaborate mechanical clocks in the seventeenth and eighteenth centuries, and I spent several years combing through scholarly articles and books about these fascinating men. As I slowly got my bearings, I became intrigued by the movement of Europeans into Asia, the means by which they got there, and the primary reasons they went. These questions led to black pepper. If you follow the early tracks of Europeans to the East, you inevitably run into the spice.

Eventually I put aside the Jesuits and focused on the spice, which opened entirely new worlds. My invaluable guides were the extraordinary historians who have written about pepper. They led me to the journals of the European traders who had traveled to Asia during the seventeenth and eighteenth centuries, which became important sources for telling the story of pepper. As much as possible, eyewitness accounts provided the historical setting and conveyed whenever possible what it was like for these Europeans to meet people from other cultures. These accounts are culled from the journals of merchants and sailors who were employed by the Dutch and English East India Companies, and from the logbooks of sailors aboard American ships that sailed to Indonesia in the nineteenth century to buy pepper.

Some of these journals have now been digitized, so it is no longer necessary to read the material in its original form. It is still thrilling, though, to hold in one's hands a journal or ship's log written hundreds of years ago. Perusing these journals is one of the pleasures of historical research: You never know what you will find. There was a perennial preoccupation with food, for instance, as revealed in European sailors' numerous, colorful descriptions of fish, birds, and other animals encountered in Asia. Like other meetings between the West and Asia, this one ended in destruction. The extinction of the dodo is related to the pepper trade, and a chapter in the book is devoted to the frenzied killing of animals in Asia by European traders.

The book follows the Portuguese, who first sailed to India around the Cape of Good Hope, and then tracks the English, Dutch, and Americans to Asia. The Indonesian islands of Sumatra and Java were essential destinations for procuring pepper, and on these islands a substantial portion of the story of pepper unfolds. The longest chapters are devoted to the English and Dutch, whose loathing for one another drove so much of the history of pepper and of empire in Asia. The two-hundred-year-long rivalry between the English and Dutch East India Companies also shaped the momentum of modern global trade with its never-ending need to exploit foreign resources to satisfy local markets. The Indiamen, as the sailing ships of the northern European companies were called, were the early forerunners of the giant container ships that today ply the world's oceans. The Strait of Malacca, a crucial waterway in the pepper trade, is still the shortest route between India and China and is still a dangerous place to move cargo. There are many other ways in which the story of pepper resonates in the modern world.

The last chapter brings the story full circle with a survey of modern-day scientific investigations of pepper's medicinal properties. Thousands of years ago, pepper was renowned as a cure-all for disease, and only later did it become a condiment. Scientists today are discovering that the spice affects human health in manifold ways, a validation of pepper's role in the apothecaries of the ancient Greeks and Romans, as well as in the medicinal systems of China and India.

Geography plays such a crucial role in the story of pepper that it would be remiss not to include maps of the Indian Ocean, India, Malaysia, and Indonesia. Many of the ports where the pepper trade was conducted are unfamiliar to Western readers. I constantly had to refer to maps in order to figure out where the story of pepper had taken me, and I hope that the maps in the book help orient readers. Nowadays, Google can find the location of nearly any place on earth, but you still have to have a reason to look. How many people in the West know where South Sulawesi and Malaysia are, or have heard of Malacca?

This book isn't a comprehensive history of European pepper trading in Asia. For those who wish to pursue certain topics in more depth, there is a rich literature. Instead, this book attempts to illuminate history through the desire for a single substance. Why pepper? Why does this common commodity, the ever-present companion of salt, merit attention? How could history be explained through pepper? I hope that this book answers these questions.

Pepper's story has not been told outside the confines of academe. It is my fondest hope that I may bring some of this story to a broader audience.

Snow is white and lieth in the dike,
And every man lets it lie;
Pepper is black and hath a good smack,
And every man doth it buy.
—A "COMMONPLACE BOOK" OF THE FIFTEENTH
CENTURY

. . . we were "not so much sub-continent as sub-condiment," as
my distinguished mother had it. "From the beginning, what the
world wanted from bloody mother India was daylight-clear,"
she'd say. "They came for the hot stuff, just like any man calling
on a tart."
—SALMAN RUSHDIE, *THE MOOR'S LAST SIGH*

PEPPER

One

Meet the Pipers

BLACK PEPPER AND ITS SIBLINGS BELONG
TO A FAMILY OF PLANTS WITH THE
MUSICAL-SOUNDING NAME *PIPER*.

•

"Pepper is the bride around which everyone dances."
—JACOB HUSTAERT, 1664, A DUTCH EAST INDIA COMPANY
GOVERNOR OF SRI LANKA.

For most of human history, pepper wasn't easy to obtain, an essential fact that led this spice to become a major force in world history. Black pepper is indigenous to India, thousands of miles from the ports of Europe. Traders had to get to the source of pepper, and that obsession led to the dawn of global trade.

Like a botanic Helen of Troy, pepper launched a thousand ships. This fiery berry from a tropical vine, a mere wrinkled ball of flavor, dragged Europe out of its medieval torpor into the cosmopolitan trading network of the Indian Ocean. Although there were other exotic spices that captivated the Western world, none was as widely used as pepper, and none can claim a wider impact on world history.

Over the centuries, pepper has become a culinary ingredient in almost every culture. Think Indian pepper chicken and shrimp, French steak au poivre, Italian pecorino pepato cheese, German pfeffernüsse cookies, and the dozens of spice blends that incorporate pepper, including most famously quatre épices from France and garam masala from India. Nearly every kind of meat and many cheeses are enlivened by pepper, and it can add a delicious sparkle to desserts and fruit. A commando spice, pepper is a take-charge kind of condiment that refuses to be subtle or delicate.

No one knows when the first human being bit into a peppercorn and decided it would taste good on a piece of meat or in a vegetable stew, but in the West it was the ancient Romans who apparently first made pepper an integral part of their meals. Food was only part of the reason for pepper's esteem; health played an equally important role. In the Roman Empire, pepper was the equivalent of aspirin, seen as the cure-all for aches and pains and many other conditions. If you had a cough or a fever, or were bitten by a poisonous snake, it was common practice to be given a drink or a salve laced with pepper. Dioscorides, a famous first-century Greek physician who lived during the time of Nero, wrote an herbal guide that was still being consulted in the sixteenth century. He praised the spice's wonderful properties: "The virtue of all peppers . . . is to heat, to move a man to make water, to digest, to draw to, to drive away by resolution, and to scour away those things that darken the eyesight."

Dioscorides influenced generations of physicians. It was he who recommended putting pepper in a drink or a salve to help calm the shakes accompanying fevers; to cure the bites of venomous animals; and to fight coughs and "all diseases about the breast, whether it be licked in or be received in drink." The spice, he noted, could be chewed with raisins to "draw down thin phlegm out of the head," drunk with leaves of the "bay tree" to "driveth away gnawing and quite dissolveth it; and mixed with sauces to help digestion." Pepper could even help remove "morphews" and other foulness in the skin by mixing it with saltpeter.

The Romans were hardly the first to embrace pepper as an elixir. Long before Roman galleys crossed the Indian Ocean, the Greeks, Chinese, and south Asians had been incorporating pepper into tonics to fight numerous conditions. Belief in the spice's considerable utility is reflected in India's ancient Ayurvedic system of medicine, which is more than three thousand years old. In Sanskrit, black pepper is known as *maricha* or *marica*, meaning an ability to dispel poison, and it is taken to aid digestion, improve appetite, ease pain, and to cure colds, coughs, and intermittent fevers, among other ailments.

During medieval times in Europe, pepper was firmly established as a culinary ingredient, and it was also a vital part of the apothecary trade, as the frequent references to the spice as a "drug" attest. An essay published in England in 1588 noted that the mixture of three peppers known as *Diatrion piperon* was famous for its ability to help "conconction, to discuss wind, to do good against the cold affects of the stomack, and yet not to heat the liver or the blood, wherein consisteth as singular propertie of this medicine." A book published in England in 1596 advised that pepper was "wholesome for the brain," and another published a year later recommended the spice alone or combined with other substances for conditions ranging from headaches and gas to leprous facial sores and tumors. Even at the turn of the seventeenth century, the naturalists who wrote these guides still relied heavily on Greek and Roman sources for their information about Asian plants.

Many of the properties attributed to pepper some four hundred years ago sound strange today, but modern scientists who are studying the spice are finding that it does improve human health. The spice is still used for a variety of medicinal purposes in Asia, especially in India, and if scientific investigations continue to be successful, pepper may eventually play a role in Western medicine as well, especially in the treatment of cancer and other life-threatening illnesses, a topic discussed in the last chapter of this book.

Black pepper's renown made it a must-have item for the wealthy, who had a mania for the spice in the Middle Ages. In those days, pepper was guarded by servants in royal households and kept in the private wardrobes of the rich. It was considered a privilege to cook with pepper. Few dishes did not benefit from large quantities, which might be considered stomach-churning today. But for most people, pepper was too expensive—in the year 1439, a pound of pepper was roughly equal to more than two days' wages in England. Meanwhile, pepper could be traded for gold and silver, and was actually used to pay for labor and goods. Pfeffersack (pepper sack) was a common expression that referred to a merchant who made handsome profits from the pepper trade. Europe itself offered relatively few indigenous spices, mainly saffron (also very expensive) and cumin.

An incredible hunger for pepper and the money it could bring spurred residents of an entire continent to risk adventure on foreign oceans and in foreign lands, and it is within this context that the story of pepper really begins. In the fifteenth century, pepper was the reason why Europeans searched obsessively for an all-ocean route to India. Although they also craved other spices, it was pepper that unleashed the age of discovery, when Europeans hoped to find a way to Asia aboard their own ships, cutting out the Arab middlemen in the pepper trade to earn all of its enormous profits for themselves. Columbus carried peppercorns with him on his 1492 voyage. He wanted to make sure that wherever he made landfall, the natives could tell him where to find pepper.

Like a giant magnet, pepper pulled the world to India, the land of black pepper. Although the Europeans loved pepper, they were the last to join the pepper trade in the Indian Ocean—Gujaratis from the northwest coast of India, Bengalis, Tamils, Arabs, Southeast Asians, and Chinese had been trading the spice for hundreds of years. The great Treasure Fleet of the Ming Dynasty, which sailed as far as the east coast of Africa in the early part of the fifteenth century, made a beeline for the southwestern coast of India to purchase pepper. Great port cities in Malaysia and Indonesia were built on the pepper trade, and thrived long before the Europeans entered the Indian Ocean. These Islamic cities were cosmopolitan places where Southeast Asians, Bengalis, Persians, Arabs, and Chinese lived. But the Europeans were a different sort of customer. They wanted to control the pepper trade, and that meant conquering the port city suppliers, setting in motion a new chapter in the history of pepper and empire.

At the end of the fifteenth century, the Portuguese became the first Europeans to sail to India when Vasco da Gama rounded the Cape of Good Hope and crossed the Indian Ocean, an incredible feat. The Portuguese then spent the next one hundred years trying to gain control of the pepper trade in India and Asia. When they failed, the Dutch and the English attempted to take it over in the seventeenth and eighteenth centuries. The history of black pepper is bound to the two companies that are synonymous with the evils of colonialism, the English East India Company and the Dutch East India Company or VOC (*Vereenigde Oostindische Compagnie*), and the spice gave birth to the insidious opium trade when the Dutch first offered the narcotic as payment for pepper grown along the Malabar Coast of India. There was a reason why Voltaire wrote that after the year 1500 there was no pepper obtained in India that was "not dyed red with blood." The rivalry between the northern European mercantile companies penetrated almost all of the pepper ports in Asia, but most notably those in Java and Sumatra in Indonesia, and deepened the trading links that had already existed in Asia. The so-called "country trade," or intra-Asia trade, was especially important to the VOC.

By the time the Americans entered the scene in the nineteenth century, they realized that the pepper trade couldn't be conquered. These sensible businessmen went about making their own fortunes from pepper, and the import duties on the spice helped shore up the economy of a young nation. When piracy imperiled the pepper trade, President Andrew Jackson sent a U.S. warship to Sumatra, resulting in the first official armed U.S. intervention in Southeast Asia.

Many people in the West today associate Sumatra with coffee, but long before coffee there was pepper. This large island that straddles the equator and nearly touches mainland Asia was the world's largest producer of pepper for more than two hundred years; hundreds of millions of pounds of pepper poured out of the numerous ports that lined Sumatra's shores. This island played the lead role in the pepper trade, and its fate influenced the history of India and Southeast Asia.

Medieval Europeans who had never seen pepper growing in the wild entertained some fanciful notions of its origins. According to Bartholomew the Englishman, who lived in the thirteenth century and wrote encyclopedias, the spice grew on trees in forests guarded by serpents. Its black color was the byproduct of fire. "Pepper is the seed of the fruit of a tree that groweth in the south side of the hill

Caucasus in the strong heat of the sun," he wrote. "And serpents keep the woods that pepper groweth in. And when the woods of pepper are ripe, men of that country set them on fire, and chase away the serpents by violence of fire. And by such burning the grain of pepper that was white by nature is made black."

This persistent myth wasn't dispelled until more Europeans began traveling to India during the sixteenth and seventeenth centuries and could see for themselves how pepper grew. An early account was given by the brilliant Portuguese physician and naturalist Garcia da Orta, who lived in Goa and published a profoundly influential treatise on the medicinal plants of India in 1563. But even da Orta believed that black and white pepper came from different climbing plants. Many scholars have published Orta's drawing of a pepper plant, which has a strangely modern sensibility, resembling the paintings of early twentieth-century cubists. Some fifty years before Orta's treatise was published, an Italian named Ludovico di Varthema is said to have vividly portrayed the pepper plantations in Calicut, a port city on the southwest coast of India, in his own account about his travels in Asia, published in 1510 to much acclaim.

One of the European travelers to the East who was delighted to see a pepper garden, and who accurately described pepper, was Peter Mundy. An astute Englishman from Cornwall, Mundy was a factor, or merchant, for the East India Company during the early seventeenth century. He spoke Italian, French, and Spanish, in addition to English, and traveled widely in Europe, India, and China, filling his journals with charming drawings. Everything interested him: pepper gardens; the clothing of Chinese and Japanese women; fishes in the Indian Ocean; houses, boats, and royal processions in Sumatra; hairstyles in Madagascar. He was a curious and keen observer who drew what was novel to him at a time when relatively few European traders went to the East.

In 1637 Mundy found a pepper garden in Surat, a city in north-western India; most likely he had never seen a pepper plant before. The long vines planted at the foot of what he called small betel nut trees immediately caught his eye, perhaps because they reminded him of England. The vines, he wrote in his journal, resembled ivy. "Att the Foote of these trees they sett the pepper plant, which groweth uppe about the said tree to the height of 10 or 12 Foote, Clasping, twyning and fastning it selff theron round about as the Ivy Doth the oake or other trees with us," he wrote. "They continue 10 to 12 yeare yielding good pepper; then they sett new plants, soe I was told. This yeares Croppe was newly gathered, some of it then lying a Drying in the sunne; yet were there a few clusters, both greene and ripe, left among the leaves on the plant. The berry when it is Ripe beecommeth ruby red and transparent cleare (I mean the substance about the kernel, otherwise greene), as bigge as small pease, sweet and hott in tast. The kernel of the said berry is the pepper indeed. The berry they putt to dry in the sunne and then that outward reddish substance drieth, rivelleth [shrivels] and becommeth black, in few daies, as wee now see it."

Mundy spent most of his life traveling, and was for a while a merchant for the English East India Company before he switched sides and worked for William Courteen, a rich merchant who established an association that for several decades challenged the monopoly of the Company. Before sailing to India in 1635 for Courteen, Mundy related with a certain wistfulness that he needed to find a ship in order to earn some money: "I had not bin longe att home, but through want of my accustomed Imployment, waistinge of meanes and some other occasions, I resolved once againe for London, to seeke some Voyage or Course to passe away tyme and provide somewhat for the future, which accordingly I performed . . ."

Aside from his extensive travels, there isn't that much that is known about Mundy. He was born around 1596 into a merchant family that sold pilchards, or sardines, and he may have married. He probably died in the late 1670s in England. Mundy's remarkable diaries were never published in his lifetime; they appeared in print for the first time in 1914.

Wild pepper can be easily overlooked amid the unruly posturing of other tropical plants. The spice doesn't advertise itself with large, vividly colored flowers, or tease the nose with delicate scents. It doesn't generate an addictive or hallucinogenic substance, a distinctive aroma, or dazzling color. Its leaves are a modest dark green, shiny on the outside and paler below. Its only small extravagance is the berries it produces. They dangle in clusters from its vines like long pendulous earrings. After drying, the green berries become black, wrinkly little balls, each harboring a single seed—the peppercorn—the jewel delivering the mouthwatering kick that is its sine qua non.

Pepper is a woody climbing vine, and it still grows wild in its original home in the monsoon forests of the Western Ghats, the mountains lying along India's southwest coast, in what is now the state of Kerala. On this coast, the pepper ports of Calicut and Cochin served traders from many faraway empires. At one time, pepper vines were planted by the people here at the onset of the monsoon in June, and nearly every household had pepper plants that trailed on jack, mango, or on any other available tree.

In the botanical world, pepper belongs to a genus of plants with the musical-sounding name *Piper*. This fifelike genus was created in 1753 by Carl Linnaeus, the Swedish botanist whose system for classifying plants is still in use today. He placed seventeen species in the *Piper* genus, and probably appropriated the ancient Greek name for black pepper, *Peperi*, as the basis for the group. The official botanical name for black pepper is the Latin *Piper nigrum* (*nigrum* is the species name). Although *nigrum* means black, white pepper comes from the same plant, a fact that confounded even the most learned observers. The difference depends on when the berries are picked and dried. Black pepper is picked when the berries are still green, while white pepper is picked later, when the berries have turned from green to red. The berries are placed in water to remove their tough outer covering, and are then dried, as Peter Mundy observed.

Pepper isn't a fast-maturing plant. It takes several years for the branching woody vines to mature, and during their growth the vines can reach up to thirty feet. Trees, wooden poles, reinforced concrete poles, and other material are used as supports. The pepper berries are handpicked when they are ready for harvesting, which usually begins some two to three years after planting. Preparing the berries for market involves a lengthy process of drying, cleaning, and sorting. The plant loves the warm, humid, rainy tropics, in a narrow band around the equator. Pepper also requires well-drained soils, and its preferred habitat is forests. Unshaded plants exposed too long to the scorching sun will not yield many berries. The colorful mixes of whole peppercorns seen in many markets today contain green and black peppercorns. Although there are pink peppercorns, the ripest berries, the sweet pink little balls in some peppercorn mixes aren't true peppers but hail from the cashew family of Brazil.

Black pepper has gotten plenty of competition from its siblings during the course of human history. In ancient Rome, Indian long pepper (botanically, *Piper longum*), was preferred. Long pepper, a shrublike plant—as opposed to a vine—displays long, dull, leathery green leaves. *Piper longum*, a native of northeastern India, was nearly twice as expensive as black pepper in Rome. Today, long pepper is rarely found in the West, although it is still used in India. Cubeb pepper, another *Piper* sibling, is called Javanese pepper, and it originated in Indonesia. Cubebs look like black peppercorns, except they have a kind of tail. Some types of gin are infused with cubeb pepper.

Yet another famous member of the pepper family, *Piper betle*, is well known today in Asia, although it is not a spice. Commonly called *paan* in India, betel is chewed like a plug of tobacco or a wad of gum, and the telltale red spittle it produces is easily spotted on the street. Betel chewers prepare the plug by spreading a thin layer of lime on a fresh betel leaf and adding a sliver of areca nut and a mixture of spices. The nuts, spices, and lime are then wrapped in the leaf. The betel sandwich is reported to aid digestion, freshen the breath, and induce euphoria—the principal reason why it is so popular today among young people in Taiwan, India, and other countries. Over the past decade, unfortunately, medical researchers have linked betel chewing to a rising incidence of oral cancer in Asia. The culprit seems to be the areca nut, not the betel.

Betel chewing isn't a modern phenomenon. The Chinese used betel leaf at least as early as the Tang Dynasty, 618 to 906 A.D., and the Europeans who made their way to India four hundred years ago often remarked on the practice, which became fashionable among some Europeans living in Asia. By the sixteenth century, betel chewing was widespread in tropical Asia, and it was considered impolite not to offer a guest a chew (and still is considered so today). A book published in Britain in 1779 on the purchasing of drugs and spices in Asia and the East Indies described chewing betel as "universal in India, as well as on the coast of China: it is produced at all entertainments and visits amongst the natives, and even to Europeans, some of whom, especially the Portuguese, have adopted the habit."

One hundred years earlier, William Dampier, an intrepid English pirate who lived from 1651 to 1715 and was the first Englishman to travel to the Galapagos Islands, vividly described people chewing betel in the East Indies in his book *A New Voyage Round the World.*

Like many people, he used betel and areca interchangeably. "The betel nut is cut in four pieces and wraped up (one each in an Arek leaf), which they spread with a soft paste made of lime or Plaifter and then chew it altogether," he wrote. "Every man in these parts carries his lime box by his side, dipping his finger into it, spreads his Betel and Arek leaf with it. The Arek is a small tree or shrub of a green bark and the leaf is long and broader than a willow. . . . It is exceedingly juicy and makes much spit. . . . tastes rough in the mouth and dies the lips red, and makes the teeth black, but it preserves them and cleans the gums. . . . It is also accounted very wholesome for the stomach, but sometimes causes great giddiness in the head of those that aren't used to chewing it."

A Frenchman traveling in Java in the seventeenth century described how "everyone knows what the Betel-Leaves and Arequa Nuts are, which all the Natives of this island both Men, Women, and Children chaw incessantly to fortifie their Gums and Stomach, for sometimes they swallow the Juice. This Juice is as red as Blood . . . when you are not accustom'd to this Drug you find its Taste insupportably sharp, but otherwise it becomes like Tobacoo, and you find it difficult to leave it."

In the eighteenth century, a Dutch sea captain noted that when ladies go out in Jakarta, they are invariably attended by four or more female slaves, one of whom bears the betel-box. The chewing of betel and areca nuts, which was called *pinang*, was a common pastime, even an "infatuation," among the ladies. The pinang was often combined with Java tobacco. The chewing, noted the sea captain, "makes their spittle of a crimson colour, and when they have done it long, they get a black border along their lips, their teeth become black and their mouths are very disagreeable, though it is pretended that this use purifies the mouth, and preserves from the toothache."

And in the nineteenth century, an American seaman in Sumatra noticed that men "wagged" their jaws over betel, the pungent leaf, "longer than the most inveterate tobacco chewer over his plug."

Other plants masquerade as pepper, but do not belong to the musical *Pipers,* the only true peppers of the world. Melegueta pepper, for instance, is a pretender belonging botanically to an entirely different plant genus called *Afromomum.* Melegueta is native to West Africa, and it was an important spice in Europe during the fourteenth and fifteenth centuries, until black pepper became more widely available with the opening of the ocean route to Asia at the end of the fifteenth century. Melegueta was known by the melodic name *grains of paradise,* a reflection of the medieval preoccupation with the Garden of Eden that so heavily influenced Europeans' yearning for the East and its spices. The Portuguese considered the African pepper inferior to black pepper, one of the reasons for its decline in popularity. However, melegueta was favored as a spice by the English until the nineteenth century, and it is still used in West African cookery today. It also is a flavoring in akvavit, the liqueur popular among Scandinavians. Grains of paradise look like small black peppercorns and have a strong peppery sweetness.

The pepper genus *Piper* bears no relationship to another famously misnamed plant, chili pepper, which was originally found in the Western Hemisphere. Chilis belong to the genus *Capsicum* and are an essential ingredient in many tempting dishes all over the world. Chilis were exported from the New World to the Old World. These hot peppers, along with vanilla and allspice, are the only spices native to the tropics of the New World, a comparatively barren part of the spice landscape. Vanilla comes from the flower of a South American orchid.

Christopher Columbus was eager to find pepper in the New

World, and the natives of the Caribbean told him the berries grew wild on the islands. It turned out the island berries were allspice, not true pepper. But Columbus didn't have a naturalist with him, and he blithely accepted their word that he had found pepper. Allspice berries look like large peppercorns and are the fruit of an evergreen tree, not of a plant. Nevertheless, allspice became known as pimento, a derivation of *pimiento,* the Spanish word for pepper. Perhaps Columbus was aware of his ignorance, but he was a shrewd man. He had been sent to find spices and other treasures, and he didn't want to disappoint his patrons, the monarchs Ferdinand and Isabella. He readily acknowledged that he could not identify the astounding variety of trees and plants he encountered on the islands, which he thought were part of Asia. "I do not recognize them, for which I feel the greatest sorrow in the world," Columbus wrote in the log of his first voyage. Afterward, one of Columbus's letters was circulated widely in Europe. In it he gushed over the islands' limitless fertility and the vast amount of spice that could be obtained. He wrote to his patrons that they could acquire "as much as they order to be shipped."

Obviously, Columbus wanted to promote his discoveries to his patrons, who he hoped would finance more voyages. In reality, the West offers few appetizing spices, while the East presents a smorgasbord. The *Oxford Concise English Dictionary* defines spice as "an aromatic or pungent vegetable substance used to flavour food, e.g. pepper." The Asian tropics, where you will find pepper, also nurtures other such notable spices as cinnamon, cloves, ginger, cardamom, turmeric, and nutmeg. Cinnamon is a native of Sri Lanka (formerly Ceylon); ginger and turmeric originate in Southeast Asia; nutmeg (and mace), the two-in-one spice—mace is the bright red, lacy membrane surrounding the nutmeg seed—is from the Banda Islands; the clove is from the Moluccas (modern-day Maluku Islands); pepper and cardamom are from India. Spices are derived mainly from the bark (cinnamon), root (ginger and turmeric), fruit (nutmeg and cardamom), or berry (pepper) of trees or plants, while herbs, which are mostly found in the temperate zones of the world, tend to be from stems or leaves.

If the New World had hosted the variety of spices found in India and Southeast Asia, the history of the world might have taken a different course.

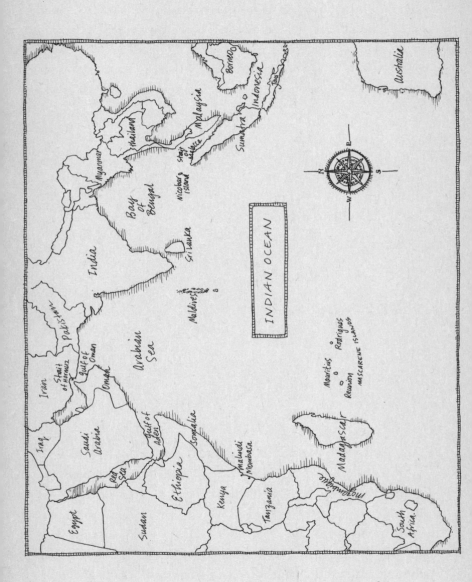

Two

The King of Spices

DURING MEDIEVAL TIMES, BLACK PEPPER WAS USED TO
PURCHASE LAND AND PAY TAXES. A MAN'S WEALTH WAS JUDGED
BY HOW MUCH PEPPER HE HAD IN HIS HOUSEHOLD.

•

"Pepper is small in quantity and great in virtue."
—PLATO

*"The King of Portugal, Lord of Spices, has set . . . prices just as he
pleases, for pepper, which, at any cost, no matter how dear, will not long go
unsold to the Germans."*
—MUNICIPAL COUNCIL OF NUREMBERG, BEGINNING OF
THE SIXTEENTH CENTURY

In 408 A.D. a barbarian army led by Alaric the Goth swept into northern Italy from the Balkans and made its way to Rome, which was ill prepared to deal with the invaders from the east. Alaric immediately laid siege, cutting off the lifelines to the city. With no assistance forthcoming from her neighbors, Rome stood alone against a formidable foe. The barbarian blockade gradually choked the city. Food became scarce and disease rampant. Starving people filled the streets, and soon corpses littered the city's elegant marble temples. Rome had become a morgue. The city was on its knees when Alaric offered the conditions under which he would withdraw his forces. Naturally, the barbarian demanded the riches of the imperial city, its gold and silver, its exquisite silk tunics, and its pepper. He knew that the Romans had great stores of pepper and other spices in special warehouses called *horrea piperataria* that stood in the city's spice quarter. The warehouses were built during the reign of Domitian, early in the first century, and held rare spices that had poured into Rome, some possibly as tribute. In the second century, during the reigns of Marcus Aurelius and his son Commodus, the famous physician Galen had his office in the spice quarter.

By the time Alaric the Goth arrived, Romans had been using pepper in their food and medicines for centuries. It enlivened a wide variety of food, and was especially prized as an antidote to poison. Pepper's worth had not escaped the Goth. His army finally left Rome, laden with thousands of pounds of gold and silver, thousands of silk tunics and scarlet-dyed skins, and three thousand pounds of pepper. The ransom mollified the Goth only briefly. Two years later, his army surrounded the city once again, and this time the city was sacked.

Although the Greeks in the fourth and fifth centuries B.C. were familiar with pepper—Hippocrates recommended mixing pepper with various herbs and other ingredients as a treatment for fever—we know that the Romans really got the pepper trade started in the West because they used the spice widely as an ingredient in food. Pepper was generously sprinkled throughout the more than 470 recipes of the famous gourmet Apicius, known for his enormous greed, elaborate banquets, and obsession with food (he was alleged to have hired a ship to look for oversize prawns off the African coast) as much as for his skill as an epicure. In his multivolume cookbook, "Apicius showed it [pepper] employed, ground or whole, black or white, in almost every recipe," writes historian J. Innes Miller. "It was used in the kitchen and also at the table," notes Miller, "where it was served in a pepper-pot, *piperatoria,* not infrequently made of silver."

As early as the first century A.D., the Romans traded at pepper ports along the west coast of India, and their ships could sail from the Red Sea across the Indian Ocean to India in as little as forty days. This busy trade was extinguished when Rome fell to the barbarians in the fifth century, but gold Roman coins, which were used to buy pepper, along with Mediterranean amphoras used to store wine and other items from that trade, are still unearthed in India today.

It was during the Crusades that medieval Europeans glimpsed the tantalizing riches of Arabia, opening their eyes to the pungency of pepper, the fine caress of silk and velvet, and the sweetness of sugar. All of these soon became luxury items in Europe, which was enthralled with the riches of Arabic civilization.

The ruling classes didn't consider a meal worth eating unless it was generously spiced with pepper, cloves, and cinnamon. Use an ounce of pepper, an ounce of cinnamon, an ounce of ginger, half a quarter of cloves, and a quarter of saffron, a medieval Italian cookbook advised. This combination, it said, will go well with "all food." The medieval palate obviously craved a peppery sweetness, and taste is heavily influenced by contemporary culture. Think of Vegemite, the jelly concoction today beloved by Australians, but reviled by almost anyone who didn't grow up on the stuff. In medieval England, it was considered a privilege to "sauce" the food of kings. For the Feast of St. Edward in 1264, Master William, a saucier, prepared a sauce that incorporated fifteen pounds of cinnamon, twelve and a half pounds of cumin, and twenty pounds (320 ounces) of pepper. Imagine dumping hundreds of modern-day pepper tins, which usually contain about 1.5 ounces of pepper, into a sauce. Two hundred years later, Duke Karl of Bourgogne, considered one of the wealthiest men in Europe, ordered *380 pounds* of pepper for his wedding dinner in 1468. Subtle flavoring wasn't fashionable in medieval times.

It is popularly believed that pepper was used in the Middle Ages to disguise the taste of rotting meat or as a preservative for meat, but that wasn't so. Wealthy families used the most spices, and they had access to an adequate supply of fresh meat all year long. They were big carnivores, and especially liked to eat birds because they believed that the animals were closer to God in heaven, while lowly vegetables in the soil were that much farther away from holiness. So they ate an incredible assortment of birds, and mammals, too—pigeons, rails, doves, peacocks, partridges, plovers, herons, cranes, swans, geese, rabbits, pigs, deer, sheep, and oxen, among others. They weren't particularly choosey. It didn't matter whether the animal flew, hopped, loped, walked, or pranced. At a feast in Canterbury during 1309 to celebrate the installation of an abbot, for example, some 1,000 geese, 24 swans, 200 suckling pigs, 200 sheep, and 30 oxen were consumed. Spices accounted for a sizeable amount, about 13 percent, of the total expense of that orgy of meat and fowl. Many meats were cooked in highly spiced sauces or ground and combined with spicy sauces, which we might find unpalatable today. In medieval times, sugar wasn't widely available in Europe. To create a fiery sweetness in their food, wealthy Europeans used a lot of pepper, cinnamon, and nutmeg. Pepper enhanced the taste of fresh meat, and it also served as a kind of after-dinner drink. Among the wealthy, it wasn't uncommon for a spice plate to be passed around for tasting after a big feast.

The less fortunate couldn't afford to buy many spices, and they did not eat much fresh meat. They bought small amounts of pepper and cumin, which came from Spain, for their meals of bread, porridge, milky cheese, and occasionally fish. Still, no matter how many times historians point out that spices didn't hide the taste of rotting meat in medieval times, this popular myth persists.

Venice, the "Queen of the Adriatic," dominated the European spice trade in the Middle Ages. As historian John Keay notes: "No less than Palmyra and Petra, the city [Venice] owed everything to its preeminence in Oriental trade—a term that was virtually synonymous with spices—and was proud to proclaim it." During Venice's glory days in the fifteenth century, pepper accounted for as much as 80 percent of the value of all spice shipments to the West. However, a complicated route combining overland and sea journeys was required. Along one such route, Arab and Indian ships crossed the Indian Ocean to the Red Sea, where pepper and other spices were offloaded at various ports and carried overland through Egypt to the Nile. There, the pepper was loaded onto boats that sailed downstream to Alexandria on the Mediterranean, the gateway to Europe, where Venetian and Genoan ships waited to carry the spice to Italy.

To break Venice's hold on the spice trade, the Portuguese had to find an all-ocean route to India. "History has shown that the hunger for spices was capable of mobilizing forces very much as the present-day need for energy sources has done," writes historian Wolfgang Schivelbusch in his enthralling book *Tastes of Paradise*. Spices, he notes with characteristic brio, "played a sort of catalytic role in the transition from the Middle Ages to modern times." After large quantities were imported into Europe in the seventeenth century by the Dutch and the English, pepper no longer played this sort of catalytic role. It became a commodity, and demand for it diminished as tastes changed and other imports from the East, most notably tea and coffee, became exceedingly popular in the eighteenth century.

Pepper's hold on the medieval imagination stemmed partly from the abject conditions of people's daily lives. Death from disease, especially plague, and from starvation brought on by horrific food shortages caused by famines were the rule of the day. Beginning in the tenth century, famines occurred regularly in Europe. Peasants in the countryside, who came to the cities to seek relief, found little respite. They begged for food and often died in public squares. Even a country as comparatively privileged as France experienced at least eighty-nine general famines from the tenth to the eighteenth centuries, an estimate that excludes the hundreds of local famines that occurred over those centuries, according to accounts cited by historian Fernand Braudel in his masterful *Capitalism and Material Life*.

Set against this grim environment, pepper offered salvation. In medieval Europe, people fixed their aspirations for a kinder life on the East, which became a sort of paradise in their minds. Europeans became infatuated with the wild notion that the alluring scented breezes of the south China Seas emanated from the Garden of Eden, which had miraculously survived the cataclysmic biblical flood that wiped out everything except Noah and his ark. "Throughout the middle ages, the Garden was believed, somehow, to have survived the flood," writes historian John Prest, "and in the great age of geographical discoveries in the fifteenth century, navigators and explorers kept hoping to find it. When they didn't, they began to think of bringing the scattered pieces of creation into a Botanic Garden or new Garden of Eden."

Since antiquity, spices had been considered part of the mythical East, a place where spices flowed like water in the surviving Garden, and wild pepper trees abounded. In the thirteenth century, cinnamon, ginger, and other spices were believed to float down the Nile from Paradise. Fishermen cast their nets into the river to gather this aromatic bounty. The desire to recreate an ideal place on earth, like the original Garden of Eden, with plants gathered from newly "discovered" lands led to the establishment of the great botanic gardens in Padua, Leyden, Oxford, and Paris during the sixteenth and seventeenth centuries.

Along with the notion of an earthly paradise, the belief that pepper and other spices existed in superabundance in the East was essential to the age of discovery. In the words of historian Paul Freedman, "fantasies of absurd plentitude" were vitally important "because it was only the expectation of magical abundance, not merely adequate supply, that drew men like da Gama and Columbus and that sufficiently excited their patrons to put up the money for these ventures."

Medieval Europeans would have been shocked by the reality of life in the land where they thought pepper trees grew. Famines wracked Asia, too, especially during the time when Europeans were first becoming acquainted with the East. The population in China, which had been growing for two hundred years, suddenly declined in the years 1620 to 1640 because of droughts and floods. India was hit by a terrible famine in 1630, and the droughts in southwest India during this period destroyed the pepper plants in what is now Kerala.

In 1631 a Dutch factor, or merchant, arrived in Surat, India, and described the devastation in a letter dated December 21, 1631. "After our departure from Batavia [modern-day Jakarta] wee arrived att Suratt the 23th October last. And going ashore to the villadg called Swalley, wee sawe there manie people that perished of hunger; and whereas heretofore where were in that towne 260 familllyes, ther was not remaininge alive above 10 or 11 famillyes. And as wee traveled from thence to the cytty of Suratt, manie dead bodyes laye upon the hyeway; and where they dyed they must consume of themselves, beinge nobody that would buirey them. And when wee came into the cytty of Suratt, wee hardly could see anie livinge persons, where heretofore was thousands; and ther is so great a stanch of dead persons that the sound people that came into the towne were with the smell infected, and att the corners of the streets the dead laye 20 togeather . . ."

People in Europe knew little about life in India and Asia. Some of their impressions were based on Richard Hakluyt's monumental book *The Principal Voyages, Traffiques and Discoveries of the English Nation*. The first edition appeared in 1589, and it was revised and greatly expanded in 1598. The book included the exploits of Sir Francis Drake, who circumnavigated the world in 1580 and was one of the greatest seamen of the Elizabethan era. Although Hakluyt never traveled to the East, his knowledge was considerable, to judge by the journals, logbooks, and other reports of voyages that he gathered and published, and he provided essential advice to convince Queen Elizabeth to allow the establishment of the English East India Company. He knew where the Portuguese traded pepper in India and where they and the Spanish did not have any exclusive claims to pepper, such as Sumatra, a piece of information that helped allay the Queen's fears that an English trading company would anger the Spanish. Hakluyt wanted to drum up interest in the East—he was one of the founders of the English East India Company—and his *Voyages* described grand seafaring epics. He was enthusiastic about expanding England's domain, but the English wouldn't be ready for empire for another one hundred and fifty years. He once wrote that it was a blessing to live in England "in an age wherein God hath raised so general a desire in the youth of this realm to discover all parts of the face of the earth." It took propagandizing to persuade men to give at least eighteen months of their lives to the round-trip journey to the East. The fantasy of the Garden of Eden and Hakluyt's adventure-filled stories helped to recruit crews for the English ships, or Indiamen, which bore names such as *Hope* and *Peppercorn*.

Pepper's link to the beginning of modern global trade is reflected in the organization required for setting the price of pepper and for tabulating its profits, which contributed to the rise of capitalism in northern Europe. Historians trace the origins of the English East India Company, the first company in the world based on stock ownership, to medieval spicers, or pepperers, who imported and distributed spices, particularly pepper. These prosperous men eventually formed guilds to protect their interests. The most important was the Pepperers' Guild of London, which held considerable political clout in the city. Some of its members served as mayor.

The pepperers established their businesses on Sopers' Lane, where apprentices dressed in blue uniforms announced to passersby the wares within. By the middle of the fourteenth century, the Pepperers' Guild had been replaced by The Grocers' Company, derived from the "Great Beam" used to weigh quantities of more than twenty-five pounds. The word grocer referred to the *peso grosso* or hundredweight of 112 pounds. Cheating the scale by adding stones, sand, or other materials—or by mixing old spice with the newly acquired— was a serious crime. A man convicted of adulteration forfeited his goods to the king. In 1428, The Grocers' received a royal charter of incorporation from Henry VI. Among other items, the charter allowed it to acquire and hold land, and conveyed the privilege of overseeing the use of the beam and weights. In 1447, The Grocers' became the official "garblers" of the land. Garblers inspected spices to ensure that they were pure, and the inspections also gave them a way to control the spice trade, which made the company even more powerful. Each year, The Grocers' Company had to submit an account of all seized goods to the royal exchequer, and in exchange, it received half of all forfeited goods. It retained the garbling privilege until 1689.

Pepper was the primary reason why the East India Company was established, and naturally, its founding members were successful grocers. When Queen Elizabeth I granted the company its charter in 1600, a major part of its mission was to bring down the price of pepper to English consumers.

During the heyday of the pepper trade, the spice was more valuable than gold and silver. In 1418, an irate English grocer reported that he had been defrauded by a man who gave him tin spoons and stones rather than silver spoons, silver, and jewels in exchange for twelve pounds of pepper. The man took off before the grocer discovered the bartered merchandise was worthless. The surviving sailors of voyages to Asia were sometimes paid for their labors in quintals of pepper and other spices. A quintal was equivalent to about 125 pounds. The spices sailors received could set them up for the rest of their lives. Pepper was considered a legitimate form of money. It was used to pay taxes, custom duties, and even dowries. When Isabella married Charles I of Spain, also known as Holy Roman Emperor Charles V, in 1526, her brother, John III of Portugal, paid part of her dowry in pepper. A man's wealth was expressed by how much pepper was in a household.

The origin of the word *spice* reflects its worth. Spice comes from the Latin word *species*, which means an item of special value. Following the defeat of the Spanish Armada by the British in 1588, King Philip II of Spain ran out of silver and couldn't pay some of his debts. In 1589, and again in 1591, he reached into his stores of pepper to square the difference.

Land was also purchased with pepper. The expression "peppercorn rent" arose to signify a fee lower than the usual rent, or a nominal fee, symbolized in some contracts by one peppercorn. In 1607 William III chartered Trinity Church in New York City (the lovely parish church in lower Manhattan near Ground Zero) and he demanded that the church vestry pay rent of one peppercorn annually to the crown. The peppercorn rent showed who really owned the property. The expression is still used in Britain today.

Nutmeg and cloves were more profitable, but pepper was used in greater quantities—six to eight times more pepper than cloves and nutmeg was shipped from Asia to Europe during the age of discovery. Historian Holden Furber, a scholar who has written extensively about the English East India Company and European trading networks in Asia, estimates that the annual demand for cloves, nutmeg (mace), and cinnamon was roughly one million pounds, compared to six to eight million pounds of pepper. In the eighteenth century, the largest quantity of nutmeg sold by the VOC in Holland was only 280,964 pounds.

The Dutch were well aware of the value of pepper, even as they obsessively pursued monopolies in other spices. This fact was not lost on their main rival, the English. During the seventeenth century, when the English and Dutch vied for control of port cities in India, Sumatra, and western Java, the directors of the English East India Company understood that pepper's value exceeded that of any other spice because it was used by everyone. Although they acknowledged that pepper was a "slight thing," a mere commodity, the directors were well aware that whoever emerged victorious from a war over pepper would control "the British as well as the Indian seas."

This insight informs the following passage from one of their letters: "If the present misunderstandings between the two nations should ferment to an open war it would thought by the vulgar, but a war for pepper which they think to be [a] slight thing, because each family spends but a little [on] it. But at the Bottom it will prove a war for the dominion of the British as well as the Indian seas, because if ever they come to be sole masters of that Commodity, as they already are of nutmegs, mace, clove, and cinamon [sic], the sole profitt of that one commodity pepper being of general use, will be more to them, than all the rest and in probability to defray the constant charge of a great navy in Europe."

From its earliest days, European pepper trading turned a profit. Historian M. N. Pearson calculates that the Portuguese, who were the first Europeans to ply an all-ocean trade route to the East, at one time made a profit of about 260 percent based on the purchase of a quintal of pepper (about 125 pounds) in India for six cruzados, and a minimum set selling price in Europe of twenty-two cruzados, the gold Portuguese coins. These numbers, however, pale in comparison to the mind-boggling profits made by American pepper traders from Salem, Massachusetts, in the early 1800s. They once made a net profit of *700 percent* on a single voyage to Sumatra. In the sixteenth century, the Portuguese received especially good prices for Indian pepper because they exchanged it for copper, much needed in India.

Around 1515 Portugal made about one million cruzados from the trade in spices, equal to all of its ecclesiastical revenues and double the value of its trade in gold and metals. Pearson calculates that *net* profits earned by the Portuguese from pepper imports in the first half of the sixteenth century were extraordinary, ranging from 89 percent to 152 percent. During the second half of the sixteenth century, European demand for spices from Asia doubled again, and prices skyrocketed, rising as much as threefold. Over this period, pepper comprised the bulk of the spices imported.

By the early seventeenth century, the Portuguese were not the only Europeans in the Indian Ocean; the Dutch and English had entered the pepper trade and the Dutch were especially successful. The demand for pepper in Europe doubled yet again, and by the 1620s the Dutch and the English had largely supplanted the Portuguese in the spice trade. The sea route around the Cape of Good Hope had replaced the Levant as the means for Asian goods to reach Europe, something which the Portuguese had failed to accomplish in the sixteenth century. The northern Europeans at this point accounted for 80 percent of the trade in pepper.

In 1622, Europeans were consuming about seven million pounds of pepper annually. By that time, the English East India Company was the only importer of the spice into England. In 1618, the *Charles*, a company ship, brought back more than 8,100 quintals (1,012,500 pounds) of pepper; in 1621, it returned to London laden with more than 6,400 quintals (800,000 pounds), and in 1625, it carried nearly 8,000 quintals (1,000,000 pounds) back to England.

Pepper dominated the Dutch trade in spices, too, even though the Dutch had built a monopoly in nutmeg and cloves after brutal campaigns to seize islands in the Moluccas, or Spice Islands, the only place in the world where clove trees grew, and the tiny Banda Islands, where nutmeg trees grew. The Hollanders, though, never lost sight of the fact that pepper was more valuable than clove and nutmeg, simply because so much more of it was used. During the eighteenth century, demand for pepper remained strong even as other commodities, particularly tea, surpassed the trade in the spice. In 1722, when tea was enjoying brisk trade, more than nine million pounds of pepper were still being exported to Europe from Asia.

The Chinese had a long and enduring appetite for black pepper. The spice was first brought into China from India as early as the second century, mainly for medicinal purposes. Under the Sung Dynasty (960 to 1127) the trade in pepper expanded and the spice was often brought as tribute from visiting Southeast Asian embassies. The Chinese were trading with Java and with Sumatra at least since the tenth century.

When Marco Polo traveled to China in 1271 during the Yuan Dynasty (1271 to 1367), tremendous quantities of pepper were being imported into the country, where the spice was used widely in cooking. In *The Travels,* the Venetian traveler reported: "At the end of the five days' journey lies the splendid city of Zaiton [modern day Quanzhou], at which is the port for all the ships that arrive from India laden with costly wares and precious stones of great price and big pearls of fine quality. It is also a port for the merchants of Manzi that is, of all the surrounding territory, so that the total traffic in gems and other merchandise entering or leaving this port is a marvel to behold. From this city and its port goods are exported to the whole province of Manzi. And I assure you that for one spice ship that goes to Alexandria or elsewhere to pick up pepper for export to Christendom, Zaiton is visited by a hundred. For you must know that it is one of the two ports in the world with the biggest flow of merchandise."

Marco Polo was also dazzled by the city of Hang-zhou, which he called Kinsai. He commented on its stately mansions and gardens, the canals crossed by numerous stone bridges, and the traders who brought supplies by carts and boats. The crowds flocking to its enormous marketplaces especially impressed the European. ". . . anyone seeing such a multitude would believe it a stark impossibility that food could be found to fill so many mouths," Polo wrote. To convey the hugh quantities of provisions, including meat, wine, and groceries, that had to be brought into the city to meet the demand, Polo quoted a customs official who told him that the amount of pepper consumed daily in the city amounted to forty-three cartloads, each weighing 223 pounds.

Marco Polo also described the size of Chinese junks, which carried a much larger cargo than European ships. He estimated that 150 to 300 men were needed to crew the Chinese vessels, and one ship could take as much as "five or six thousand baskets of pepper."

The consumption of pepper in China expanded even more following the extraordinary voyages of Zheng He during the Ming Dynasty (1368 to 1644). In the early 1400s, this commander began his historic voyages for the Emperor Zhu Di. Pepper was one of the primary reasons for the voyages of the magnificent Chinese Treasure Fleet of the Dragon Throne. A man named Ma Huan accompanied the fleet on three of its seven expeditions, acting as the official translator of either Arabic or Persian. He wrote about visiting Calicut, Malacca, and the port city of Pasai in northern Sumatra, where a large number of foreign ships came to buy black pepper.

In Calicut, pepper was extensively cultivated by the people living in the mountainous countryside who had established gardens, Ma Huan wrote in *The Overall Survey of the Ocean's Shores.* "When the period of the tenth moon arrives, the pepper ripens; [and] it is collected, dried in the sun, and sold," he wrote. "Of course, big peppercollectors come and collect it, and take it up to the official storehouse to be stored; if there is a buyer, an official gives permission for the sale; the duty calculated according to the amount [of the purchase price] and is paid in to the authorities. Each one *po-ho* of pepper is sold for two hundred gold coins."

Zheng He's fleet sailed widely in the China Seas to Korea and Japan and in the Indian Ocean to India, the Persian Gulf, and the east coast of Africa. For the voyages of the Treasure Fleet, the Chinese built the biggest wooden sailing ships the world had ever seen. The largest were four hundred feet long. By comparison, Columbus's *Santa Maria* was tiny, measuring only eighty-five feet long.

The Chinese implemented an extraordinary campaign to obtain the wood for their massive ships by planting more than fifty million trees in the Nanking area in 1391. Calicut was the destination of the first voyage of 317 junks in the fall of 1405. Outfitted with a crew of more than 27,000, and on later voyages with hundreds of medical officers and pharmacologists, the Chinese ships had watertight bulwark compartments and balanced rudders for steering, technical innovations that would not be incorporated into European shipbuilding until the late eighteenth century. The Chinese already had a long maritime history, and at various times had the finest boats sailing the Indian Ocean, but none could compare with the Treasure ships, which could be identified easily by the brightly painted dragon eye on their prows.

The affinity for pepper among the Chinese was well known among the Europeans in Asia. A Portuguese merchant based in Malaysia in the sixteenth century noted that the Chinese wanted pepper more than anything else, and were willing to buy as many boatloads as were available. He also noted that in the early 1500s, a quintal of pepper was worth four ducats in Malacca, but sold for fifteen ducats in China. And an Italian observer named Andrea Corsali reported in 1515 that there was "as great profit in taking spices to China as in taking them to Portugal."

When the Ming dynasty, the last native rulers of China, fell in 1644 to the marauding Manchus, many southern Chinese fled overseas to Malaysia, where they took up pepper farming. By the end of the seventeenth century, the Chinese had established themselves as prominent pepper traders there. Their presence in Malaysia was noted by Charles Lockyer, an independent English merchant who traveled widely in Asia. In 1711, he described the city of Malacca as a "healthful place" where "the houses in the town make a good appearance, are built with stone, and ranged in streets, much like our small seaports in England." He noted especially that the Chinese "keep the best shops in the place, which are well filled with the manufactures and produce of their own country . . ." The Chinese especially liked tea and sugar candy, and some had set up teahouses in the town.

In the succeeding centuries, overseas Chinese continued to play a major role in the pepper trade, and China remained a large consumer of pepper.

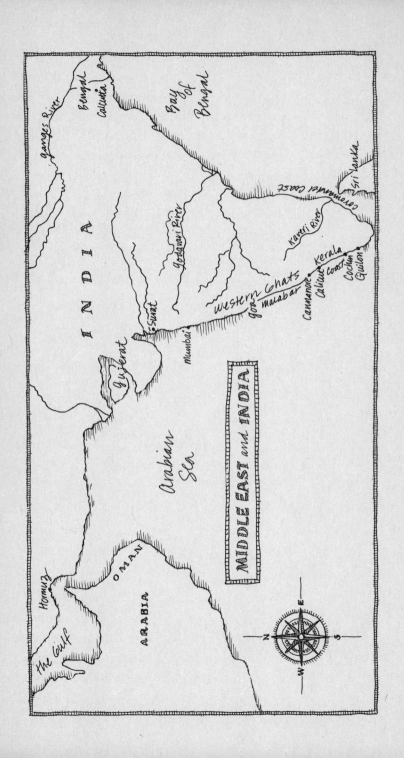

Three

Drugs and Souls

EUROPEANS ORIGINALLY SAILED TO ASIA TO BUY PEPPER
AND TO SPREAD CHRISTIANITY. THE PORTUGUESE, RULED
BY A CATHOLIC MONARCHY, WERE THE FIRST TO SUPPORT
THE JESUITS, THE CATHOLIC ORDER MOST OFTEN
ASSOCIATED WITH EUROPEAN EXPLORATION.

Boast no more about the subtle Greek
Or the long odyssey of Trojan Aenas;
Enough to the oriental conquests
Of great Alexander and of Trajan;
I sing of the famous Portuguese
To whom both Mars and Neptune bowed.
Abandon all the ancient Muse revered,
A loftier code of honour has appeared.
—LUÍS VAZ DE CAMÕES, *THE LUSIADS* (1572)

Vasco da Gama's small fleet of Portuguese ships sailed around the Cape of Good Hope in early 1498 and then headed north along the coast of East Africa, taking the inner passage between Madagascar and the coast. No other European ships had ever sailed this far around the Cape, and they stopped for provisions in Mozambique, Mombasa, and the nearby town of Malindi before sailing across the Indian Ocean. It was in these port towns that da Gama first encountered thriving settlements that had prospered because of trade with India, and his behavior set the tone for the hundred or so years that the Portuguese attempted to dominate the pepper trade. Along the coast of Africa, the people were Muslims who spoke Arabic. When asked about their religious beliefs by local royalty, da Gama and his crew were evasive, lest they be identified as Christians, and they took hostages to protect themselves against what they perceived as hostile locals. When they reached Malindi, everyone in the town already knew that the Portuguese quickly resorted to force in unfamiliar situations. This pattern of hostage taking and the impulsive use of force would be repeated often in the years ahead.

Finally, da Gama sailed into Calicut, a vibrant pepper port on the southwest coast of India, fulfilling a long-sought dream immortalized in *The Lusiads*, a book-length poem published in 1572 by Luís Vaz de Camões. The effusive poem created the grand legend of da Gama as a hero for the ages, whose courage surpassed even the daring of the ancient Greeks. The Portuguese had been steadily making their way south along the west coast of Africa throughout the fifteenth century, hoping to find sources of African gold. They traded their saffron, copper, and wine for melegueta pepper, cobalt, animal skins, and cotton. In 1488 Bartolomeu Dias at last rounded the Cape, but after brushing the Indian Ocean, he turned back.

After so many decades of Portuguese exploration, da Gama dearly wanted to reach India, but his paranoia overcame his sense of occasion. Fearing for his own life, he sent ashore a convict from his fleet to make the first contact with the subcontinent. To this day, historians don't know the convict's name. The fellow was asked by two men in Calicut why he was there, to which he replied famously,

"Christians and Spices." This oft-told tale is supposed to provide a rationale for Portuguese exploration and exemplify a first encounter between East and West. But it is partly a joke, for two reasons. First, the convict wasn't greeted by Asians. The two men who met him were from Tunisia in North Africa, and they were traders. This was hardly a momentous meeting of East and West. Instead, the encounter reveals the sophisticated existing network of trade in the Indian Ocean during the so-called age of discovery. The Portuguese, it turns out, were rather late to the party. Da Gama didn't even navigate his own ships to India from the east coast of Africa. In Malindi, he brought on board a Muslim from Gujarat, a region in northwestern India, who piloted the ships to India.

Second, the Portuguese weren't looking to convert anyone; these sailors weren't missionaries. Da Gama and his men were seeking the legendary Prester John, the medieval Christian king who supposedly ruled in the East in unimaginable splendor. This widely believed fairy tale resembled the equally preposterous notion that the East harbored the Garden of Eden. Both held sway for hundreds of years, and helped induce Europeans to travel to the East.

Da Gama's behavior in Calicut on his first voyage created quite a stir. He complained about the way he was treated, disregarded court etiquette, and was paranoid and irritable. Calicut was the home of the Zamorins, merchant Hindu rulers who maintained a vast trade in the Indian Ocean, extending west to Africa and east to the islands of Indonesia and beyond. Even the Chinese respected Calicut's importance. This port city boasted a sophisticated court and culture, and was incredibly tolerant.

A glimpse of Calicut's wealth and cosmopolitan atmosphere is provided by a French seaman named François Pyrard, who survived a shipwreck off the Maldive Islands and imprisonment by the Portuguese. Describing Calicut as a kind of paradise on earth, he wrote in his journal: "Between the town and the king's palace there is nothing but houses and there is no place in all India where contentment is more universal than at Calecut, both on account of the beauty and fertility of the country, and of the intercourse with men of all races, who live there in free exercise of their own religions." The delightful quarters of the city, which include its bazaars or "little towns," were so full of people all day long, he reported, that they were difficult to pass through. The buildings in the bazaars were "very large and well constructed of stone and wood, and supplied with shops, warehouses, and yards, all securely enclosed . . ." The houses in the city had gardens and porches, which served to receive passing strangers "both for giving them meat and drink, and also a place to rest and sleep . . ." Pyrard spent eight months in Calicut until he was kidnapped outside of the city by the Portuguese, who took him to Cochin as a prisoner.

Pyrard's story is among the more colorful adventures to emerge from the time when Europeans began to sail to Asia to procure pepper for commercial companies. He had originally set out in 1601 as part of the crew in two vessels, one of which was named *Croissant*, financed by prosperous French merchants who were inspired by the success of the Dutch and English in the East Indies. It was not an especially well-planned voyage. Almost from the beginning, the ships encountered difficulties, not the least of which was, as Pyrard observed, the "bad order and discipline in the ships; for there was no piety or devotion, but plenty of oaths and blasphemy, disobedience to officers, mutiny and carelessness, and every day quarrelling, assault, thefts, and the like vices." Carelessness and drunkenness caused the ship carrying Pyrard to be wrecked off the Maldive Islands. Only he and three other men survived. Incredibly, Pyrard quickly endeared himself to the islanders because of his ability to learn their language. He was treated well. He lived on the islands for four years, and his detailed observations of the habits of the people are recorded in his journal. Pyrard didn't return to France until 1611, when he published the first edition of his travels in Asia.

When da Gama arrived in Calicut in 1498, the people remembered stories of sailors who had arrived on their shores more than ninety years earlier. They told the Portuguese that these sailors "wore their hair long and had no beards except around their mouths. They landed wearing cuirass, helmet and vizor, and carrying a certain weapon (sword) attached to a spear. Once every two years they returned with 20 to 25 ships." These sailors were the Chinese. Unlike Zheng He, the commander of the Treasure Fleet, da Gama wasn't known for his tact or diplomacy, and he had trouble negotiating in this kind of environment. His offensive behavior in India left a mark. According to one anonymous report, "The entire land wished him ill." His behavior on his first trip to India was mild compared to the debacle on his second expedition, when he held the lofty title "Admiral of the Indies." On this infamous voyage, he encountered a ship returning to Calicut from Mecca that carried some 380 Muslim men, women, and children. The women offered their jewels in return for their lives and begged the Portuguese to at least save their innocent babies. Da Gama ordered the ship to be burned, and everyone on board perished.

The Portuguese monarchy was enthralled with da Gama's first journey, even though his ships were nearly blown onto the coast of Brazil (in 1500, the Portuguese fleet led by Pedro Álvares Cabral would "discover" Brazil on the way to India), only fifty-five of his crew of 148 men survived, and he had to burn one of his ships. Nonetheless, some twelve thousand pounds of pepper were brought home aboard the two ships that made the round-trip journey, so the trip was profitable. However, the Hindu Zamorin leader made it very clear that the Portuguese would have to bring something of value on the next visit. "And what I want from your land is gold and silver and coral and scarlet [cloth]," he wrote to the Portuguese king.

Da Gama's journey was the first time that pepper had been imported directly from India to Europe via an all-ocean route, a great achievement that received widespread acclaim. Da Gama didn't return to Lisbon with the remnants of his fleet on that first journey because he had to bury his brother Paulo in the Azores. Paulo died on the long voyage and his ship was burned in Mombasa, since there weren't enough men to sail her. Scurvy—which turns the skin into a patchwork of ugly purple dots, painfully distends hands and feet, and makes the gums bloat so massively that eating becomes impossible—had killed nearly two-thirds of da Gama's crew. (Scurvy remained a major cause of death among sailors until well into the mid-nineteenth century. It wasn't until the early twentieth century that Axel Holst and Theodor Frölich proved definitively the cause of scurvy was a lack of ascorbic acid—vitamin C.)

Those who survived da Gama's voyage were well compensated. They received their pay in "drugs," read spices. Nicolau Coelho, the captain of the first ship of the expedition to reach Lisbon, received a quintal, or some 125 pounds, of all the drugs brought back, and each pilot and sailor was given a half quintal.

The Portuguese monarch, Don Manuel, richly rewarded da Gama and his descendants with a yearly allowance of one-thousand cruzados, a sum of money roughly equal to the annual revenues of a large property. Don Manuel wasted no time in broadening his own domain. After da Gama's first voyage, he was not only "King of Portugal and the Algraves on this side and beyond the sea in Africa, and Lord of Guinea," but he also became "Lord of the Conquest, Navigation and Commerce of Ethiopia, Arabia, Persia and India." Even today, da Gama is considered a national hero in Portugal, and his legend lives on as the navigator who "discovered" the sea route to India from Europe.

Vasco da Gama and Prester John

By the time da Gama left Lisbon, the Prester John fable had been around for more than 300 years. Marco Polo and other travelers in the thirteenth century set out to find the Christian king, but no one could locate him. Then, someone came along who claimed to be Sir John Mandeville, an English knight who spent more than thirty years wandering in Arab lands and in the East during the fourteenth century. This clever, anonymous author recharged the spirit of Prester John by reporting that the king was alive and well and living lavishly as emperor of India. At his court, he entertained and fed more than thirty thousand people each day at tables made of emeralds. The main gates of his palace were made of precious stones, and the halls and the chambers of his palace were made of crystal. His throne was encrusted with onyx, crystal, and jasper. Two great gold balls topped the towers of his palace, and they shone brightly in the night. When he went into battle, three large gold crosses preceded him. The crosses were guarded by tens of thousands of men at arms and a hundred thousand foot soldiers, who were not counted as part of the emperor's main army.

Travels of Sir John Mandeville was published in Europe around 1372 and was enormously popular. By 1500, more than twenty-five editions had been published in Spanish,

English, German, Czech, Dutch, and Danish translations. Columbus read Mandeville's travels and noted the abundance of spices in the margins of his copy of the book. Mandeville's literary hoax was widely held to be true well into the seventeenth century. The identity of the author is unknown, although over the years some scholars have argued that he was Jean de Bourgogne, a physician who died in Liège in 1372.

By the time da Gama went to India, the story of Prester John was as intractably implanted in the European imagination as a splinter. Da Gama carried a note from King Manuel to Prester John. The Portuguese desperately wanted to find the king and enlist him as their ally in their fight against their enduring enemy, the Moors. They convinced themselves that the people they met in India were bona fide Christians and were quite willing to superimpose Christian iconography and practices on Hindu temples and forms of worship. When da Gama and his retinue were taken inside a Hindu temple in Calicut, they believed it was a church, even though the "saints" painted on its walls had large flaring nostrils, bulging eyes, and numerous flailing arms. Da Gama dutifully reported that India was filled with Christians.

Despite this deliberate mischaracterization, Christianity does have deep roots in India, planted most likely by missionaries who arrived in the subcontinent in the fourth and fifth centuries, and not, as often stated, by the apostle Thomas, or "doubting Thomas," who was said to be taken as a captive to South Asia much earlier and to have preached there. In some areas of Turkey and in what is now Iran, Nestorian

Christianity was more widely practiced, although this Eastern brand of Christianity was condemned by Rome in the fifth century because it separated the divine and human natures of Christ.

The pepper route was filled with misery and death for the Europeans. In addition to the hazards of navigating by dead reckoning, men sailing to Asia had to travel thousands of miles in unsafe ships plagued by frequent leaks and loose rigging, and outfitted with anchors that were easily lost because they were too light. A Portuguese writer named Figueiredo Falcão, who had access to official records, wrote in 1612 that some thirty-five Indiamen were wrecked in the years 1580 to 1610. Other observers have estimated that between 1550 and 1650, some 130 Portuguese ships were lost either through shipwrecks or enemy attacks. Likewise, between 1601 and 1620 the English sent out eighty-one Indiamen and only thirty-five of the ships returned to England, a dismal record.

The crew also had to endure each other; drunkenness abounded and reckless behavior sent quite a few ships up in flames, as Pyrard related when his ship was wrecked off the Maldive Islands. The voyages were always accompanied by the deaths of fellow travelers from scurvy and dysentery, another major killer. The ships stank. Hygiene was awful and the sick would often lie in their own excrement. Cockroaches, rats, and other vermin abounded. It isn't known exactly how many European sailors perished during the early days of Indian Ocean sailing, when a round-trip voyage could take up to two years—including a layover in India of three to four months to load spices—but the losses were great. Among the Dutch, only about one in three sailors survived the ordeal of travel to

Asia, and the Portuguese, Spanish, and English probably fared no better.

In the journals that survive of these voyages, deaths were recorded, and the cause was usually "flux" or "bloody flux" (dysentery). Oftentimes men died on consecutive days, as is evident in the dreary roll call of names in the following journal entry of a merchant on one of the early voyages: "The sixteenth day our general departed Bantam and came aboard to proceed on his voyage to the Malucos; this night died Henry Dewbry of the flux . . . The seventeenth day died of the flux William Lewed, John Jenkens, and Samuel Porter."

Even if they survived the voyage, the Bombay proverb, "two monsoons were the life [of] a man" described the fate of many Europeans in Asia. Unless one had a serious death wish, why would anyone want to leave Europe under these circumstances? The usual answer is money (spices) and religion. They were going to strike it rich or they were sailing for the glory of God, and riches usually preceded the harvesting of souls. The Portuguese and the Spanish, the first European countries to entertain ocean exploration, were not timid about their aspirations. The Portuguese rallied to "Species and Souls," while the Spanish adopted "Gold, Glory, and Gospel" as their motto.

The Portuguese, ruled by a Catholic monarchy, were the first to support the Jesuits, the Catholic order most often associated with European exploration. Therefore, it is generally assumed that the purchase of pepper—and by extension conquest—was mixed up with missionaries and the pursuit of souls from the beginning of ocean travel. In some ways, it clearly was. In the early days, the Jesuits, regardless of their nationality, sailed to Asia aboard Portuguese carracks. Wherever the traders went, the missionaries followed. When new lands were "discovered," the Portuguese and the Spanish claimed the divine right to convert the "conquered," finance missionary activities, and provide transportation to new territorial acquisitions. These rights, called *Padroado* by the Portuguese and *Vicariato Regio* by the Spanish, solidified the grip of the Catholic monarchies on missionary activity, which even Rome could not pry loose. But the missionaries and the spice traders never mixed very well, even though the Jesuits engaged in the spice trade to shore up their own shaky finances in Asia. Nearly 16 percent of the Jesuits' annual income in the seventeenth century was derived from Eastern spices, and spices continued to be a source of income for the order into the eighteenth century. The Jesuits, however, never liked the European traders in their midst, especially the Portuguese. In the beginning, the Jesuits were quite careful to distinguish themselves from the Portuguese traders in Macao. They didn't want the Chinese to mistake them for coarse, uneducated traders. Nevertheless, the Jesuits had to rely on the Portuguese, and the first Jesuit foray into mainland China from Macao, a Portuguese territory, was made by accompanying Portuguese traders to Canton in 1583.

The Portuguese and Spanish, the first out of the gate in terms of discovery, argued like schoolchildren over how to divide what they considered the unexplored world. Finally, in 1494, they signed the Treaty of Tordesillas, named after a town in Spain, which modestly divided up the world between them. This agreement moved their previous line of demarcation seventy miles to the west so that Portugal could pocket Brazil in South America, as well as all of Africa, and India, Japan, China, and the Philippines. Spain received the rest of the Americas, but in 1565, it violated its own treaty when it invaded the Philippines. Of course, the English and the Dutch—Protestant countries—and the Asians ignored the Catholics' treaty.

In the sixteenth century, the Portuguese were the dominant Europeans in Asia, and they were the first to establish forts there. It was their extraordinary good luck that they entered the Indian

Ocean some sixty-five years after the Chinese abruptly quit official maritime trade. At the end of his reign, the Ming emperor Zhu Di, an ardent supporter of oceanic trade, suffered a series of calamities that led him to suspend future voyages of the Treasure Fleet. When his son, Zhu Gaozhi, became emperor in 1424, his first order was to stop all voyages and to send home immediately all foreign officials in the capital. He never explained his decision. Some historians suggest he was following the precepts of a rigid Confucian system that had placed great store in social and familial relations, and played down the value of trade. However, there was one more voyage of the great fleet. In 1432, Zheng He led the seventh and last voyage to Calicut with more than a hundred ships and 27,500 men. The great commander died on that journey at the age of sixty-two. Although the Chinese continued to trade unofficially for many centuries through their southern ports, they never regained mastery of the ocean. In 1525, an imperial edict ordered the destruction of all ocean-bound ships and the arrest of all merchants who sailed on them. It's always tempting to speculate that world history would have proceeded along a different course if the Chinese had remained a dominating maritime power.

The sudden withdrawal of the Treasure Fleet had a huge impact, leaving a gaping hole in trade in the eastern half of the Indian Ocean. Bengalis, Tamils, and especially Gujaratis from the west coast of India—who traded widely in the Indian Ocean—wasted little time in filling the void left by the Chinese.

It was also lucky for the Portuguese that the Indian Ocean could accommodate many more traders, and that the reliable monsoons acted like a giant conveyor belt, pushing ships back and forth across the ocean with relative ease. During the summer, the powerful southwest monsoons helped propel ships from Africa to India and beyond to Southeast Asia. In the late fall, the more benign northeast monsoons swept the ships back to Africa. The monsoons were the reason why Arab traders called Southeast Asia "The Land below the Winds." The pattern of the monsoons obliged ships to sail only during certain seasons lest they be caught in the tropical storms that raged off the Cape of Good Hope. So, ideally, ships leaving Lisbon before Easter would round the Cape after the stormy season, leaving an adequate amount of time to ride the southwest monsoon to India in September or October.

On the return trip, the ships would leave India in late fall or around Christmas and reach the Cape before May when stormy weather emerged. In practice, many of the Portuguese ships were delayed because of administrative problems, the prolonged wait for a full cargo of pepper, or lack of cash to buy pepper ahead of time. The delays often were disastrous for the ships, and led to many shipwrecks off the Cape. The sailors who plied the Indian Ocean long before the arrival of the Portuguese carefully guarded their knowledge about the monsoons. The Portuguese did bring cannon and firearms into the trading network of the Indian Ocean, which probably wasn't novel. But it was their willingness to use force, and their desire to claim territory, that brought a new, unwelcome dimension to trade. Cruzado, the Portuguese gold coin bearing the distinctive cross of St. George, means crusade.

It didn't take long for the Portuguese to become the most reviled Europeans sailing on the Indian Ocean. Many travelers to the East expressed their scorn. "The Portuguese, as at other places in India, are a degenerate race of people, well stocked with cunning and deceit; instead of that courage and magnanimity their own writings are so full of," wrote English trader Charles Lockyer in 1711, echoing the distaste for the Portuguese that had become widespread by that time. Toward the end of the seventeenth century, the English pirate William Dampier noted that the Portuguese had "insulted" the natives, and "being grown rich in trade, they fell to all manner of looseness and debauchery; the usual concomitant of wealth, and as commonly the forerunner of ruin." Dampier also had heard that in Malacca the Portuguese made use of native women "such as they liked they took without control."

Relatively few Portuguese women ventured to Asia; most married men left their wives at home, preferring a household of slave girls while stationed in Goa and elsewhere in Asia. From time to time, the Portuguese crown encouraged their men to have liaisons with native women, and many European observers reported that mixed marriages were not uncommon, although Dampier clearly implied that the Portuguese took native women by force: "they as little restrained their lust in other places; for the breed of them [the children of Portuguese men and Asian women] is scattered all over India." It should be remembered that the Portuguese recruited grave robbers and other criminals to serve as crew for their ships. Da Gama had sent ashore a convict in Calicut. These men, if they survived, were far beyond the reach of Lisbon, and they behaved according to their own standards. As news spread about the hazards of the voyages to Asia, it became increasingly difficult to recruit enough Portuguese men for the Indiamen. The voyages were so unpopular that in 1623 it was reported that sailors had to be abducted and kept in irons until an India-bound ship had sailed. They must have known that their chances of surviving were slim.

The monster carracks of the Portuguese, reaching some two thousand tons, suffered great losses. François Pyrard described a fleet of four carracks, each carrying about a thousand soldiers, sailors, and passengers, which departed Lisbon in 1609. When the ships arrived in Goa, only three hundred men were alive on each of the ships. On the ships that were overcrowded, mortality was especially high. A report from a Jesuit in the late 1500s underscores the appalling number of deaths on these voyages: On one ship more than five hundred of 1,140 people and on another three hundred of eight hundred people perished. In the seventeenth century, the Portuguese sent thousands of soldiers to replenish their garrisons in India. Between 1629 and 1634, only 2,495 of 5,228 soldiers who left Lisbon survived the trip to Goa. Survival was hardly guaranteed once they got to India. In the seventeenth century, Europeans survived an average of three years in India. In Goa, some 25,000 Portuguese soldiers perished from cholera alone between 1604 and 1634. Is it any wonder that men had to be put in leg irons to ensure that they would sail to the East?

The Portuguese did attempt to monopolize the pepper trade in the Indian Ocean, but they were only partially successful. In 1510, they captured Goa, famous in our day for the hordes of hippies it attracts. The city on the west coast of India lies some 318 miles north of Calicut, 240 miles south of modern-day Mumbai, formerly Bombay, and 10,450 miles from Lisbon via the Cape of Good Hope, a long way from the clutches of the Portuguese monarchy and the pope in Rome. Since it has one of the finest harbors in India, Goa became the center of Portuguese enterprise in Asia in terms of trade and missionary work. The first Jesuit to reach the East, Francis Xavier, arrived in Goa in 1541.

After capturing Goa, the Portuguese quickly stretched eastward in their quest for greater control of the spice trade. Naturally, they looked to Malacca, the great port city on the southwest coast of the Malay Peninsula that controlled the sea lane connecting the Indian Ocean to the South China Sea and the Pacific Ocean, and which enjoyed unusually mild weather. As one observer noted: "The country abounds with timber and is fruitful in other respects; the air is wholesome, the heat moderate, and every thing else, as agreeable to European constitutions as can be expected in a climate within 2 deg. 30 min. of the equator." Malacca was the crucial transit point for spices and many other commodities heading east to China and west to India and Europe, and a port city quite dependent on the trade in pepper. It also relied on trade for its survival, since food-stuffs such as rice and fruit had to be imported into the city from Java and Siam (today Thailand); Malacca was truly a port city since it could only be reached by water. Fish, however, were plentiful. Like the ports along the west coast of India, Malacca's trading seasons were dictated by the monsoons, and ships could not arrive or depart from May to the end of October.

Malacca in the fifteenth century was at the height of its power as one of the greatest seaports in the world—a cosmopolitan place where Africans, Gujaratis, Tamils, Bengalis, Chinese, Javanese, Persians, and Malaysians traded and lived together. Historian M.A.P. Meilink-Roelofsz describes how Malacca rose from provin-cial backwater to powerful sultanate in less than a hundred years in her classic work on the impact of Europeans on trade in the Indo-nesian archipelago. The population of the port city reflected the reach of the Indian Ocean from the east coast of Africa to the Per-sian Gulf, India, the Malay Peninsula, and the island of Sumatra. China and Japan lay to the east of the Strait of Malacca. Zheng He, the commander of the Treasure Fleet, visited Malacca in 1409; sub-sequently it became a tribute nation to China.

The Europeans who visited Malacca in the following century were awestruck. "This city of Malacca is the richest seaport with the greatest number of wholesale merchants and abundance of shipping and trade that can be found in the whole world," gushed Duarte Barbosa, a Portuguese sea captain, in 1517. "No trading port as large as Malacca is known, nor any where they deal in such fine and highly prized merchandise. Goods from all over the East are found here; goods from all over the West are sold here," wrote Tomé Pires, a hapless Portuguese ambassador who offended the emperor of China and eventually died in a prison in Canton in 1524.

Pires arrived in Malacca eleven months after the Portuguese conquered the city, and he spent two years and seven months there. He allegedly coined the famous phrase, "Whoever is lord of Malacca has his hand on the throat of Venice." In those days wild elephants and tigers, as well as deer, roamed the port city. Pires's renowned *Suma Oriental*, an account of Asian trade that he wrote between 1512 and 1515, was the first description of Malaysia by a European. He also has the distinction of being the first European to describe the use of chopsticks. The Portuguese were notorious for holding on to information about their "discoveries." King Manuel I decreed in 1504 that all information about exploration was a state secret. It wasn't until 1944 that Pires's journals were published in their entirety.

In 1522 the Portuguese conquered Malacca under the command of the fierce Alfonso de Albuquerque. It was a brutal campaign. A Malaysian observer of the invasion described the incessant bombardment of the city. "And the Franks engaged the men of Malaka in battle, and they fired their cannon from their ships so that the cannon balls came like rain," he wrote. "And the noise of the cannon was as the noise of thunder in the heavens and the flashes of fire of their guns were like flashes of lightning in the sky: and the noise of their matchlocks was like that of ground-nuts popping in the frying-pan." Among those who overtook the city was Ferdinand Magellan.

In a city where most of the buildings were made of wood, the Portuguese quickly went about constructing an enormous medieval-style fortress on the banks of the Malacca River and alongside the sea to fortify their position and make sure that ships could still supply the garrison even during a siege. Built with slave labor on the ruins of a great mosque, the fortress was constructed in part with stones from the mausoleums of former Malaysian sultans and from religious buildings. The imposing A Formosa, or The Famous, had walls eight feet thick. "The walls of the fortress are of great width; as for the keep, where they are usually built, you will find few of five storeys like this," wrote Tomé Pires in his *Suma Oriental*. "The artillery, both large and small, fires on all sides."

This commanding fortress, a symbol of Portuguese might, served as the residence of the various Europeans who controlled Malacca, and it also accommodated two hospitals, five churches, a palace for the governor, a prison, and other buildings. Surrounded by a wall nearly one mile long, the fortress was believed to be impregnable. In the nineteenth century it was destroyed by the British. A prominent Malaysian scholar who witnessed the demolition described elephant- and house-sized pieces of the fort blown into the air and cascading into the sea. "Everyone was startled," he wrote, "when they heard the noise, their surprise all the greater because never in their lives had they heard such a sound or seen how the power of gunpowder can lift bits or rock as big as houses." The stones from the fortress were carried away to build houses, and the British used pieces to make warning buoys.

Once the Portuguese secured the port city in 1511, they cast their eye farther east to the Spice Islands, or the Moluccas, the little volcanic islands that transfixed the world as its only source of clove. These islands—Ternate, Tidore, Moti, Makian, Bacan—lie some two thousand miles east of Malacca, and their names were well known during the age of discovery, although few sailors knew their exact location.

The islands were immortalized by the poet John Milton in *Paradise Lost* (1667):

. . . the Iles
of Ternate and Tidore, where Merchants bring their spicie
Drugs . . .

The Portuguese poet de Camões described them more closely in *The Lusiads*:

Look there, how the seas of the Orient,
Are scattered with islands beyond number;
See Tidore, then Ternate with its burning
Summit, leaping with volcanic flames.
Observe the orchards of hot cloves
Portuguese will buy with their blood;
And birds of paradise, which never alight,
But fall to earth the day they end their flight.

Even the Chinese had not ventured to the Moluccas, partly because their junks were too large to travel among the islands. Some historians argue that even Arab traders did not go to the Spice Islands before the arrival of the Europeans. Javanese and Malaysian sailors most likely transported the aromatic spice from the Spice Islands to Java, where it was purchased by the Chinese and by Indian and Arab traders. The Chinese had been using cloves since at least 300 B.C. as a perfume and breath freshener. In the West cloves were known since at least the time of the ancient Romans, when the physician Galen recommended using the dried flower buds in prescriptions for ointments. Cloves, saffron, pepper, and other aromatic spices were said to have been presented in gold and silver caskets to a bishop in Rome in the fourth century. Cloves were especially prized for their superb ability to mask odors.

Only four months after Malacca was conquered, Albuquerque dispatched three ships to the Spice Islands. The islanders weren't overjoyed to see the foreign ships on their shores, and they resisted these unusual interlopers who, unlike Malaysian and Javanese traders, were clearly interested in subjugating them. The Spice Islands were ardently pursued because cloves, like pepper, were used as a spice and as a medicine, and the spices' geographic isolation made them even more valuable. Magellan took cloves on his round-the-world voyage in order to show locals what he was after, and when the only ship of his fleet to have survived the harrowing voyage returned to Lisbon in 1521, it carried a skeleton crew and some 53,000 pounds of cloves, which earned a profit of some *2,500 percent*. Nearly sixty years later, England's great seafaring hero Sir Francis Drake circumnavigated the globe, and he was the first Englishman to import cloves directly to England.

Along with Goa and Malacca, the port of Hormuz on the Persian Gulf was an important hub for Indian and Indonesian spices transported in the Indian Ocean. The Portuguese conquered Hormuz in 1515 but failed to capture Aden at the entrance to the Red Sea, the key to the traditional spice trade in the Levant. The old trade route through the Levant, which encompasses the eastern Mediterranean, parts of the Middle East, and Turkey, persisted and thrived. In the middle of the sixteenth century, according to the estimates of some historians, almost half of Europe's pepper was still being supplied by ships via the Levant, an indication of the relative inability of Portugal to assert itself in the Indian Ocean and force all trade around the Cape. Muslim merchants, bypassing areas in the Indian Ocean dominated by the Portuguese, simply shipped their pepper to ports on the Red Sea, as they had for centuries, where the spice was taken overland to ports in Syria and Egypt on the Mediterranean and from there to ships that would finally take the spice to Venice.

There were other holes in the Portuguese net. Muslim traders, too, could bypass the Strait of Malacca altogether by shipping spices from the far eastern Spice Islands through the Strait of Sunda. Consequently, the Portuguese never had complete control of the spice trade, and what they did control was challenged by Arab, Indian, and Malaysian traders—and later by the Dutch and English. Portugal did try to assert its power by setting up a system of passes for all ships sailing the Indian Ocean, but this system was barely functional. Because of the long distances and huge expense involved in shipping spices from India, Sumatra, and the Spice Islands, the Portuguese conducted much of their trade with Asians. Most of the Portuguese ships had Asian crews because there weren't enough Portuguese sailors. The Portuguese did not dominate the spice trade for a long time. By the early seventeenth century, they were already beginning to lose their footholds in East Asia, and by the 1620s they had already been eclipsed by the far more successful English and Dutch, who accounted for most of the pepper trade. By the time Dampier traveled in Asia in 1688, the Portuguese had lost control of Malacca in Malaysia and of Ternate in the Moluccas.

Nevertheless, historian A. J. R. Russell-Wood points out that the Portuguese influence was extraordinary. Linguistically, the Portuguese language has had a more far-reaching impact than the Dutch language, even though the Dutch largely usurped the Portuguese in the pepper trade in the seventeenth century. Portuguese was for many years the dominant language in most of the maritime ports of Asia, and vestiges of the language could still be heard in Malacca and along the Malabar Coast in the twentieth century.

The Portuguese held on to Goa until 1961 and didn't relinquish their grip on Macao, the little island off the southeast coast of mainland China, until 1999. In the sixteenth century, the Chinese allowed the Portuguese to settle on the island in exchange for their help in defeating pirates. By 1562, historians estimate that Macao had about 800 to 900 Portuguese, and a few modest churches. In his journals, Matteo Ricci, the phenomenally gifted and indefatigable Italian Jesuit who lived in China for twenty-seven years, from 1583 to 1610, described Macao as a place where people gathered "eager to barter for all sorts of merchandise brought from Europe, India, and the Islands of the Moluccas. The prospects of quick fortunes were an enticement to the Chinese merchants to take up residence on the island, and in the course of a few years the trading post began to assume the appearance of a city. Numerous houses were built when the Portuguese and the Chinese began to intermarry, and before long the rock point was developed into a respectable port and a prominent market."

The number of Jesuits who went to Asia was small compared to the number of ordinary people who sailed to the East. The Jesuits were inveterate letter writers, in part because they were obliged to report on their activities, and their words are preserved. But the voices of ordinary people tend to be lost to history. Who would want to venture out on an unknown ocean, surrounded by filth, ragged men, and the prospect of disease? Surely, convicts had little choice in the matter, but families went, too. The voyage to the East must have been especially difficult for the few women who accompanied their husbands to India, although little is known about them. On the rare occasions when Portuguese vessels bound for Goa from Lisbon carried women, there were no more than twenty. Some bizarre solutions were put forth to remedy the chronic lack of European women in Portuguese strongholds. A Jesuit in the sixteenth century in Brazil suggested sending prostitutes. Convents were popular among married European women who needed a refuge while their husbands were away. The Augustinian convent of Santa Monica, established in Goa during the early seventeenth century, would far exceed its capacity of one hundred nuns.

Despite the obstacles, some European women managed to establish themselves in Asia in the early days of European exploration. One of them was an Englishwoman named Judith who survived a shipwreck off the coast of China. Judith was the maidservant of an English family sent to the East in 1619. She accompanied Richard Forbusher, a master carpenter for the East India Company, and his wife and two young sons aboard a ship named *Hope*. Only a sketchy account of their ordeal survives. Forbusher is mentioned several times in the company's court minutes, which provide details of transactions brought before the court. We know that he was an able carpenter. In the company's court minutes dated February 26, 1619, Forbusher was described as an "old servant who built a pinnace in the Somers Islands, and is known to be very skilful, and willing to go and live in India for seven years with his two sons."

When they arrived in Bantam, the family and maidservant debarked and were apparently put on the *Unicorne*, which was bound for Japan. This ship was wrecked off the coast of China, where they were taken captive by the Portuguese and shipped off to Malacca. At some point, Forbusher was slain, the children "detained," and Judith turned "Catholic," according to the company's records. On October 25, 1626, Forbusher's wife, Johan Cranfield, petitioned the company for her husband's wages. She related that she was ransomed for two Portuguese men and had made it all the way back to London. Her children had apparently died. Only Judith remained in Malacca. We do not hear again about this family in the company's records. It isn't known whether Johan ever got her money, although the company did pay a widow her husband's wages.

In 1637 Judith suddenly appears in the journal of Peter Mundy. He arrived in Malacca in May of that year and describes "an Englishwoman Married to a Portugall Mestizo of some quallity, are well to live, and have beetweene them one pretty boy." He relates that when Judith arrived in Malacca she went to live with the "Misericordia," an order that takes care of orphans. "She was called Judith and now Julia de la gracia." We don't know much more about Judith, but we can imagine that she might have found a measure of happiness in Malacca.

In later years some women risked their lives to go to Asia and earn their fortunes by disguising themselves as men. Johan Splinter Stavorinus, a captain for the Dutch East India Company from 1768 to 1778 who made several voyages to Africa and Asia during his employment, describes in his richly detailed journal a woman named Margaret Reymers who dressed in men's clothes and enlisted as a solider aboard the ship *Schoonzicht*.

A farmer's daughter in her early twenties, Margaret left the duchy of Oldenburg because of "ill treatment," according to Stavorinus. She met a Dutch recruiting officer in Hamburgh, who advised her to don men's clothes and go to India, where she would make her fortune. Margaret was tall and "of a large and coarse make, by which she could easily pass for a man, in her soldiers' uniform," Stavorinus observed. She remained unnoticed for two months on the *Schoonzicht*, but after her subterfuge was discovered, she was put ashore at the Cape of Good Hope and kept there in order to be sent back to Holland with a homeward bound Dutch Indiaman. When Stavorinus's ship arrived at the Cape, Margaret was put aboard. An arrangement was made for her to serve as a maid to a lady on the ship who was sailing from Batavia (modern-day Jakarta) to Holland. Nothing seemed amiss until she suddenly gave birth. Margaret told Stavorinus that while she was at the Cape, a surgeon's mate had seduced and abandoned her. Six months pregnant when she came aboard Stavorinus's ship, Margaret had "hoped that the ship would have reached its destination before the time of her delivery."

Another woman who disguised herself as a man, Dona Maria Ursula de Abreu e Lencastre, had an unusually adventurous life. Born in Brazil, Dona Maria escaped an odious marriage by enlisting as a marine on a Lisbon-bound warship. She then sailed in 1699 to India, where she served valiantly as a soldier. Dona Maria kept her true sex a secret for fourteen years, until she was wounded while rescuing her captain. When she recovered, the captain married her and they had a child named João.

The Jesuits and Pepper

Along with conquest, the history of black pepper is entwined with the Jesuits, the Catholic order most often associated with the European age of discovery. The Jesuits certainly went to Asia to win souls, but they usually followed in the footsteps of the pepper traders and traveled to their posts aboard pepper ships. Ignatius Loyola, the Spanish nobleman who founded the Jesuits in 1534, made traveling in the service of God one of the touchstones of the new order. Jesuits were expected to serve anywhere the pope or superior general requested. They had to function without a great deal of financial support or direct supervision, which landed them in quite a few awkward situations when they encountered civilizations far more sophisticated than their own, such as in Japan and China. In some ways, the Jesuits who went to China were the most sympathetic of all the Europeans who came to Asia in the heady early days of pepper-inspired ocean travel.

The Jesuits were not the first Christians to enter China. Nestorian Christians had established a church in China during the eighth and ninth centuries, and they became more numerous during the Yuan Dynasty, when openness toward foreigners resulted in more religious freedom. The Mongols were particularly attracted to this Eastern variant of Christianity that was condemned by Rome. Both Khublai Khan's mother and the wife of his brother Hülegü, who founded the Ilkhanid dynasty in Iran in 1259, were Nestorians. In the mid-thirteenth century, the pope in Rome sent out unsuccessful diplomatic missions to China, partly to persuade the Mongols to become allies against the Muslims, but Western Christianity only established itself in China near the end of that century when the pope appointed the Franciscan John of Monte Corvino archbishop of Beijing. Corvino reached China in 1294 (when Marco Polo was there) and built two churches during the thirty years that he spent in China, but his influence was limited. Both the Nestorians and Western Christians were swept out of China when the Ming dynasty, the last native dynasty to rule China, began its reign in 1368. Throughout Chinese history, periods of religious toleration alternated with xenophobia, when Muslims, Christians (Western and Nestorian), and Buddhists faced persecution.

In the sixteenth century, the peripatetic Francis Xavier,

one of the first Jesuits, traveled throughout Asia and the Far East and even spent time in the remote Spice Islands. His travels largely mirrored the path of spices through India and Asia. However, Xavier never made it into China, the country he considered most important for his mission. He dreamed of converting the Chinese emperor to Catholicism. At the end of his life, he fervently believed that if the emperor could be converted, then China and all of its tributary port cities and kingdoms would become a Catholic realm. He wrote: "I hope to go there [China] during this year, 1552, and penetrate even to the Emperor himself. China is that sort of kingdom, that if the seed of the Gospel is sown, it may be propagated far and wide. And, moreover, if the Chinese accept the Christian faith, the Japanese would give up the doctrines which the Chinese have taught them." He only knocked at China's door, leaving the job of converting the emperor to others. Xavier died on a small island near mainland China in 1552, and was buried in Goa, India, in 1554. Over the next two centuries, some two thousand Jesuits followed him to the East.

The Jesuit who is most often associated with China is Matteo Ricci, a tall, blue-eyed Italian, who was the first Jesuit to serve at the court of the Chinese emperors. An extraordinary polymath and a deeply compassionate man who truly wanted to understand China and its people, he adopted the garments of a Confucian scholar and spent five years translating into Latin the books of Confucius—the first time Chinese was translated into a European language. He eventually served at the court of the reclusive Emperor Wan Li in Beijing, who reigned from 1573 to 1620. Many of the Jesuits who followed Ricci served at the court of the emperor as well, and they, too, adopted the dress of the scholar in order to make themselves acceptable to the court and to elite Chinese society. In one of his reports to Rome, Ricci wrote that he had "two silk garments made, one for formal visits, and the other for ordinary wear. The formal robe, worn by scholars and notables, is of dark purple silk with long, wide sleeves; the hem, which touches my feet, has a border of bright blue silk half a palm in width and the sleeves and collar, which drops to the waist, are trimmed in the same way.... The Chinese wear this costume on the occasion of visits to persons, formal banquets, and when calling on officials."

The Jesuits' presence at the court was largely tolerated because of their knowledge of Western science, notably astronomy and mathematics, and their ability to regulate and repair clocks. Exquisite and elaborate mechanical clocks, many of which were made by the finest clockmakers in England and France as gifts for the emperor, were festooned with jeweled toy animals and figures that moved and filled the air with warbling of birds and with melody. A famous automaton clock in the emperor's palace was named The Conjurer after the sleight-of-hand artists who had been enchanting the Chinese since the days when acrobats and magicians from Greece and Syria traveled to China along the old Silk Road. The clock featured a Greek temple with doors that opened when music played to reveal a figure seated before a table with two cups. The magicians's head and lips moved while he performed tricks with the cups. At the close of his act a small box appeared on the table and a bird popped out and sang.

The clocks especially fascinated the two Manchu emperors who, between them, ruled China for nearly 120 years—Kangxi (from 1662 to 1722) and his grandson Qianlong (from 1736 to 1795)—during the Qing dynasty. At one time more than four thousand clocks filled the halls of the emperor's palaces in northern China, the Forbidden City, and the Summer Palace in Beijing, and Jehol, the lavish palace northeast of the imperial city that was used for hunting expeditions and to escape the summer heat.

The idea of Jesuits wearing elaborate Chinese gowns wasn't entirely accepted by the powers in Rome, although Ricci did originally receive approval from his superiors in Macao and Rome to change his attire from that of a Buddhist monk to that of a Chinese scholar. To the uninitiated, it could be quite shocking to see a Jesuit wearing the garments of a Chinese scholar, the most elite class in China's rigid hierarchial society. In 1699, Father De Prémare, a French Jesuit, met Father Joachim Bouvet, a French Jesuit who famously served at the court of the Kangxi emperor and personally tutored the emperor in astronomy and geometry. De Prémare wrote in a letter that Bouvet "had all the Marks of Distinction . . . which . . . Envoys of the court . . . have in this Empire; our Countrymen were not a little surprised when they saw him . . . "

Like Xavier, the Jesuits living in China believed that they could convert the emperor to Catholicism. So they quietly performed their scientific work in the hope that one day the emperor would be persuaded to convert, an astonishing expectation given that the emperor was considered the Son of Heaven, the intermediary between heaven and earth, and the supreme ruler of a civilization more than three thousand years old. Many Jesuits lived among the elite and had privileges that grew out of their personal relationship with the emperor, although some of the Jesuits were not welcomed at the court, and there were periods when they and other Christian missionaries were persecuted in China and its neighboring kingdoms. Then, churches would be destroyed, books burned, and missionaries thrown in prison or banished, although there were worse punishments. Some missionaries were killed by strangulation or were beheaded.

Converts received particularly bad treatment. A French Jesuit named Father Pelisson, who was based in Canton, describes a period of persecution that he had learned about from a Spanish Jesuit named John Anthony Arendo, who lived in the capital of Cochin-China, a kingdom between what is now North Vietnam and Thailand. The ruler of that kingdom, "who is but young, and extremely superstitious," the Jesuit wrote, "is wholly devoted to the Chinese Bonzes, or idol-Priests, whom he invited into his kingdom. He has two uncles; and these he consults on all occasions. One of them is a professed enemy to our religion." In early 1700, the king ordered the destruction of all churches, the Father related, and the houses of the five missionaries in the city were ransacked and their servants seized. All of the missionaries were imprisoned except the Spaniard Arnedo, who was given a little garden near the palace and the title of "mathematician."

He was allowed to go wherever he pleased. Obviously, there were certain advantages to being a scientist-missionary.

Despite the occasional backlash against Christians, the Jesuits' relationships with Chinese emperors in Beijing generally saved them from harsh treatment. Kangxi was particularly close to his Jesuits, and the French Jesuit Father Bouvet, who looked like a member of the emperor's court, was among those who tutored Kangxi and traveled with him. Another polymath Jesuit named Father Dominique Parennin, a Frenchman, accompanied Kangxi on hunting and military expeditions and persuaded the ruler that more accurate maps of the empire were needed, prompting the emperor to order the French Jesuits to survey the entire Chinese empire to produce a map. Still other Jesuits were court painters and architects who attended the Qianlong emperor and helped design some of the buildings in the famous Summer Palace in Beijing. Ultimately, it wasn't the Chinese who banished the Jesuits, but the Catholics in Rome.

The brouhaha erupted over something called the Rites Controversy, an extraordinarily long-running and ultimately ruinous debate over Chinese offerings to the dead, part of the ritual for venerating ancestors. Scholars also performed such ceremonies to honor Confucius, which usually included dedicating a tablet to him. Rome saw the practices of burning paper money and offering food and incense to the dead as forms of pagan worship and great offenses to Christianity. Rome wanted the rituals banned. At its core, the debate was about the Church's ability to accept cultures other than those of Western Europe. Ricci and many of his successors believed that the rites were not religious and therefore should be tolerated. They understood that in order to convert the Chinese to Christianity some sort of accommodation was necessary, especially rituals at the heart of an ancient moral and ethical system involving Confucius. Ricci was a rare proponent of multiculturalism, a man four hundred years ahead of his time. The controversy raged for years, and finally, in 1742, Pope Benedict XIV issued a bull, a solemn edict, confirming that he would never allow the rites to be put into practice. There could be no commingling of Chinese culture and Catholicism. No other pope challenged his ruling until the twentieth century.

The Jesuits created quite a few enemies among the other Catholic orders. Thirty-one years after the Chinese rites were forbidden to be practiced, Rome banned the Jesuit order altogether, and it was not reinstated until 1814. An oath against the Chinese Rites was required by missionaries until well into the 1930s. It wasn't until 1938 that the Church changed course and finally allowed the rites to be practiced by Chinese Christians.

Four

___

Golden Elephants

DURING THE GOLDEN AGE OF BANDA ACEH IN THE EARLY 1600S,
DAYLONG FEASTS WERE HELD IN SHALLOW RUNNING STREAMS
AND CROWDS WATCHED FIERCE ANIMAL FIGHTS. HERE ON THE
NORTHERN TIP OF SUMATRA THE TYRANT ISKANDAR MUDA
RULED WITH AN IRON HAND. SOON EUROPEAN TRADERS
LOOKED ELSEWHERE ON THE ISLAND TO BUY PEPPER.

•

*"The Situation of the Port of Achen is admirable, the Anchorage excellent,
and a healthful Air all along the Coast."*
—JESUIT FATHER DE PRÉMARE, FEBRUARY 17, 1699

In the early sixteenth century, the newly conquered city of Malacca offered the Portuguese a unique chance to tighten their grip on the Indian Ocean pepper trade. Strategically, Malacca controlled commerce between the Indian Ocean and the China Seas; just across the Strait of Malacca, tantalizingly close, the vast island of Sumatra, the westernmost part of the fabled East Indies, beckoned.

Sumatra spreads across the equator, its northern half reaching toward mainland Asia and its southern half stretching toward Java. Towering mountains carpeted with lush tropical forests hug its west coast, and from these mountains innumerable cascading rivers flow into the pepper-rich central highlands. Along these waterways, natives brought their precious cargo of pepper to foreign traders, who had long been drawn to the island's marshy eastern shores on the Strait of Malacca. As early as the tenth century, the Chinese had sailed to Palembang in southeast Sumatra seeking the tailed cubeb pepper, (not black pepper) to flavor their food and improve (as they believed) their sex lives. In the fourteenth century, they also sailed to the northeastern part of the island to purchase pepper in the newly established port city of Pasai. Like Malacca, this port city was Islamic, a result of Muslim traders, who had been plying the Indian Ocean for hundreds of years, establishing themselves in these and other ports in Southeast Asia in the fourteenth and fifteenth centuries.

Soon after conquering Malacca in 1511, the Portuguese found themselves embroiled in the courtly intrigues of the Malaysian world, where rival rulers jockeyed for position and occasionally usurped one another. The Portuguese were generally reluctant to intervene unless their trade was threatened, and they usually did not understand the politics that led to these conflicts. One of their interventions, an attempt to mediate a conflict between Pasai and Pidië, another port city lying along Sumatra's northeastern shores, backfired badly. Instead of welcoming the Portuguese mediators, the people of northern Sumatra united under a new sultanate—Aceh, which would become the most-feared power in the Strait. And Banda Aceh, the site of the sultan's palace, would become one of the world's great pepper ports and a celebrated center of Islamic learning.

Known mostly in the West today because of the catastrophic tsunami in 2004 that killed 118,000 people in northern Indonesia, Banda Aceh was at the height of its power in the sixteenth and early seventeenth centuries. Called Achin by the English, the town was brimming with everyday pleasures, from the banks of its clean flowing rivers filled with bathers to its bustling marketplaces offering aromatic spices and diverse goods. The journals of foreign visitors provide glimpses of its wealth and beauty, and their delight seems genuine. After the filth and misery of ocean travel, Aceh must have appeared as a kind of paradise. Surrounded by water and trees, the town was wrapped in a green mist, a tropical verdure that extended far beyond the bounds of the town to the countryside. Residents enjoyed unusually good health, and pepper and gold abounded. The port "At first appeared to me like the landscapes framed by the Imagination of some painter or poet . . . whatever is most delightful in a County Prospect . . . ," observed a French Jesuit named De Prémare who visited Aceh in 1699. "The gold of Achin is thought to be the purest in the world," he wrote.

In the sixteenth century, Aceh's might surpassed the strength of Pasai and Pidië combined, and even the Portuguese had to acknowledge its supremacy as a pepper port. Aceh attracted the Muslim traders who could no longer do business along the southwest coast of India or in Malacca because of the Portuguese. In Aceh these traders purchased pepper and other spices, camphor, as well as gold. In the early seventeenth century, the Dutch and English followed when the market for pepper exploded in Europe.

Acehnese marketplaces also offered large amounts of betel, the chewing gum of Southeast Asia that is mixed with lime and areca nuts; betel grew well in Sumatra. Precious nutmeg and cloves reached the port city via the narrow Sunda Strait separating Sumatra and Java. Using this route, the Acehnese had found a way to ship these spices to Sumatra, avoiding the Portuguese in Malacca altogether. The Sunda Strait was where Krakatau erupted in 1883, killing 36,000 people in Java and Sumatra.

Aceh's reach extended throughout the Indian Ocean, the East Indies, and the China Seas. It was the most accessible port in the East Indies, an entrepôt where cloves and nutmeg from the remote Moluccas and Banda Islands and pepper grown in Sumatra and Java could be purchased by foreign traders, and where the fine woven cloths of Gujarat, Bengal, and the Coromandel Coast of southeast India could be sold to the Acehnese. The textiles of India, much in demand in Indonesia, were widely traded for pepper. In the early seventeenth century, Aceh was described by an English merchant as a port that "lieth well to answere to the trade of all Bengala, Java, and the Moluccas, and all China . . . to the decrease and diminishing of all Portugals trade, and their great forces in the Indies."

The first English sailor to record his impressions of Sumatra was the brilliant Arctic navigator John Davis, who also piloted ships to the East Indies for the Dutch at the end of the seventeenth century, an unusual job for an Englishman. The island of Sumatra, he wrote in his journal, appeared to be "a garden of pleasure." The land was "pleasing and fertile. . . . Of pepper they have exceeding plentie, Gardens of a mile square." Sumatra also had "plentie of Gold and Copper Mines, divers kinds of Gummes, Balmes, and many kinds of Drugges [spices], and Indico." Like many of the European men who traveled to the East Indies in the seventeenth century, Davis's observations read like an advertisement for trade, an invitation to bring more ships to the far corners of the globe.

In Aceh, Davis encountered a thriving, prosperous port, packed with merchandise, in an unusually hospitable climate, where "the Ayre is temperate and wholsome, having everie morning a fruitfull dew, or small raine." The spacious port city, he observed, was "built in a wood, so that wee could not see a house till we were upon it.

Neither could wee goe into any place, but we found houses, and great concourse of people: so that I think the town spreads over the whole land. . . . I saw three great marketplaces, which are every day frequented as fairs with all kinds of merchandise to sell." Dwellings were spread among forests of bamboo, banana, coconut, and pineapple trees.

In 1598 Davis served as the chief pilot for the second Dutch expedition to Indonesia. It was led by Cornelius Houteman, who was infamous; his pioneering voyage three years earlier was an orgy of destruction. Offering an early example of Dutch brutality that would be repeated often in the centuries ahead, Houteman's well-armed ships, financed by a group called the Compagnie van Verre (Company of Far Distant Lands, one of the companies that subsequently formed the VOC) bombarded Bantam, the rich pepper port in northeastern Java, and other ports, and he and his men executed prisoners in gruesome rampages. Although scurvy and other diseases killed more than two-thirds of his crew—only eighty-seven out of 240 men survived the twenty-eight-month voyage, an abysmal death toll even by the low standards of the late sixteenth century—Houteman was sent out on another expedition because he proved that Dutch ships could sail to Asia and return with pepper.

When the ships on the second voyage under Houteman's command reached Aceh after a grueling two-year voyage, the Englishman Davis noticed "foure Barks riding in the Bay, three of Arabia, and one of Pegu [Burma], that came to lade Pepper." During their three-month stay, the aging Sultan Ala'ud-din Ri'ayat Syah took a measure of the strange men who had ventured so far from their homes to buy pepper. This wily, tyrannical sultan, who rose to power in 1588, did not know of the land where the Dutch came from, but to everyone's surprise he had heard of England. While wining and dining the visitors, the sultan made it known that he wanted to meet an

Englishman, a request that surely was not welcomed by the Dutch. When the sultan persisted, the Dutch relented and allowed Davis to meet the sultan.

Davis described the ruler as "a lustie man, but exceeding grosse and fat," aged one hundred year "as they say." The sultan asked a lot of questions about England, and especially about "the Queene, of her Basha's, and how she could hold warres with so great a King as the Spaniard? (for he thinketh that Europe is all Spanish)." Apparently, news of England's victory over the Spanish Armada in 1588 had reached Sumatra through the far-flung network of traders who visited Aceh. (The remark about all of Europe being Spanish is understandable, since Portugal had relinquished its crown to Spain in 1580, the Netherlands was under Spanish rule, and the Dutch and the English had yet to make a mark in maritime Asia. Portugal did not free itself from the Spanish yoke until 1640, and the Netherlands finally freed itself from Spain in 1648.) Davis's responses pleased the sultan. One month later, however, the sultan laid a trap for his unwary visitors, and Davis and a handful of men were lucky to escape with their lives and one of their ships. Cornelius Houteman wasn't so fortunate. He was killed by poison and his brother taken prisoner.

The sultanate of Aceh ruled over northern Sumatra with an iron hand, and in its prime controlled ports far down the east and west coasts of the island as well as villages in the central highlands of Minangkabau where gold was mined. Other sultanates, especially Johore in the southern Malay Peninsula, feared Aceh's territorial ambitions, and warfare broke out regularly among all of the rulers in the Strait of Malacca. Alliances shifted and sometimes Islamic sultanates allied themselves with the Portuguese to fight Aceh. Whenever the Portuguese in Malacca felt their trade threatened, they attacked neighboring Johore and the kingdom of Aceh across the

Strait, although they did not try to capture the city of Banda Aceh itself after an attempt failed in 1521. The Portuguese launched more than fifteen invasions against these sultanates. Meanwhile, large Acehnese war fleets besieged Portuguese Malacca at least four times in the sixteenth century, and the Acehnese even called on the faraway Turks to help their cause. Aceh continued its campaign against Malacca in the early decades of the seventeenth century.

In the late seventeenth century, Banda Aceh was still a thriving port, but the power of the sultanate had diminished under a series of female sultanas. The wide-ranging adventurer William Dampier spent six months in Aceh in 1688 after becoming shipwrecked. He commented on the generally high standard of living and on the continual influx of foreign visitors. The houses, Dampier observed, were built on poles in the same fashion as those he had seen in Mindanao (in the Phillipines), but in Aceh, "by reason of their gold mines, and the frequent resort of strangers, they are richer, and live in greater plenty." He described the city as seated on the banks of a river, near the northwest end of the island, and about two miles from the sea. "This town," he wrote, "consists of 7 or 8000 houses and in it there are always a great many merchant-strangers, viz. English, Dutch, Danes, Portuguese, Chinese, Guzarats, etc. The houses of this city are generally larger than those I saw at Mindinao, and better furnished with household goods."

Foreign traders flocked to Aceh to buy pepper. The peppercorn was the first cash crop to be exported by Southeast Asia. Sometime during the fifteenth century, Muslim traders first brought black pepper from India to northern Sumatra. Historians aren't sure of the precise date, but there is no doubt that the black pepper vine flourished in Sumatra, as well as in Vietnam, the Malay Peninsula, and northern Java.

The plant was easily cultivated in well-drained tropical soils cleared of forest, and by 1500 black pepper was traded in port cities along the northeastern coast of Sumatra, especially in Pidë and Pasai, and in parts of Malaysia. At first pepper gardens weren't common in Sumatra, but cultivation extended south and inland as consumption of black pepper rose in Europe. In the sixteenth century, pepper gardens proliferated along parts of the west coast of the island.

In 1598 Davis described an abundance of pepper in northern Sumatra growing "like hops from a planted root, and windeth about a stake set by it until it grow to a great bushie tree." Soon after the market for pepper surged in the early seventeenth century, pepper gardens spread almost everywhere in Sumatra, which became the world's largest supplier of pepper. Even India imported pepper from Sumatra, where the spice was less costly to produce, when pepper was in especially high demand.

The Dutch and English entered the pepper trade at the beginning of the seventeenth century, causing pepper production to expand. Although the Portuguese still played a role in the trade, their impact diminished. In the sixteenth century, they had kept the price of pepper artificially high by keeping supplies deliberately low. As supplies of pepper increased, the price went down and it became even more popular.

The northern Europeans hastened the development of pepper gardens in Sumatra, which became a virtual pepper mill. Pepper was transported from all of its shores—Aceh in the north, Jambi and Palembang in the east, Priaman and a host of smaller ports in the west, and the Lampongs in the south. Most of the island's pepper was grown in the central highlands, which is penetrated by interconnecting, meandering waterways. Natives brought pepper by boat from upstream villages to downstream ports twice a year. No European could navigate these waterways. When the pepper harvests came in, hundreds of lightweight rafts carrying thousands of bags of pepper would emerge noiselessly in the early morning hours in the ports where Chinese junks, Portuguese carracks, and Dutch and English East Indiamen awaited.

The spread of pepper in Sumatra, the world's sixth-largest island, mirrored the seemingly insatiable demand for the spice in Europe and the expanding market for Indonesian pepper in China. The total quantity of pepper shipped to Europe reached a peak of some fourteen million pounds in the 1670s, nearly double the amount from earlier decades. By this time, pepper was mainly shipped via the Cape of Good Hope, which had finally replaced the traditional Muslim trade route through the Levant. Total exports of pepper from Southeast Asia ebbed somewhat by the turn of the eighteenth century, but soared to thirty million pounds by the turn of the nineteenth century and to fifty million by 1900. Some 80 percent of this pepper came from Sumatra. Through the years, Sumatrans adapted to the market by clearing more forest for pepper gardens, and moving their gardens once the soils were exhausted. Historian Anthony Reid estimates that roughly 7,600 square kilometers, or about 1.6 percent of the land, were cleared of forest to make way for pepper during the centuries when Sumatra was the leading producer of the spice. Today, grasslands cover the land where pepper gardens once flourished.

The craze for black pepper in Europe transformed the fortunes of Sumatra.

On February 13, 1601, four ships—the *Red Dragon*, the *Hector*, the *Susan*, and the *Ascension*—set out from Woolwich on the Thames River bound for Aceh. Led by the six-hundred-ton *Dragon*, the small fleet was the first of the English East India Company. James

Lancaster, a respected seaman who had fought against the Spanish Armada and had successfully raided Portuguese ships in a Brazilian port, was in charge. But until then, neither Lancaster nor any other English captain had much luck charting a safe course to the East Indies. An expedition Lancaster had joined ten years earlier met with disaster, and he and his surviving crew had been brought back as castaways to England. In 1596 another attempt was made under a different captain, but all the boats and men were lost. Meanwhile, the Dutch, financed by companies that would soon unite as the VOC, had successfully reached Bantam, the pepper port on the northeastern end of Java, and left merchants there and at Aceh and other ports in Indonesia.

More than twenty Dutch ships had been outfitted for Asia, and those that returned brought back fully laden cargoes of pepper and other spices. Probably all of the Dutch merchants and captains had studied Jan Huyghen van Linschoten's enormous *Itinerario*, published in 1596, the fruit of this Dutchman's years of service in Goa, India. A comprehensive merchant and seafaring guide to Asia, Linschoten's tome enticed traders with vivid accounts of abundant pepper along the Malabar Coast of India, and Java especially, where ". . . there is much pepper, and it is better than that from India or Malabar, so much that yearly one should be able to load four or five thousand quintals of pepper, Portuguese weight."

The fear that the Dutch would dominate the pepper trade once again spurred English merchants in London to press their cause with Queen Elizabeth for an expedition to the East Indies, despite the dismal track record of previous voyages. She finally agreed in 1600, and the East India Company was chartered. The merchants raised money for the expedition, and Lancaster became one of the first directors of the fledgling mercantile company, which would later embody the British Empire. He wisely hired John Davis as the pilot on the *Dragon*. At the time, Davis was the only living English navigator who had been to the East Indies. Although he is mentioned very briefly in the surviving narratives of the voyage, Davis must have been indispensable.

The voyage didn't have an auspicious beginning. Lancaster's fleet lingered for weeks in the Thames and the Downs (an anchorage off the southeastern coast of England) because the small, unstable ships could not maneuver without favorable winds. Their progress was stalled again around the equator by adverse winds, although they did overtake a Portuguese ship and plunder her, taking away a "hundred sixe and fortie buts of wine, an hundred threescore and sixteene jarres of oyle, twelve barrels of oyle, and five and fiftie hogsheads and fats [vats] of meale, which was a great helpe to us in the whole voyage after. The generall divided these victuals indifferently to all the ships; to every one his proportion without partialitie." Nevertheless, the crew paid a heavy price for the delays. It took seven months for them to reach Table Bay in South Africa, and by that time scurvy had taken its grisly toll. The surviving men were so weak they could barely handle the sails or throw down an anchor. Merchants, who considered themselves above sailors, had to pitch in. In three ships, merchants took turns with the topsails, a job normally reserved for common mariners.

The only ship largely unaffected by the disease was the *Dragon*. Lancaster, a veteran of long voyages to the tropics, had taken along "certain bottles of the juice of limons [lemons]" and gave "three spoonfuls each morning" to each man on the ship. By the time the fleet left Table Bay at the end of October, the death toll on the other three ships was horrific—one hundred and five men had died, or more than one-quarter of the crew. But the survivors had rested, and food was obtained for the ongoing voyage from the natives the Englishmen met. Unfortunately, Lancaster's cure for scurvy didn't carry forward on other East India Company expeditions.

Although the ships encountered adverse winds after passing the Cape, they were anchored safely in Antongil Bay near Madagascar by Christmas Day. Here Lancaster traded for provisions while disease claimed the lives of twenty more men in his small fleet. In March 1602, the ships left the bay, and in May reached the Nicobar Islands. In June, sixteen months after leaving England, they finally sailed into Aceh. Scurvy and dysentery had taken many lives, but none of the ships had to be scuttled for lack of crew.

The English found some "16 to 18 ships from many nations" anchored in Aceh, including vessels from Gujarat, Bengal, and Calicut, Pegu, and "Patanyes" (Patani, a port on the east coast of Malaysia). In precolonial, preimperial days, the English were just another group of traders endeavoring to do business with pepper-rich Sumatra. They came as supplicants bearing a letter. Lancaster was entrusted with a lengthy handwritten missive from Queen Elizabeth I to the "great and mighty King of Achem." The rambling letter, laced with broadsides against the Spanish and Portuguese, the enemy of the English as well as the Dutch, asked for permission to buy the commodities of their land. Nearing the end of her long reign, Elizabeth knew that trade in such a faraway place was a gamble, so she sought to win over the sultan with flattery and endearments. Her letter reflects the mind of a shrewd monarch who acknowledges the paucity of spices and other goods in her own lands compared with the wealth of such products in another, and she is well aware of the hazards of obtaining them.

Elizabeth's letter is a remarkable document that begins with a rationale for trade based on the premise that God decreed that the "good things of his creation," are dispersed "into the most remote places of the universal world . . . he having so ordained that the one land may have need of the other; and thereby, not only breed intercourse and exchange of their merchandise and fruits, which do so superabound in some countries and want in others, but also engender love and friendship between all men, a thing naturally divine." Ironically, the letter frequently states that love will flow from trade. To underscore the notion that the English are trustworthy, she solemnly promises that the dealings of the English merchants "shall be true, and their conversation sure, and we hope that they will give so good proof thereof, that this beginning shall be a perpetual confirmation of love between our subjects on both parts, by carrying from us such things and merchandise as you have need of here." The wily queen also assures the Acehnese king that the English will be much better trading partners than the Spanish and Portuguese. She notes: "So that your highness shall be very well served and better contented than you have heretofore been with the Portugals and Spaniards, our enemies . . ."

Soon after Lancaster's little fleet arrived in Aceh, the sultan sent two Dutch merchants to the ships. Luckily, the aged Sultan Ala'uddin was still reigning and was still interested in the English queen, as he showed during his conversation with John Davis three years earlier. The Dutch merchants told Lancaster that indeed the Queen of England was famous in Aceh for her victories over the Spanish king.

Apparently, Davis's interview with the sultan had made a lasting impression. Lancaster promptly sent John Middleton, the captain of the *Hector*, and four or five others to the sultan to ask for an audience to deliver his letter. The meeting went well. The sultan kindly entertained the men and gladly granted their request. It isn't known why the sultan was so favorably disposed toward these particular English traders, but certainly the enduring enmity of the Acehnese for the Portuguese might have played a role.

On the third day, Lancaster went ashore accompanied by thirty of his men. They met the Dutch merchants, who took them to their house, where they waited for word from the sultan. When the sultan's envoy arrived, Lancaster refused to give him the letter, explaining that it was the custom of his country to deliver such important missives himself. The envoy looked carefully at the seal of the letter, wrote down the queen's name, and quietly left.

After a while, the Englishmen were startled by a great noise from many trumpets and drums. They looked outside and saw six huge elephants and a large crowd of people approaching. His transportation to the palace had arrived. "The biggest of these elephants was about thirteen or fourteen feet high, which had a small castle, like a coach upon his back [a howdah], covered with crimson velvet. . . . In the middle thereof was a great basin of gold, and a piece of silk exceedingly wrought to cover it, under which her majesty's letter was put." Lancaster was mounted upon another elephant and he and his men, and the great crowd of townsfolk, went off to the sultan's court. The letter had become an occasion for a merry procession.

At the court Lancaster delivered the letter and some presents from the queen: a silver basin and cup; fine daggers; an embroidered belt to hang a sword in; and a plume of feathers, the gift most pleasing to the sultan. Then the festivities began with a banquet where meat was served on golden dishes. Even though Islam forbids wine, the sultan drank a rice wine called arak during the meal. This wine was "as strong as any of our aquavita: a little will serve to bring one asleep." With the sultan's permission, Lancaster diluted his own wine with water. Afterward, "damsels" danced to music, "and these women were richly attired and adorned with bracelets and jewels; and this they account a great favor, for these are not usually seen of any but such as the king will greatly honor."

Whether the merchant who had witnessed these events felt anything as he watched these women dance, we will never know. Like most merchants and captains who kept journals, this anonymous diarist kept his feelings to himself, though he dutifully noted what had transpired. All of the captains and other ranking crew members of the Company's voyages were instructed to document their experiences to benefit others on later expeditions. These men knew that their journals weren't private, and they carefully avoided emotional embellishments.

Lancaster left the feast carrying presents from the Sultan Ala'uddin Syah: a fine white calico robe "richly wrought with gold"; an ornate Turkish belt; and two creeses, the distinctive daggers worn everywhere in Aceh. The first official encounter between the English East India Company and the sultanate of Aceh had ended with a satisfying exchange of gifts. The gold threaded calico robe must have been especially beautiful.

Sultan Ala'ud-din soon granted the English request for free entry into the port, along with custom-free trade and other provisions, but the crafty sultan did not allow the English to build a factory—a trading agency, and warehouse—in Aceh, nor did he sign an exclusive trade treaty with the English. Perhaps the sultan had heard through the Indian Ocean grapevine of Muslim traders that the Portuguese had set up factories along the southwest coast of India and had used these facilities to establish territorial strongholds. His reluctance to afford foreigners a permanent base of operations in Aceh was prophetic: The northernmost region of Sumatra remained an independent kingdom until almost the end of the nineteenth century.

Although the English were disappointed with the sultan's decision, they could not afford to belabor their case and began the business of buying pepper, the reason why they had traveled to the East Indies. Two problems immediately arose: There wasn't enough pepper to fill their ships, and the spice was far more expensive than what John Davis had told them it would be. Worried, Lancaster hatched a plan with the sultan to plunder Portuguese ships in the Strait of Malacca to find additional goods for his ships. Before sailing, Lancaster dispatched the *Susan* to Priaman, a pepper port on the west coast of Sumatra, and he left some merchants in Aceh to continue buying the spice that was available.

In early September, the *Dragon, Ascension,* and *Hector,* along with a pinnace and a Dutch ship that wanted to join the adventure, set out for the Strait of Malacca. Reaching the waterway, they came upon a large Portuguese carrack, the *Santo Antonio,* bound from India to Malacca. Ordnance was exchanged, but the big ship couldn't fend off her many pursuers, and the Portuguese surrendered. She was loaded with calicoes, rice, and other goods, and carried more than six hundred men, women, and children. The English unloaded the prized calicoes, which were eagerly sought in the Indonesian archipelago and could be traded for pepper, and the rest of the goods, but left the passengers and crew alone. Lancaster returned to Aceh in late October, where he found that his merchants had been well treated and had bought enough pepper, cinnamon, and cloves to almost fill the *Ascension.*

The old ruler was overjoyed with Lancaster's "good success" against the Portuguese. He even teased the English navigator about forgetting the most important piece of business—procuring "a fair Portugal maiden" for the sultan. Lancaster replied that "there was none so worthy that merited to be presented." This reply elicited a big smile from the sultan, who said: "If there be anything here in my kingdom may pleasure thee, I would be glad to gratifie thy goodwill." It isn't likely that Lancaster took him up on his offer. From the narrative of the voyage, it appears that Lancaster was a practical man entirely absorbed in lading his ships and returning safely to England. He gave the sultan presents from the Portuguese booty and said good-bye.

In early November, the *Ascension* was sent back to London, and the *Dragon* and *Hector* sailed south along Sumatra's west coast for Bantam in Java, where the Englishmen heard that pepper could be bought at a much more reasonable price than in Aceh. Before leaving Sumatra, they stopped in Priaman, where the *Susan* was lading pepper. The pepper here, they learned, was cultivated in the interior of Sumatra in a region called Minangkabau. The English merchants also heard about a "good store of gold, in dust and small graines, which they wash out of the sands of rivers, after the great flouds of raine that fall from the mountaines, from whence it is brought."

The *Susan* was sent back to England, and Lancaster sailed ahead with the *Dragon* and *Hector* to Bantam, which they reached on December 16. They shot off a great bombard to announce their arrival, and went to see a boy king and his entourage of noblemen. Lancaster produced another letter from Queen Elizabeth, and the parties quickly came to an agreement allowing the English to buy great amounts of pepper at very reasonable prices. By February 1603, the two ships were fully loaded and ready to depart. Meanwhile, John Middleton, the captain of the *Hector*, had fallen sick and died, which was a great blow because he was well liked and came from a distinguished family of seamen who played leading roles in the early history of the East India Company. When the captain aboard the *Susan* died, Henry Middleton, John's brother, assumed the post and sailed the ship back to London. Henry would later return to the East Indies for the Company. Lancaster left three merchants in Bantam, who were to set up a factory to provide lading for the ships' return.

The voyage back to London was as treacherous as the outgoing journey. The *Hector* and *Dragon* got caught in a horrific storm somewhere south of Madagascar, causing leaks for the remainder of the voyage. The men barely had time to gather their rattled wits when another huge storm broke in early May. This violent maelstrom shook the rudder loose from the ironworks on the *Dragon*. With her rudder lost, she was at the complete mercy of the ocean, carried wherever by the wind. At some point the ship was nine or twelve miles from the Cape, but the winds pushed her south, where hail, snow, and sleet brought more misery. Meanwhile, the *Hector* remained close by. To save themselves, the desperate men on the rudderless *Dragon* wanted to be put on the *Hector*, but Lancaster refused to abandon the ship. After several solutions to the ship's predicament proved useless, Lancaster told the captain of the *Hector* to leave the *Dragon* and sail on.

But the next day, the *Hector* was still in sight; the men on the ship would not leave Lancaster stranded in the ocean. Within a few days, the carpenter aboard the *Dragon* managed to salvage the rudder, and with the help of the *Hector*'s men, the *Dragon* was finally able to sail. On June 6 they passed the Tropic of Capricorn, and ten days later they reached the island of Saint Helena, some 1,150 miles off the west coast of Africa in the southern Atlantic Ocean, where they could finally come ashore and replenish their water and food.

The *Dragon* and *Hector* arrived in England in September 1603, but it was politically and economically a different country from the one Lancaster had left. During his voyage, Queen Elizabeth had died and James I had ascended to the throne. Plague had broken out and the market for pepper was stagnant. The Company merchants couldn't sell their pepper on the continent because of Dutch competition, and they discovered that their new sovereign had a great store of pepper, probably as a result of a raid on a Portuguese carrack a year earlier. The crown's pepper had to be sold first. Consequently, it took years for the Company's merchants to sell their pepper.

The long voyage around the Cape of Good Hope to the far side of the Indian Ocean had cost many lives. Only half of Lancaster's original crew of 480 men survived. The death rate hadn't improved much since da Gama had rounded the Cape more than a hundred years earlier. Nevertheless, Lancaster proved that English ships could bring home the pepper—his four ships brought back one million pounds—and plunder Portuguese ships in the Indian Ocean. He was knighted for his services and, despite the glut, the East India Company made plans for another expedition to the East Indies. The English had entered the pepper trade.

Only a few years later, the Company sought the exclusive right to import pepper into England, a request that the English merchants did not make initially to Queen Elizabeth when they asked permission to found the Company. Once again, the merchants used the Dutch to make their argument. They noted in a petition to the king that Dutch competition would lead to its downfall. ". . . [the Dutch] will so watch their times as they will hurt us either by affording to our people bad pepper better cheap, to beat down the price of our better pepper . . . or by some other device as by experience we daily find." In November 1609, the king issued a proclamation forbidding anyone from buying pepper except from the East India Company. With a lock on the domestic market, the Company went on to develop a valuable and robust reexport market to continental Europe, a far larger market than England by itself. The Company had its foundation commodity, a spice used by everyone, and it also served quite nicely as ballast in the East Indiamen returning to Europe from Asia.

Treasure hunters today wouldn't find many valuable items in the wrecks of pepper ships. In 1606 a Portuguese carrack returning with a cargo of peppercorns from Cochin, India, went down near Lisbon, sending out a long plume of black pepper, which people along the coast risked their lives to salvage. When the wreck was excavated in

1993, archeologists found a few silver and gold objects, Chinese porcelain, and other items all buried underneath a thick layer of black peppercorns.

Lancaster's welcome banquet in Aceh set the stage for envoys in the years to come: Foreign merchants often received a royal welcome. Letters would be placed ceremoniously in golden basins atop elephants. Envoys would proceed to the palace as part of a parade. Great feasts would follow, and perhaps an animal fight would be staged for the visitors. This was a time of wealth and sensuous pleasures, of blood sport and pageantry, when the power of the Acehnese sultanate was at its height under the rule of Iskandar Muda, who came to power in 1607. He was the grandson of Sultan Ala'ud-din Syah, whom Lancaster had befriended.

Iskandar Muda made Aceh even more powerful than his grandfather had by uniting the central growing regions in Sumatra. He set the terms for a large portion of the pepper sales in northern Sumatra, and merchants could not proceed to many other ports in Sumatra without his permission. By the early seventeenth century, the pepper gardens around Aceh were already becoming exhausted, and merchant ships had to visit other ports, such as Priaman and Tiku on the west coast, to obtain additional pepper.

This sultan wasn't easily cowed by the brass cannons of the Europeans. Iskandar Muda used his own heavily armed ships to bring his pepper to India to sell at the highest prices. In 1622 he even shut the Dutch and English out of the Acehnese pepper market, which included the important west coast ports.

Gold was another source of Aceh's fabulous wealth—the raw material for the gold dishes mentioned frequently in merchants' journals. In the central region of Sumatra, gold was sieved from rivers and mined in the hills of Minangkabau. Lancaster heard about river gold when the *Hector* and *Dragon* stopped in Priaman to meet the *Susan*. Iskandar Muda was said to have one hundred bahars (about 41,200 pounds) of gold and employ three hundred goldsmiths. He also was reported to have at his disposal thousands of women who formed part of his female guard. In the nineteenth century, Aceh's fierce women would play a role in defending the kingdom's northwestern shores against the United States, one of the newcomers to the pepper trade.

A tyrant, Iskandar Muda annihilated anyone who got in the way of his plans for expanding his domain or enriching himself. Far-reaching raids by his great fleet of ships struck fear in the hearts of Malaysians everywhere. On the Malay Peninsula, he conquered the cities of Pahang in 1618 and Kedah in 1619, and Perak on the island of Banka, valued for its tin, in 1620. Considering his mighty fleet, armed with cannon, it is surprising that he never secured Malacca or its neighbor Johore, though he tried in 1629.

Iskandar Muda assembled an enormous fleet of some 236 ships with nearly twenty thousand men and sent the great armada to Malacca to assault his longtime enemy, the Portuguese. The flotilla of thirty-six large galleys and other Acehnese ships landed in early July off of Malacca and laid siege. For as far as the eye could see, wrote a Portuguese observer, "nothing but the ships covered the sea . . ." Nevertheless, the Portuguese had prepared and put up a valiant fight, even though they were vastly outnumbered. In August, the Portuguese were obliged to burn down the convent of Madre de Deus, lying outside the city walls, after an Achenese assault, but the fortified walls of Malacca were not breached. The tides of war began to turn in October, when the Portuguese, aided by five relief ships that had come from Sri Lanka, stockaded the mouth of a river about four miles from the city, where almost the entire Acehnese fleet had put in. The Acehnese ships were harried by an almost continuous bombardment from which there was no escape.

At the end of November, the sultan of Johore, an ally of the Portuguese, arrived with some sixty boats and thousands of warriors to reinforce the blockade, causing some four thousand Achenese to flee into the jungle, which was so rugged that the Portuguese did not send men in pursuit. "They [the Acehnese] left the whole of their fleet bottled up in the river with many cannons great and small, and many sick, and some spoil which the lord governor allowed the soldiers to sack," wrote the Portuguese Captain-General of Malacca António Pinto da Fonseca. In the following months, some Acehnese men emerged from the jungle to surrender to the Portuguese. The great sea battle diminished the ability of Aceh to wage war, and Iskandar Muda never again assaulted Malacca.

The punishments meted out during the sultan's long reign were particularly brutal. Cornish merchant Peter Mundy visited Aceh in 1637 and 1638, and he saw people without limbs, noses, and lips, and "privities" (genitals). "These maimed and dismembred people wee saw some about the towne," he wrote, "the stumpes off their legges putt into bigge bamboes or canes, wherewith they goe as on stilts." Before he died, Iskandar Muda had all of his male heirs killed. His son-in-law Iskandar Thani, who succeeded him, proved equally brutal during his brief reign. When he first came to power in 1638, the new ruler suspected treason and had four hundred people put to death in "inhumaine and bloudy executions," which Mundy described in his journal. He wrote of "sundry sorts off exquisite torments, viz., Divers Cutt in peeces; others sawne in 2, being made fast to tymbers, and as the wood is cutt soe goeth the saw through their Bodies by little and little; some hung on Iron hookes by the heeles, stretched wide abroad, and Molten lead powred into the Fundamentts of the Men and privities of the weomen to cause them [to] Conffesse where their Masters or husbands treasure lay." Could any man endure molten lead in his throat or any woman molten lead in her vagina?

The rampages of these rulers caused fear and disgust among the Acehnese. After Iskandar Thani died, the leading chiefs of Aceh decided that they did not want any more bloody executions, and during the remainder of the seventeenth century, from 1641 to 1699, they placed four women in succession on the throne of Aceh.

Yet the Acehnese witnessed some joyous spectacles during the rule of the bellicose Iskandar Muda and his son-in-law. These Acehnese sultans staged opulent feasts, parades, blood sport, and hunting, and their subjects were well aware of these activities and even joined in on occasion. During Iskandar Muda's nearly thirty-year reign, royal feasts and ceremonial processions and the events staged for foreign visitors were quite elaborate. He amused his visitors with lavish banquets that offered hundreds of plates of food and enormous quantities of rice wine. He impressed his own people as well with his wealth and might by staging royal marriage celebrations that lasted for months, daylong water feasts and, most notably, animal fights involving elephants, buffalos, and rams. The forests of northern Sumatra were filled with the sounds of horns and the roars of elephants when the sultanate was at the height of its glory.

A man's wealth was measured by how many elephants he owned, and naturally Sultan Iskandar Muda made sure that he had more than anyone else. He was believed to have some nine hundred elephants, and each had a name. Most of the captive elephants in northern Sumatra belonged to him, and the sultan often sent elephants to envoys during their stay in Aceh, a considerable honor. At the time of his reign, elephants roamed widely in the forests of northern Sumatra. He had a passion for hunting elephant, a fact well known to foreign traders wishing to procure pepper in Aceh.

Not surprisingly, elephants figured prominently in the extraordinary royal processions that occurred in Aceh during the peak of the sultanate, when European traders vied for the privilege of buying pepper in the port city and along the west coast of Sumatra. These elaborate parades often incorporated a mind-boggling assortment of richly draped elephants, horses, noblemen, lancers, retainers, slaves, and thousands of soldiers. The sultan himself would ride on an elephant fitted with a howdah (saddle) of pure gold.

During one of the major feasts of Islam in April 1637, Peter Mundy witnessed a huge noisy procession of elephants and men going to the mosque from the palace during the rule of Sultan Iskandar Thani, who owned a thousand captive elephants. He described in great detail this marvelous parade, and it is worthwhile to glimpse the festivities through his eyes to get a sense of these royal processions: ". . . Then came a squadron of Elephantts with certain things like little low turretts on their backes, and in each of them a souldier in redde with a launce in his hand standing uprightt, a shash [turban] on his head part gold . . . ," Mundy wrote. "The first rancke of Elephantts (they going by 4 in a rank) had each of them 2 greatt swords, or rather long Iron Sithes Fastned to their tusks. . . . Next after these came another Number of Elephantts with little turretts or Cradles on their backes allsoe, somewhatt high railed, whereon were placed smalle gunnes . . . with a man to manage them. Affter these other elephantts with more turretts with 2 men in each . . . then other Elephantts with long flags . . . Affter these came a Multitude with gunnes, and then as many with very long pikes . . . Amongst all were led many good horses with ritch saddles and Furniture; then a guard of Eunuches on horsebacke withoutt saddles . . . Then commeth the King on a greatte and stately Elephantt, richly adorned and covered all downe to the Feete. . . . Hee was mounted alofft on a ritch seatt which was covered overhead with a very ritch high Double Pavilion or arche . . .

"Att his Issuing Forth the Musick played, some of them by turnes and others alltogether . . . all the afforesaid musick Discordantt, Clamorous, and full of Noise. The Marche was alsoe very confuzed and on heapes, there beeing scar[c]e room and tyme For order. However, it was all rare and straunge to behold, *viz.*, the Multitude of greatt Elephantts accoutred and armed after severall Manners, Weapons and Ornamentts, costly Furniture, ett., there beeing Nere as Many More Elephantts allsoe fitted for this shew (thatt could nott Marche with the rest For lack of roome) which stood in sundry places by while the others passed."

Once again Mundy provides a clearly written, eyewitness account of life in Aceh. He must have spent a good deal of time watching the jostling crowd of men and elephants pass, although he doesn't mention how long it took for the parade to reach the mosque. Mundy drew the procession, and he even included the hordes of onlookers at its edges. His drawings are like postcards from the seventeenth century.

The next day the sultan invited Mundy and other foreigners to an animal fight featuring elephants. Nearly one hundred and fifty were arranged in a circle, and pairs of furious elephants fought in the middle of the ring. Mundy wrote that the elephants were: "Doing their uttermost to hurt each other and Drive backe by shooving and setting their huge Massy bodies one against the other, soe thatt one or the other Must give ground att last."

Elephants were part of the blood sports enjoyed by the Acehnese, who seemed to have plenty of leisure time on their hands. Among the other Englishmen who observed animal fights in Aceh was William Keeling, an extraordinary seaman who was only twenty-four years old when he served as captain of a ship for the Company's second voyage to the East Indies in 1604. He saw a contest of a hundred elephants and described the fight of buffalos as ". . . full of strength and sleight, seeming therein to have a kind of discourse, and was indeed the most pleasing fight twixt beasts I ever saw." Keeling commanded the tumultuous third voyage to the East Indies in 1607, when it took his ships sixteen months to reach Priaman in Sumatra. He then sailed to the far eastern Spice Islands, where the Dutch accused him of conspiring to kill a group of VOC men. He survived and subsequently led another Company expedition in 1615 at the age of thirty-five.

Keeling was unusually devoted to his wife. He did not want to be separated from her when he was told to remain in Bantam or in Jakarta to take charge of the Company's business in the East Indies. The Company turned down his petition to have her travel with him. Hanging on as long as she could, she remained on his ship until the last moment it left the Downs. The Company later rescinded its instructions to Keeling and he returned home with his fleet from Bantam.

Another captain who witnessed animal fights in Aceh was Thomas Best, a veteran seaman who led the Company's famous tenth voyage in 1613. The animal fights began with six elephants, followed by four buffalos, "which made a very excellent and fierce fight. Their fierceness such that hardly 60 to 80 men could part them, fastening ropes to their hind legs to draw them asunder," Best wrote. The entertainment finished with ten to twelve rams pitted against one another "which likewise made very greate fight; and so continued till it was darke, that wee coulde not see longer." Sultan Iskandar Muda then gave the Englishmen a "bankett of at least 40 dishes, with such plenty of hott drincks as might have suffized a druncken armye."

Although Keeling and Best returned with pepper to England, neither could persuade the sultan to sign a trade treaty. The crafty sultan had wined and dined them, and provided them with riveting spectacles, but he refused to give away his pepper exclusively to any foreign country.

The spectacular animal fights staged during the reign of Iskandar Muda and his son-in-law fell out of favor among the sultanas who succeeded them over the following fifty years. Today, the Asiatic elephant (*Elephas maximus*), which made its home in Sumatra, Southeast Asia, and India, is considered a threatened species, a victim of the export trade, the reduction of their forest habitats, and disease. Nowadays it is mostly the tourists who ride elephants in Asia.

Feasts in Flowing Water

The sultans of Aceh enjoyed feasting, but flowing water probably offered the most pleasant setting for dining grandly in Aceh. Imagine being fêted all day in a shallow river of clear, cool running water, as merchant traders regularly were, amid the splendors of the tropics. You drink rice wine while servants offer food on golden platters. At the end of the day, you return to your quarters for a nap. In the seventeenth century, these men, who bathed infrequently on their long voyages to the East, emerged in Aceh into a land where fresh water was abundant—probably one of the reasons why the Acehnese especially liked to bathe, as historian Anthony

Reid has noted. The city is located on the Aceh River and faces the Andaman Sea. The English pirate Dampier noted during his stay in Aceh that "They are here, as at Mindanao, very superstitious in washing and cleansing themselves from defilements, and for that reason they delight to live near the rivers or streams. . . . The river of Achin near the city is always full of people of both sexes and ages. . . . Even the sick are brought to the river to wash."

This was a land where baths and pleasure gardens dotted the banks of the river, where cleanliness was desired and appreciated. Few Europeans of that time would have understood the benefits of bathing. Modern plumbing and modern hygiene didn't exist. Human waste was flung out the window from a chamber pot. The water for baths had to be hauled from wells, and bathing was a low priority compared to all of the other chores that had to be done.

In 1613 Thomas Best and some of his men were with Iskandar Muda when he sat in a river for five or six hours while his nephew poured water over him from a bucket made of pure gold. An English merchant who observed this scene wrote that Best and some Dutch merchants were taken to the river, which was six or seven miles from the town, with the King, who was riding an elephant. "They came to a place wher they washed themselves; the King sitting upon a seatt in the midst of the river, with our Generall and the Dutch merchants and all his nobles aboutt him in the watter, with aboundance of people that were spectators on the shoare; his nephew poureing watter upon him as he satt, with a golden buckitt, for a space of 5 or 6 houres. Then afterwards they had a great banquett, with aboundance of food and arack, dressed after their manner. Having ended the banquett, they retourned to the Kinges pallace, with our English trumpetts sounding before them, and women playing and singing before the Kinge."

Another daylong fête was described by William Keeling in May 1616. In Aceh Keeling was entertained in a river during the early rule of Iskandar Muda, and his sense of sheer joy offers a rare insight into his feelings. "At the King's commaund," he related, "I . . . attended him to the spring of the river about 5 or 6 mile from the towne where we dyned w[i]th him & and his nobilitie sitting above the waist in water, the cleerest and coolest I ever saw or felt." At the time, many of Keeling's men were dying of dysentery, and Keeling himself eventually became sick. Meanwhile, he was constantly concerned with the lading of pepper, which pressed on him as the days went by and more of his men died. "I sent to the King and bought 300 bayars of his pepper from Pryaman, the bahar is 395 English pounds," he wrote in his journal. ". . . I came aboard the *Dragon* as well to prepare the Peppercorne to her speedy lading [of] pepper as for my health, now too impaired by a long flux [dysentery]," he noted in another journal entry. Yet, despite his preoccupations, he could still revel in water "the clearest and coolest" he had ever seen or felt. After Keeling returned to England in 1617, he never went to sea again. Dysentery had taken a toll on his health, and he died at the age of forty-two in 1620.

As the seventeenth century unfolded, the joyous processions and feasts staged for the English and Dutch traders who sailed to Sumatra to buy pepper became mere memories. Merry scenes of Europeans aloft sacred elephants dissolved into armed conflict for trade, profits, and control as the Dutch, in particular, pushed to establish spice monopolies throughout Asia. In this century, the Dutch dominated the Asia trade with their fast ships and brutal focus on establishing spice monopolies in cinnamon (Sri Lanka), cloves (the Moluccas), nutmegs, and mace (Banda Islands). They made sure no one else had access to these spices, and deliberately kept supplies low to raise purchase prices in Europe. The penalty was death for anyone caught buying these spices from anyone other than the Dutch. When sultans in maritime ports would not agree to the terms set by the Dutch to buy spices, the northern Europeans would blockade the ports. Aceh, for example, was the target of a crippling Dutch blockade in the 1650s. Since many Asian spice ports were dependent on boats to bring in food, the blockades effectively starved the local population.

In the early seventeenth century, English and Dutch traders sought to buy pepper from regions in Sumatra that were not controlled by either Aceh or Bantam, the pepper-rich sultanate in northeastern Java that also held sway over the pepper trade in southern and southwestern Sumatra. There was only one area that was independent— Jambi on the east coast of the island. It has been estimated that each raft reaching downstream ports in Jambi could carry 150 piculs (about 19,950 pounds), and that forty thousand to fifty thousand bags of pepper were taken annually from the Jambi highlands. Both the English and the Dutch, along with the Portuguese, Chinese, Malaysians, and Javanese, flocked there to buy pepper even though the settlement of Jambi was difficult to reach, lying more than eighty miles upstream along a navigable but dangerous river.

It took great skill to maneuver lightweight boats laden with pepper through the dangerous rapids of inland rivers and their tributaries, so the Europeans left this part of the business to the natives, whose skill with rafts was legendary, although their rafts occasionally overturned in the turbulent waters. Luckily, hardy pepper berries are not damaged by water. The Europeans negotiated prices with the downstream rulers, but upstream villages were responsible for bringing the pepper to the port. In turn, the Europeans cut deals with local rulers to ensure that the pepper was grown and transported.

It was an unusual situation in eastern Sumatra, and for a while the English and the Dutch tolerated each other because there was pepper in Jambi, as well as in neighboring Palembang. Elsewhere the Dutch weren't as open-minded.

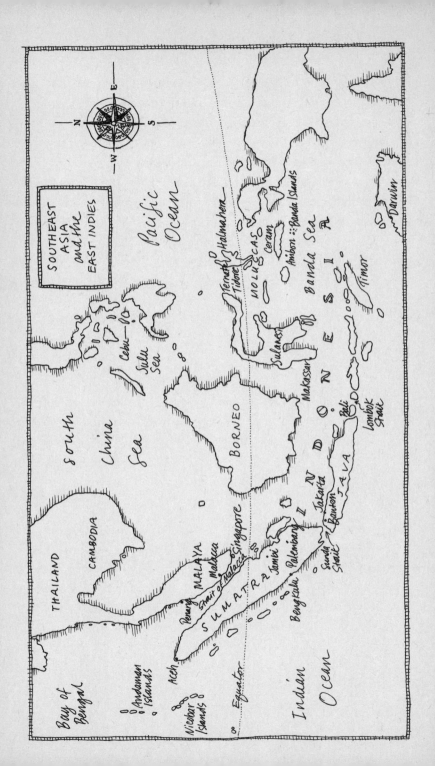

Five

The British Invade

IN 1685 THE ENGLISH EAST INDIA COMPANY FOUNDED A
PEPPER COLONY IN BENKOOLEN ON THE TREACHEROUS
SOUTHWESTERN COAST OF SUMATRA. AFTER YEARS OF
FINANCIAL LOSSES, THE NATIVES WERE FORCED TO PLANT
PEPPER BUT THE COLONY WAS NEVER PROFITABLE. EVEN SO,
THE ENGLISH STAYED FOR 140 YEARS.

•

*"Of those productions of Sumatra, which are regarded as articles of
commerce, the most important and most abundant is pepper. This is the object
of the East India Company's trade thither, and this alone it keeps in its
own hands; its servants, and merchants under its protection, being free
to deal in every other commodity."*
—WILLIAM MARSDEN, 1811

*"This [Benkoolen] is without exception the most wretched place
I ever beheld. I cannot convey to you an adequate idea of the state of ruin
and dilapidation which surrounds me. What with the natural impediments,
bad government, and the awful visitations of Providence that we have
recently experienced in repeated earthquakes, we have scarcely a dwelling
in which to lay our heads . . ."*
—SIR STAMFORD RAFFLES, 1818

Unlike the spices of the far eastern islands, black pepper could not be confined to any one region, and the burghers in Amsterdam knew that a pepper monopoly would be hard to obtain. Nevertheless, in the late seventeenth century, it appeared that the Dutch were making a bold attempt to bring pepper under their exclusive control, at least in India. Under VOC military commander Rijklof van Goens, the Dutch had greatly expanded their presence along the Malabar Coast, usurping many of the strategic strongholds of the Portuguese and their allies in India, including Quilon and Cannanore. And in 1663, he conquered the crown jewel—the pepper port of Cochin. But his campaign wasn't a complete success—Calicut would not bow to the Dutch. Instead, the powerful Hindu Zamorin leader of Calicut invited the English to establish a factory in the historically important port. Some twenty years later, the English also opened factories in other towns along the Malabar Coast, most notably Anjengo and Tellicherry, which is still known today for its outstanding pepper. The Dutch tried to remove the English by bombarding their pepper boats. Meanwhile, the English worried "how long we may be able to keep our station . . . on the coast of Malabar if the Dutch resolve to pursue their long laid design of engrossing all the pepper trade in India by armes which our duty to our king and country obligeth us to prevent to the utmost of our power."

Despite their aggression, the Dutch could not dislodge the English from the Malabar Coast. In 1701 VOC Commander Magnus Wichelman reprised a famous phrase about black pepper to express the displeasure of the Dutch. Pepper, he wrote, is "the bride around which everyone dances on this coast and she has many lovers, namely the English, Danish, Portuguese and Surat traders, etc. . . . But the most important competitors the Company must face in this trade are the English, the biggest and most harmful of them all."

. . .

Although the English were on the Malabar Coast of India, the pepper trade there was less important than the trade in Indonesia. By 1672, a particularly robust year for pepper, the English East India Company was enjoying a huge increase in its pepper imports, shipping more than seven million pounds of the spice from Indonesia to Europe, compared to only 465,000 pounds from the Malabar Coast. Nine years later, despite the ups and downs of the pepper market, the Company still imported more than four million pounds from Southeast Asia—roughly half of the consumption of black pepper in Europe. The Company was quite dependent on Indonesian pepper and, as we know, most of this pepper came from Sumatra and from Bantam in Java, where the Strait of Malacca flows into the Sunda Straits separating Java and Sumatra. Bantam was less than fifty miles away from Batavia, the Dutch East India Company's formidable headquarters in Asia.

Bantam welcomed English, French, Danish, and Chinese traders, who all had factories or warehouses there. The English even sold beer and wine to the Dutch in Batavia. Although the Dutch had tried to crush Bantam's other foreign trade earlier in the century, the sprawling port town recovered and even prospered. The town boasted a large Chinese population, who lived in a section lined with brick houses and shops, markets, a royal square, and even cabarets and other amusements geared to foreigners.

In 1671 the English had built two new factories for pepper, and over the next four years their pepper business boomed. By the late 1670s, Bantam was a free port right under the nose of the Dutch, and the largest foreign factories belonged to the English. Even though the Dutch had a factory in Batavia, its main purpose was for collecting political information rather than for trading pepper. This situation did not please Cornelus Speelman, the VOC's governor-general in Batavia. A hardworking, educated man who spoke Malay, Speelman was also a bellicose and corrupt administrator who had been suspended early in his career for trading on his own behalf. Before he became the highest ranking VOC official in Asia in 1681, he had served as governor of the Dutch factories along the Coromandel Coast of India, rife with double-dealing Europeans, and waged war against the Makassar people of South Sulawesi, securing a key Indonesian spice port for the Dutch. The war redeemed Speelman's reputation, and sowed fear in his enemies.

The English East India's factory in Bantam was its oldest in Asia. It had been operating since James Lancaster established a trading post there in 1602, and had become an official "presidency" in the Company's administrative hierarchy. The Bantam factory also housed a large portion of the English Company's pepper from Jambi on the eastern shores of Sumatra as well as from Bantam itself, a rich source of pepper controlled by the sultan. However, the flow of Jambi pepper was staunched after Malaysians from Johore crossed the Strait of Malacca, attacking and destroying the British factory in Jambi in 1679. From then on, the English were almost entirely dependent on the pepper from Bantam, and they worried that their position was becoming precarious. Batavia wasn't far away.

The Dutch in Batavia were never happy about the English factory in Bantam, and their annoyance only increased after Speelman was installed in Batavia. When civil war broke out in 1681 between the aging sultan of Bantam and his son, Speelman jumped at an opportunity to banish the VOC's main rival in Indonesia.

In the battle for control of Bantam in 1682, the sultan's son and a few hundred of his men had barricaded themselves inside the city's fort as his father laid siege. At the shelled English warehouse or factory, a terrified merchant worried that the tides of war would certainly turn if the Dutch arrived in the city, for the Dutch supported the son. " 'Tis said the Dutch have more Forces coming and if they land their men, undoubtedly Bantam is theirs," wrote the English merchant. "We stand to the fate of War, our Factory being in the midst of danger; which we keep with Guard and constant Watch: We have each our Muskets, with such other Arms as we could get for our defence; and in this posture we stand expecting the sudden (but dreadful) Assaults of the Enemy."

The Dutch attacked Bantam and overwhelmed the sultan's forces. The anonymous English merchant observed that the Dutch "soon Routed all the Javas, and received a welcome Admission into the Fort of the Young King (then drove to so great a streight by the Siege of his Fathers Army, that he could not have held out many days longer . . .) they immediately hoisted the Standard, and what remained undestroyed by the Old King's Forces, they that day mostly burnt, and Marched in Triumph through every part of Town: We kept our Factory Gates shut, and were by them unmolested; as likewise the French, Danes, and Chinese . . ." These foreign merchants might have already known that their presence would not be tolerated by the Dutch.

The newly installed young sultan, a Dutch puppet, soon ordered the British and the other Europeans, except the Dutch, of course, to leave Bantam. The English were told to abandon the town and with "all possible speed to get our Goods aboard our Ships, and depart his Countrey . . ." They hastily gathered what they could and sealed the factory with its remaining merchandise valued at 22,000 royals of eight. (The Spanish real, or piece of eight, was one of the most widely used currencies in the age of discovery. It was equivalent to 0.0255 kilograms of silver, the value of a Portuguese cruzado.) "So ended the Honourable Companies ancient Factory of Bantam, where the English have been settled, and have had a constant Trade about this 70 years," wrote the English merchant. "I cannot say they departed thence like Hannibal out of Africk, accusing both Gods and Men, with imprecations on themselves for any omissions of their own; but truly did severely repine at the Kings ingratitude to (as I may call us) the Nurses and Father of his Country, the English being by his Father and all the Inhabitants generally so acknowledged; and not undeservedly, having by their Trade enrich'd it, and brought it to what it was." That sentiment, smacking of colonial paternalism, would become the prism through which the British justified their imperium in the following centuries. Unlike the Dutch, the English liked to think of themselves as a benevolent presence only interested in enriching countries by trade, echoing Queen Elizabeth's sentiments in the letter that Lancaster had carried on the first voyage of the English East India Company.

The Dutch made sure that Bantam would never again threaten their commercial interests. Under the Dutch, all of the pepper grown in the sultan's territories in southern Sumatra and other areas had to be sold to the VOC at a contracted price and the sultan had to pay a yearly tribute of one hundred bahars (about 37,000 pounds) of pepper to the Dutch company. Bantam became the largest supplier of pepper to the VOC and a sort of vassal state. The Dutch built Fort Speelwyk, named in honor of Speelman, an impressive fortress with high, thick walls mounted by some forty-eight cannons and surrounded by a moat. The sultan was continually "guarded" by a force of some 130 Dutch soldiers in a garrison inside his palace. "This force serves nominally to defend the person of the king from all hostile attempts; but, in fact, to have him always in the Company's power," wrote Johan Splinter Stavorinus, a perspicacious Dutch naval officer who served the VOC as a captain of an East Indiaman. In 1769

Stavorinus sailed from Batavia to Bantam, where he loaded onto his ship some 1,200,000 pounds of black pepper and three thousand pounds of white pepper purchased from the sultan. "None of his [the sultan's] subjects, either high or low, not even his sons, are allowed to approach his person, without the knowledge of the captain of the Dutch military, who received information respecting the king's visitors from the guard at the gate, and transmits it, from time to time, to the commandant at Fort Speelwyk," Stavorinus wrote. "No Javanese or Bantammer is ever allowed to pass the night within the walls of the fort."

Bantam lay at the bottom of the bay where many large ships could safely anchor. Like Aceh, the Javanese town was nestled in groves of coconut trees, its houses scattered amid the forest.

In the immediate aftermath of the Dutch takeover of Bantam, the English Company's pepper imports from Southeast Asia fell substantially. Not only had the new sultan given the Dutch exclusive rights to the trade in Bantam, he also gave the VOC the same rights to the pepper in the Lampongs, an area in southern Sumatra near the Sunda Strait that belonged to the Bantam sultanate. At this point, the English had to find another pepper port in Indonesia. The Dutch had already brokered an exclusive contract for pepper in Jambi and Palembang, the rich pepper region on the east coast of Sumatra lying adjacent to Jambi, so the east coast of Sumatra was not an option. National pride and an appetite for profits (a portion of which went into the pockets of merchants for their "private trade" rather than the company itself) wouldn't let the English leave altogether and allow the Dutch to control Indonesian pepper. To the English, the Hollander's bid to occupy Bantam was another naked attempt to dominate the pepper trade, reminiscent of the VOC's campaign along the Malabar Coast. Much was at stake for the English; the market for pepper was far greater than for any other spice in terms of volume of trade, and pepper had a sentimental appeal as the foundation commodity upon which the East India Company was built.

Their dismissal from Bantam did teach the English a valuable lesson—if they wanted to establish another factory in Indonesia, they had best build a real fortification. Although there were English forts in St. Helena, Bombay, and Madras (Fort St. George) along the rest of the spice route, most of the Company's factories employed only a few men. The Dutch factories were defended by soldiers, and they had built a large castle in Batavia in addition to forts in the far eastern Spice Islands. If the English wanted to retain a presence in the spice trade, and the growing trade in other commodities, such as tea, they almost certainly would have to build forts and employ soldiers, a big expense, especially in light of the Company's shaky finances. This was a crucial turning point in the history of the Company, a time when commerce began to give way to colonialism.

The English hadn't considered Benkoolen (modern-day Bengkulu), a port on the southwest coast of Sumatra, as a promising option for a costly fort, but spurred by the actions of the Dutch, this remote settlement about three hundred miles south of Priaman became inextricably, and infamously, tied to the fortunes of the East India Company. In 1684 Elihu Yale, a native of Boston who worked for the Company in Madras, India, was temporarily in charge of this main port, from which ships were sent to Sumatra for pepper. He sent two Company employees, a former soldier and teacher named Ralph Ord and a man named William Cawley, to Aceh to negotiate with the sultana to reestablish a factory there. Zaquiyat ud-udin Inayat cordially received the English visitors and politely listened to their request, but she seemed most interested in the periwigs that the gentlemen wore and asked Ord if he could take his off. He obliged.

Like her predecessors, the sultana relished Aceh's independence and could not assent to an English fort made of brick in her domain. Even if the governor of Madras filled her palace with gold, she told Ord and Crawley, she wouldn't permit the building of a fort or even a house with brick. A permanent edifice, she knew, could be used as a base for territorial expansion. The sultana told them that a fort made of timber and plank would be the "utmost indulgence" that could be allowed, an indication of the anxiety European incursions in Sumatra had already provoked. Nevertheless, the trip wasn't entirely fruitless for the two men.

A group of chiefs from Priaman and other settlements on the west coast happened to be in Aceh when Ord and Cawley visited the sultana. Happily for the English, these local rulers were in Aceh to ask the sultana for protection from the Dutch. The Sumatrans quickly seized the opportunity to ask the Englishmen to set up a fort in their territories to help fend off the Hollanders. In return, they offered exclusive purchase of their pepper, a proposal guaranteed to be accepted. Arrangements were made and an agreement was signed in Madras with Elihu Yale leading the negotiations for the Company. But a day or two before an expedition was to sail to Priaman, the Company received an invitation from the rulers of Benkoolen to establish a factory there. It seems likely that the Company officials in Madras accepted this invitation because the Dutch had already sent a party to occupy Priaman.

Perhaps their reluctance to confront the Dutch made Benkoolen especially appealing to the English, but in fact it was impossible to avoid the Dutch, even in this relatively isolated settlement. All of the southern ports of Sumatra were within reach of Bantam and Batavia, which were controlled by the Dutch. Benkoolen was also near Sile-bar, a major supplier of pepper to Bantam.

Although the Dutch hindered attempts by the English to establish themselves in several villages to the north of Benkoolen along the west coast, the English prevailed through sheer perseverance. In 1685 they set their base of operations in West Sumatra in Ben-koolen, where they built Fort Marlborough and stayed for 140 years. Ironically, the "John Company," as the East India Company came to be called, was to rue its decision to occupy Benkoolen until its final days.

Elihu Yale, the Boston black pepper trader who led the ill-fated negotiations for a fort in Priaman, became President and Governor of Madras, and donated the fortune he earned on his private trading account to establish Yale University. He apparently never visited Sumatra but did have a hand in establishing a factory in Aceh in 1688. Ousted from his post in Madras in 1692, he was jailed on charges of profiting through private trade with Aceh. After his release, he again traded on his own behalf in Madras, and finally left India in 1699.

Years after the English first came to Benkoolen, the directors of the Company wrote: "It was a fatall and never enough to be re-pented errour of our President and Council of Fort St. George [Ma-dras] to break all our orders for a settlement at Pryaman upon a caprice of their owne to send our ships, spend our strength, our money and soe many men's lives upon settlement at such an unhealthful place as Bencoolen, because they heard there was more pepper there, which was noe news to us before wee writt a line concerning Pryaman, but wee avoided that place and others neare Sillebar because they were too neare Batavia and that we knew by long and ancient experience that they were unhealthful and, therefore, did purposely direct and enjoin Pryaman to be yet principall place of settlement and first se-cured and made as strong as Fort St. George."

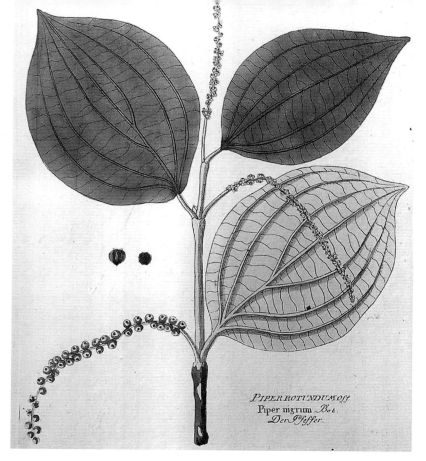

PIPER ROTUNDUM off.
Piper nigrum Bot.
Der Pfeffer.

A pepper plant from the monumental work of a nineteenth-century Austrian physician named Ferdinand Bernhard Vietz, who published an eleven-volume encyclopedia describing medicinal and culinary plants. Ignaz Albrecht, a well-known engraver, worked on the more than one thousand hand-colored copperplate engravings. THE LUESTHER T. MERTZ LIBRARY OF THE NEW YORK BOTANICAL GARDEN, BRONX, NEW YORK

Betel (*Piper betle*) leaves, often called paan, displayed at a market in Kandy, Sri Lanka.

MARGOT GRANITSAS / PHOTO RESEARCHERS, INC.

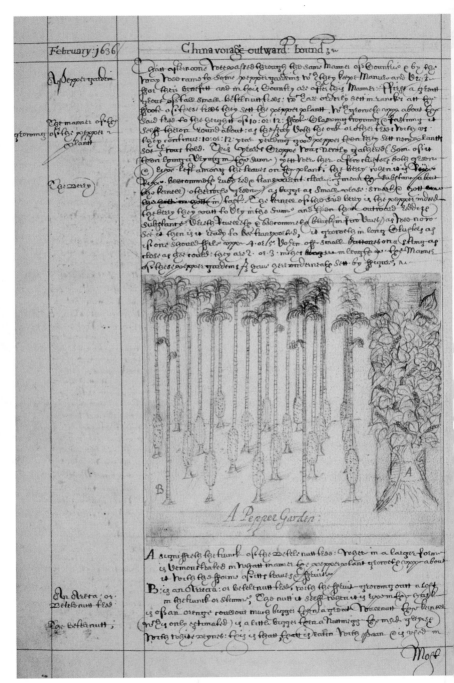

Peter Mundy's drawing of a pepper garden in Surat in northwestern India. BODLEIAN LIBRARY,
WITH PERMISSION

Long pepper (*Piper longum*), preferred by ancient Romans. GEOFF KIDD / PHOTO RESEARCHERS, INC.

Tailed Javanese pepper (*Piper cubeb*)
GEOFF KIDD / PHOTO RESEARCHERS, INC.

The spice called grains of paradise, melegeuta, or guinea pepper (*Afromomum melegueta*), native to West Africa, was widely used in Europe during the fourteenth and fifteenth centuries. GEOFF KIDD / PHOTO RESEARCHERS, INC.

Top left: Allspice, from the plant *Pimenta dioica*, is one of the few spices native to the New World. Columbus believed these berries were peppercorns. TH FOTO-WERBUNG / PHOTO RESEARCHERS, INC.

Top right: A drawing of a black peppercorns from the first edition of Charles Lécluse's Latin version of Garcia da Orta's masterwork, *Conversations on the Simples, Drugs and the Medicinal Substances of India*. The book, originally in Portuguese, was published in Goa, India, in 1563. THE LUESTHER T. MERTZ LIBRARY OF THE NEW YORK BOTANICAL GARDEN, BRONX, NEW YORK

Bottom: Black pepper (*Piper nigrum*) SCIMAT / PHOTO RESEARCHERS, INC.

Top: A hand-colored engraving of an Indian betel dealer weighing his goods, published in 1822. IMAGE ASSET MANAGEMENT LTD./SUPERSTOCK

Bottom: Peter Mundy's drawing of an elephant fight in Banda Aceh. BODLEIAN LIBRARY, WITH PERMISSION

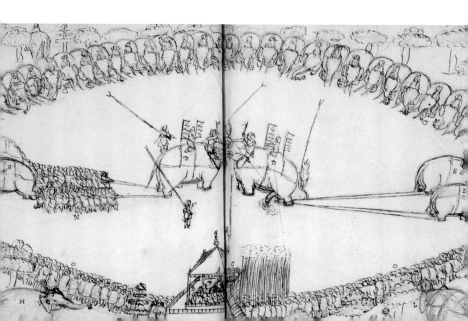

A drawing from *Linschoten's Itinerario*, published in 1598, features the lush flora of India. Notice the pepper (peeper) vine climbing the palm tree in the far right. THE HUNTINGTON LIBRARY, WITH PERMISSION

"In the Land of Pepper," a woodcut published in Germany in 1904, shows how pepper was cultivated in small gardens and brought downriver by rafts to waiting ships. Pepper leaves and berries adorn the engraving, and the poles at each side depict climbing pepper vines. Photo:

A drawing from a widely circulated pamphlet describing the torture and beheading of ten Englishmen in Amboyna in 1623. THE HUNTINGTON LIBRARY, WITH PERMISSION

Acclaimed Dutch cartographer Johannes van Keulen's seventeenth-century map of the Indian Ocean, India, and the East Indies. The map, published in 1680, shows many of the pepper and spice ports in India and Indonesia that were part of the VOC's vast trading network in Asia. BRITISH LIBRARY, LONDON, UK/ © BRITISH LIBRARY BOARD. ALL RIGHTS RESERVED/ THE BRIDGEMAN ART LIBRARY

. . .

If Aceh was a kind of Eden, then Benkoolen could only be described as a kind of hell. Remote, damp, and difficult to approach by ship because of dangerous surf, the village truly was an unfortunate place for the East India Company to establish itself in Indonesia. York Fort was built on a knoll near the mouth of the Benkoolen River, surrounded by swamps that were breeding grounds for malaria. It soon had to be rebuilt with convict and local labor in a more suitable location two miles away, and the new Fort Marlborough was poorly constructed. Meanwhile, there was a chronic shortage of military supplies, and relatively few English soldiers had signed on for service in Benkoolen. The Company bolstered its small force with Bugis people from South Sulawesi, Indian soldiers, and "Topazes," men of Portuguese descent who practiced Christianity. At one time the English even considered using slaves from Madagascar as soldiers.

The small number of defenders made the fort vulnerable, and it had to be abandoned twice—in 1719 when much abused Indonesians attacked the still-unfinished Fort Marlborough and set fire to the town, driving the British onto a Company ship in the bay; and in 1760 when the humiliated English, who could not rally the Indonesians to their side, surrendered to a squadron of French ships led by French Brigadier-General Comte d'Estaing. Disease quickly overwhelmed d'Estaing's crew of 150 men, and he quit the settlement after only a few months.

Benkoolen again became a British possession, but Company officials could not restore order. They found "many of the pepper gardens in ruins, the people restless, and in many cases unwilling to commence cultivation," wrote William Marsden, a scholar and Company man who lived in Benkoolen from 1771 to 1779, in his epic history of Sumatra. The sultan of Moko Moko, an important chief in a region north of Benkoolen, also had ordered the destruction of his territories, and the pepper gardens in Benkoolen and Silebar were ruined.

From the very beginning, Benkoolen was a graveyard. Only four months after setting up the trading post, disease had already spread like wildfire through the small settlement. The desperation of the men is evident in their letters. ". . . Wee are by Sicknesse all become uncapable of helping one another & ye great Number of people that came over not above thirty men [are] well," wrote Benjamin Bloome, who was chief of the settlement from 1686 to 1690, to Company officials in Madras. The mounting death toll was awful, he confided to Ralph Ord in Indrapurna, a settlement to the north of Benkoolen. "Our people dayly die & now we are in worse Condition then ever, for wee have now neither men to Make a grave to bury ye dead & none to carry the dead corps out of the towne." The situation in Indrapurna, Ord replied, was equally dire. "We are sorry to hear ye Sickly Condition you are in though are little better or Rather worse our Selves," Ord noted. "There is not one of our black people well, some dead, and many near dying; the Rest alltogeather disabled from any service . . ." Ord, the founder of the English settlement in Benkoolen, died in Priaman in 1686. It was rumored that he was poisoned by the Dutch.

Along with the dying and the sick, the officials constantly worried about Dutch assaults on the settlements. Bloom appealed to a rajah whose territory was near Seblat, a pepper-growing region some seventy miles north of Benkoolen. "At our first Settlement here, you Promised at all time to Stand by & assist us, when ever any Occasion required it," Bloome wrote. "Now therefore, as before there was Never any Occasion, Soe now Your constancy must be tried. For as ye Dutch & Javas are come to Sillibar, and undoubtedly with a designe to assault this Place, as you are Senicble [sensible] of . . . I desire that you will come back with all Speed, for . . . your presence now here is much more requisite then at another time." Although the Dutch were indeed near, they never attacked Benkoolen.

Despite the number of deaths, the fledgling settlement managed to survive, and residencies to the north and south became part of the British domain. But life in Benkoolen was confined. Sumatra's formidable mountains and treacherous jungles did not inspire exploration. Those who had to make annual inspections of the pepper gardens in the so-called outer residencies dreaded the task. Many turned to drink to help them get through the days, which wasn't unusual among Company men. During July 1716, the nineteen "covenanted" civil servants of Fort Marlborough imbibed ". . . 74 dozen and a half of wine [mostly claret], 24 dozen and half of Burton Ale and pale beer, 2 pipes [each 105 gallons] and 42 gallons of Madeira wine, 6 Flasks of Shiraz [a Persian wine], and 164 gallons of Goa [toddy] . . ." The bill for the wine alone was said to exceed the value of all pepper exports from West Sumatra in 1716.

It wasn't easy to recruit men to a remote garrison infamous for being a death trap. So it isn't surprising that many of the fort's administrators were despicable characters. The pirate trader William Dampier, who spent five months in Benkoolen as a fort gunner in 1690, described James Sowdon, the "Chief" from 1690 to 1692, as a detestable petty tyrant. Sowdon possessed "so much Insolence and Cruelty with respect to those under him, and Rashness in his management of the Malayan Neighbourhood, that I soon grew weary of him . . . under a Man whose Humours were so brutish and barbarous," wrote Dampier. "I forebear to mention his name after such a Character; nor do I care to fill these Papers with particular stories of him: But therefore give this intimation, because as it is the interest of the Nation in general, for it is especially of the Honourable East India Company, to be informed of abuses in their Factories."

On occasion, an administrator's behavior was so outrageous that he was suspended and imprisoned, which was the fate of Deputy Governor Richard Farmer in 1718. In 1807 Resident Thomas Parr was beheaded by enraged Malaysians after he tried disbanding the men of the Bugis Corps, the refugees from South Sulawesi who formed the so-called country guard, and instituting forced cultivation of coffee. Even Joseph Collett, an administrator who is credited with more humane treatment of the local inhabitants, seems like a typical British colonial who treats his charges like children. Collett, who was Deputy Governor of Benkoolen from 1712 to 1716, boasted in a letter about his approach: "I treat them as a wise man should his wife, am very complaisant in trifles, but immoveable in matters of importance."

Collett's day in Benkoolen started with a good breakfast of bread and butter and Bhoea tea, a popular black tea from China, at about seven o'clock. He worked until noon, and then dined on boiled chicken, pigeon, crawfish, crabs, or prawns, "all excellent in their kind, or some good relishing bit," along with "a good Draught out of the Punch-Bowle." After taking a "Pipe for Digesting," he goes back to work. "If I find it possible to get so much time, I go out at 4 and either ride or walk till six. If I ride I have a Horse Guard attending me and the Union Flagg carry'd before me. I have also a foot Guard of Buggess [Bugis] Soldiers who generally keep way with me." The Bugis were especially recruited by the British in West Sumatra to supervise pepper planters and to serve as soldiers because of their reputation as good fighters.

In fact, Collett was accompanied by guards wherever he went. "If I walk, I have 4 men with Blunderbusses go before and a Guard of Buggess to bring up the rear," he wrote. "If I dine abroad or shou'd lye out of the Fort, which I have not yet done, the number of my Guard is increased."

Collett closed his office at six and came home to "sitt again and then to Supper. I take a Pipe or two with a chearfull Glass and then to my Chamber, where I either sit to business or what else is proper before my going to bed. I have two servants and two slaves of my own, one of them a female too, but not a present of any king . . . However to prevent scandal I keep her in another Family where she works for me, ironing, etc. but never comes into my house. . . . The Mallay Town adjoining to our Fort consists of seven or eight hundred houses full of Inhabitants."

As Collett was sitting down for his fine meals attended by servants and slaves, the natives in the so-called British residencies didn't have enough to eat. British policies in Benkoolen were starving the population, and it started with the number of vines that the inhabitants were forced to plant and then sell at a contracted price.

Only ten years after Benkoolen was founded, officials on Leadenhall Street in London, the headquarters of the English East India Company, were aware of the faltering pepper trade in southwest Sumatra. Losses mounted year after year, and little could be done to offset the considerable expense of building a fort and provisioning soldiers. The entire operation was proving a drain on the Company's finances. Spurred into action, officials in Benkoolen decided that forced cultivation, a euphemism for slavery, would increase pepper production and ensure a regular, reliable supply of the spice, thereby improving the Company's ledger sheets. The result was part reservation, part plantation, and a disaster for the people of southwest Sumatra, where pepper cultivation relied on families in upstream villages to plant the vines and maintain the pepper gardens. Men usually cleared the jungle forests for the gardens while women and children planted and harvested. Women sold the pepper in local markets.

The English largely destroyed this system of agriculture and even the social fabric of West Sumatra by striking deals with local chiefs for the delivery of contracted amounts of pepper. In 1695 the chiefs agreed to "bind their subjects to plant 2,000 pepper vines annually, and to give their assistance to the English officials to see that the terms were enforced." Unmarried men over the age of sixteen had to grow half as many vines as married men. When the imposed quotas failed to be met, the number of vines was reduced in 1724 to one thousand for families and five hundred for single men. It was an overwhelming amount of work. Many single men simply left their villages rather than face the daunting prospect of planting twice as many vines upon getting married. During the British occupation in southwest Sumatra, many historians have noted, it was said that single women greatly outnumbered single men. Married women found that they were no longer welcome in local markets to sell their family's pepper because the English did not think this was an appropriate job for women.

The penalties for families that didn't make the quota were harsh. Men and women would be fined or thrown in prison, and over the years the punishments became more severe. Pepper wasn't necessary for survival, and yet as early as 1690, only five years after the establishment of Benkoolen, William Dampier observed that two chiefs were in the stocks "for no other Reason but because they had not brought down to the Fort such a quantity of pepper as the Governour had sent for."

Families still had to plant rice to survive. Over the years, British demands for pepper led to a critical shortage of rice and near starvation as people neglected growing food while they struggled to meet the Company's pepper quotas. ". . . the scarcity of rice such as was never known here before has forced People to quit their Habitations to go 6 to 7 Days Journey inland to procure Provisions for their

Families, many of whom for several Months together had had no other Sustenance than Roots and leaves of Trees; and the Misery they have undergone is almost inexpressible," wrote a Company official in Benkoolen in 1741.

The overriding concern of the British was profits, and despite increasing efforts to force people to cultivate more pepper, the Company continued to lose money. A typical dispatch from the Company in 1755 complained of the drain on funds following another disappointing pepper harvest. Company officials wrote to Fort Marlborough: ". . . encreasing the investment of pepper is the material point in view for the interest of the Company, and if a sufficient quantity is not procured for loadings for two ships in a year at least, notwithstanding the great care and economy in your management and the reduction of expences to the utmost prudent extent, we are satisfied our settlements on the West Coast will be a continual drain [on] our estate . . ."

The Company men in London pressed for more frequent surveys of the residencies to ensure that production would meet quotas. Yet such efforts proved fruitless; the pepper enterprise in southwest Sumatra did not turn a profit for the Company. National pride and an unwillingness to cede the region to the Dutch kept the English Company in Sumatra year after year.

The Company never lost its conviction that the failure to grow enough pepper stemmed from the inherent laziness of the inhabitants. Letters from Fort Marlborough were filled with accusations about indolent and lazy "Mallays," and threats about disciplinary actions against the most recalcitrant. In 1746 Company officials in Fort Marlborough asserted: "The People of Manna and Laye [Lais] Residencies have really been remiss [in cultivating pepper], and as the mallays are a stubborn, ignorant people, it is very Difficult task to make them sensible of their Interest. . . . We find by experience that the Lenity which Your Honours have always recommended to us hath [no] Effect upon such Illiterate Dispositions, and that it is highly Necessary [that] We should for once Act with some Strictness towards the most undeserving."

The same letter laments that several Bugis people had quit and returned to their homeland. "They are reported to be a bold Trusty people when employed at Ceylon, The Malabar Coast, or other places where the Dutch use them, but here they intermix with the Mallays and soon Contract their Lazy, Idle, Disposition, which was not at first Apprehended."

Even the scholar William Marsden, who studied the Malay language and was a more sympathetic observer, refers to the "natural indolence of the natives," although he at least acknowledges the "smallness of the advantage" pepper cultivation brought to them. The price paid for pepper in the British districts was quite low, Marsden observed, "affording to each man an income of not more than from eight to twelve dollars yearly . . ." He attributed the cheap price to Benkoolen's isolation, and noted that pepper cultivation was more successful in other parts of Sumatra. "In the northern countries of the island, where people are numerous and their ports good," he wrote, referring to the pepper ports that had sprung up along the northwestern coast of Sumatra, "they are found to be more independent also, and refuse to cultivate plantations upon any other terms than those on which they can deal with private traders."

The Benkoolen settlement and its residencies were difficult to approach by boat. This had deterred the Chinese and other Eastern merchants from buying pepper in southwest Sumatra. Without competition, the British could pay low prices for pepper. The British did attempt to attract the Chinese to Benkoolen, hoping that it would be seen as an alternative destination to Batavia, where a large number of Chinese immigrants had settled. Although Benkoolen never became an important destination for the Chinese, the settlement did have a "China bazaar" and tea shops and other businesses, and under Joseph Hurlock, the governor of Benkoolen from 1746 to 1752, most of the pepper grown in the English residencies was sent to China rather than to Europe. In the 1750s, exports resumed to Europe.

Company men couldn't imagine that their own disastrous policies caused their economic problems in Benkoolen. To boost pepper production, they entertained the bright idea of relocating people from the hills to the coastal areas to cultivate pepper. "This country being very thinly inhabited," officials wrote in 1754, "it should be strongly recommended to the gentlemen in the management of affairs here to encourage the people from the hills to come and settle upon the sea coast. We have been treating with two of their chiefs, who have promised to bring down all their subjects to the number of about five or six hundred families."

When relocation proved futile, another bright idea was hatched—plant valuable nutmeg and clove trees from the Banda Islands and the Moluccas in Benkoolen. This was one of the great dreams of all rivals in the spice trade who wanted to break the Dutch spice monopolies. The English and the French had each schemed to steal seedlings from the far eastern Spice Islands and plant them elsewhere. Finally, a one-armed Frenchman named Pierre Poivre (Peter Pepper; yes, this really was his name), a missionary-turned-botanist who wrote some of the earliest works about forest conservation, successfully accomplished this act of botanical piracy, smuggling nutmegs and cloves to the island of Mauritius in the 1750s. Another European adventurer in Asia, Poivre came from a wealthy family of silk merchants in Lyons and at one time worked for the French East India Company, which was founded in 1664. As a young man, he traveled as a missionary to China and Southeast Asia, and later lost an arm in a battle in Batavia. In the 1760s he was the administrator of Mauritius and Réunion, two islands in the Indian Ocean that were frequented by pepper traders on their way to India and Indonesia.

The British had their chance to transplant nutmeg and clove seedlings from the far eastern islands when they temporarily wrested control of the Moluccas from the Dutch in 1796. They brought the seedlings to West Sumatra. Earlier attempts to grow the spices in Benkoolen had failed, but now large numbers of seedlings could be transported without fear of Dutch reprisals. Although the horticultural experiment was a success—between 1811 and 1816 some 42,390 pounds of nutmeg and 6,155 pounds of cloves were shipped from Benkoolen to India and England—the costs of obtaining the spices from the spice islands and establishing plantations in Benkoolen outweighed profits. However, until the very end of the Company's involvement in Benkoolen, officials at Fort Marlborough hoped that the nutmeg and cloves planted in Company and privately owned plantations could save the pepper residencies.

The settlement was in especially bad shape when Sir Stamford Raffles and his second wife, Sophia, arrived in Benkoolen in 1818, and the new Lieutenant Governor was deeply shaken by what he saw. The system of forced cultivation had long failed to meet the demands of the Company, and the people of southwestern Sumatra had been crushed. Soon after arriving in Benkoolen, he wrote to the Company's directors in London: "It will be pretty obvious that the population is for the time as effectually enslaved to the local Resident as the Africans of the West [Indies] are to their proprietors with this difference only that the former having no permanent property in the people, and only a temporary interest in their services, has consequently a great inducement to exact them with severity."

Encountering a desperate, depopulated country, Raffles immediately attributed the loss of its inhabitants to the Company's harsh policies. "Of the desolating effects of this system I can hardly convey to your Honble. Court anything like an adequate idea," he wrote. "The country has been nearly depopulated, and the remaining labourers charged with the additional duties of those who are no more to be found have nearly lost all character and energy. If a planter does not cultivate his stipulated number of vines, or deliver his proper produce of pepper, he is punished corporally or otherwise at the discretion of the local Resident, without any reference to the chief authority at Bencoolen. Such, in short, have been the results of this system that latterly the Government have been obliged to bring down rice at an enormous expense from Bengal [India] for the support of these poor wretches. Under such a system where is the motive for energy or industry!"

An abolitionist, Raffles was particularly upset by the slaves in Benkoolen, and he ended his letter with an urgent appeal "in favor of the unfortunate African. I allude to the Company's public slaves, of whom there are men, and women, and children, upwards of two hundred now at this settlement—most born at Bencoolen, being the children of slaves originally purchase by the East India Company. They have hitherto been considered as indispensable for the duties of the place, and it has been asserted that they are happier than free men. I cannot be expected to concur in either of these views. They are employed in loading and unloading the Company's ships, and other hard work, for which free labourers ought to be engaged. No care having been taken of their morals, many of them are dissolute and depraved—the women being in promiscuous intercourse with the public convicts for the purpose (as I was informed by the superintendent) 'of keeping up the breed'—and the children left to a state of nature, vice and wretchedness."

Finally, an intelligent, thoughtful Company man who could

acknowledge the evils of the British system had arrived in West Sumatra. With his characteristic energy and dedication to "liberal" imperialism—that empire was of the greatest benefit to those natives under the care of the "enlightened" British—Raffles abolished slavery in West Sumatra and set up a system of "free" pepper cultivation, although natives who didn't grow pepper still had to pay an annual tribute of two dollars, a huge sum of money to them, or deliver fifty pounds of pepper to Company storehouses.

Raffles went about reforming the residencies with the zeal of a headmaster, modifying harsh laws regarding debtors; removing British officials from the southern residencies and replacing them with Bugis people; abolishing cockfighting; and rescinding regulations banning men from bearing their creese, the long dagger, often with a wavy blade. Lancaster had received one as a gift from the sultan of Aceh in 1602. Charles Lockyer, an independent trader who traveled to Sumatra, had written in 1711 that "Mallayans, at work or play are never dressed till their naked daggers are in their girdles. Nor do they ever walk abroad without swords and targets, or other weapons in their hands, besides the daggers." Raffles only learned of this after local chiefs told him that it was a disgrace to be prohibited from showing their weapons.

The story of Raffles in Benkoolen is a grace note in the otherwise miserable story of the English East India Company's 140-year rule in West Sumatra. Although he was an imperialist, his genuine interest in the people of Malaysia and Indonesia is remarkable for a Company man. "What saves him is the large proportion in his make-up of humanitarian principle," wrote Emily Hahn, one of his biographers. "He provides what excuses there are for the imperialistic pattern. His appearance coincided more or less with a merging of the Crown and John Company's interests. Perhaps because of this he was a departure from the type of man who, before him, enlarged the influence of the East India Company abroad."

Raffles was not a stranger to Indonesia. He had previously spent nearly five years as Governor of Java, which the British had seized from the Dutch during the Napoleonic Wars. The British held on to the island until the French were defeated, and then gave Java back to the Dutch, which put Raffles out of a job. This bizarre situation arose because the British fear of imperialist France outweighed their mistrust of Holland. In some ways, Benkoolen resembled Java, where Raffles had endeavored to reverse forced cultivation and other vicious Dutch policies by instituting a more humane and equitable system of government and work.

Based on his upbringing, Raffles seems like an unlikely candidate for knighthood. The son of an impoverished sea captain, he was born in 1781 on a boat off the coast of Jamaica. Although he received little formal education, he managed to find work as a clerk with the Company at the age of fourteen. Over the next ten years, he rose through the ranks, based on his studiousness, intelligence, and ability to cultivate relationships with influential men. The young Raffles got a big break in 1805, when he was sent to Penang, an island off the west coast of Malaysia that the British called Prince of Wales Island, as a member of the new governor's staff. The British hoped the island would become a major pepper-producing colony, a replacement of Malacca, but its fortunes never amounted to much. (Aceh, in fact, offered a better location than Penang for the British to refit their fleets and to procure pepper, betel, and other goods. In 1762, the British appealed to the Acehnese sultanate to allow a trading base, but after repeated rejections of the Company's proposals, Penang was established in 1786.)

In Penang, the ever-studious Raffles learned how to speak Malay, which few other company men had even attempted. He also became indispensable to the workings of the colony, and most important, won the patronage of Lord Minto, governor-general of India, with his incisive argument against relocating the inhabitants of Malacca to Penang. The Penang Council had wanted to move everyone out of Malacca and destroy the city in the hopes of reviving the fortunes of Penang. Raffles's persuasive arguments convinced them otherwise.

In 1810 Lord Minto recruited his protégé to serve in Malacca, where Raffles was expected to gather information on Java and help plan its invasion to rid the island of the then-menacing French. Fifteen years earlier, the British had wrested Malacca from the Dutch when France invaded Holland and annexed the country. The British suspected that the French, whose fleets were now in Java, would use the island as a launching pad to take over Indonesia and Malaysia. Lord Minto had already put a stop on French designs to raid India when he handily dispatched the French from the islands of Mauritius and Reunion off the coast of Madagascar. Now he wanted to do the same in Java.

It is back in Malacca that we catch a glimpse of Raffles thanks to Abdullah bin Abdul Kadir, who became one of Malaysia's leading literary scholars. Abdullah was only about thirteen years old when Raffles gave him a job as a copyist in his office. The young boy, who had already earned money by writing Koranic texts and teaching religion, was enthralled by Raffles and his first wife, Olivia. His description of Raffles, published in his autobiography, *The Hikayat Abdullah*, offers one of the most affectionate portrayals of the man.

"Now as to Mr. Raffles's physical features I noticed that he was of medium build, neither tall nor short, neither fat nor thin. He was broad of brow, a sign of his care and thoroughness; round-headed with a projecting forehead, showing his intelligence. He had light brown hair, indicative of bravery; large ears, the mark of a ready listener. He had thick eye-brows, his left eye watered slightly from a cast; his nose was straight and his cheeks slightly hollow. His lips were thin, denoting his skill in speech, his tongue gentle and his mouth wide; his neck tapering; his complexion not very clear, his chest was full and his waist slender. He walked with a slight stoop.

"As to his character, I noticed that he always looked thoughtful. He was very good at paying due respect to people in a friendly manner. He treated everyone with proper deference, giving to each his proper title when he spoke. Moreover, he was extremely tactful in ending a difficult conversation. He was solicitous of the feelings of others, and open-handed with the poor. He spoke in smiles."

An avid collector of animals and plants, Raffles amassed a veritable museum of natural history wherever he went. In Malacca, he paid "good money" to Malaysians to search for "creatures of the sky, the land and the sea; of the uplands, the lowlands and the forest; things which fly or crawl; things which grow and germinate in the soil; all these could be turned into ready cash," wrote Abdullah. "There were also people who brought Malay manuscripts and books, I do not remember how many hundreds of these texts there were. Almost, it seemed, the whole of Malay literature of the ages, the property of our forefathers, was sold and taken away from all over the country."

In Sumatra, Raffles was equally avid to indulge in exploration, and there he could turn his full energies to his favorite pastime. He probably was the first Company man to travel to Sumatra's interior with the sole aim of enjoying himself, although he had hoped to visit some villages in the interior where the people were said to be antagonistic to the British. Raffles had previously explored Java in grand imperial style, and he wanted to do the same in Sumatra. Soon after arriving in Benkoolen he set off with Lady Raffles and a handful of native officers to the southern British residencies. Fifty porters carried their food and luggage.

A newspaper sponsored by the East India Company and published in London hailed their three-week excursion as a great "discovery" of an island of immense wealth "abounding in precious metals." *The Asiatic Journal* earnestly reported: "Sumatra has hitherto been very little known. . . . The European establishments are entirely on the coast; Europeans had never penetrated into the interior. All attempts to do so, indeed, were reckoned desperate; no European would embark in them. The population of the interior were considered as savages, and the mountains impassable . . . The Governor felt there was but one alternative, and that was to open the road by going himself. His enterprise was crowned with success."

More than one million people lived in Sumatra, the Company newspaper estimated (an inaccurate figure, but one possibly supplied by Raffles himself), and dutifully noted that in the governor's opinion "with a little encouragement, far greater resources are to be found in Sumatra than the British could have derived from Java . . ." Raffles fervently wished to "save" Sumatra and waged a spirited but abortive campaign to prevent the island from falling into the hands of the Dutch. Who else would entertain the possibility of making Sumatra a British colony in order to save it from the Dutch? "Sumatra should undoubtedly be under the influence of one European power alone and this power is of course the English," Raffles once declared. Despite the Company's disapproval of negotiating a treaty with the Sultan of Aceh, Raffles forged a treaty promising the independence of the Acehnese. The treaty was part of his plan for securing British control of the fastest ocean route to China from India, namely the Strait of Malacca. Aceh sat at one end of the strait, Singapore at the other end. In 1819, the same year that Singapore became a British free port, the sultan of Aceh signed a treaty that promised a "defensive alliance" between Britain and Aceh, allowed no foreign residents or treaties without the consent of the British, and permitted the Company to trade at all Acehnese ports.

A man of seemingly boundless energy, Raffles did explore Sumatra and wrote about his travels to the southern residencies in his extensive correspondence, which his wife published after his death. In these letters he doesn't appear as the Company man intent on extending the crown's influence. Instead, he is an intelligent traveler exploring and reporting on his surroundings.

After many days of strenuous hiking over mountains and through riverbeds, he wrote to the Duchess of Somerset, one of his favorite correspondents, "our view opened up on one of the finest countries I have ever beheld . . . We found ourselves in an immense amphitheatre, surrounded by mountains ten and twelve thousand feet high, the soil on which we stood rich beyond description and vegetation luxuriant and brilliant in every direction." Although Raffles is enthusiastic, he does not hide the difficulties of the journey. "After breakfasting at Lebu Tappu . . . we proceeded to a place called Pulo Lebar, where it was arranged we were to sleep. . . . During the night we were awakened by the approach of a party of elephants . . . fortunately they kept at some distance . . .

"I must not omit to tell you, that in passing through the forest we were, much to our inconvenience, greatly annoyed by leeches; they got into our boots and shoes, which became filled with blood; at night too, they fell off the leaves that sheltered us from the weather, and on awaking in the morning we found ourselves bleeding profusely—these were a species of intruders we were not prepared for." Despite such "inconveniences," the intrepid couple didn't abandon their journey, but maintained a bruising schedule of daily hikes.

The Raffles party left Pulo Lebar and walked some twelve hours to reach their next destination, one of the most arduous days of their journey. "Neither on this nor on the preceding day was there a vestige of population or cultivation; nature was throughout allowed to reign undisturbed; and from the traces of elephants in every direction, they alone of the animal kingdome seemed to have explored the recesses of the forest," Raffles related.

"We got on, however, very well; and though we were all occasionally much fatigued, we did not complain. Lady Raffles was a perfect heroine. The only misfortune at this stage was a heavy fall of rain during the night, which penetrated our leafy dwelling in every direction, and soaked every one of the party to the skin. We were now two days' march beyond the reach of supplies; many of our Coolies had dropped off; some were fairly exhausted, and we began to wish our journey at an end. We, however, contrived to make a good dinner on the remaining fowl, and having plenty of rice and claret, did not complain of our fare."

The World's Largest Flower

It was at Pulo Lebar that Raffles and Dr. Joseph Arnold, a surgeon and naturalist who accompanied the couple, stumbled on a botanical marvel—the world's largest flower. "The most important discovery throughout our journey was made at this place; this was a gigantic flower, of which I can hardly attempt to give any thing like a just description," Raffles wrote. "It is perhaps the largest and most magnificent flower in the world, and is so distinct from every other flower, that I know not to what I can compare it—its dimensions will astonish you—it measured across from the extremity of the petals rather more than a yard, the nectarium was nine inches wide, and as deep; estimated to contain a gallon and half of water, and the weight of the whole flower fifteen pounds."

Indeed, Raffles had seen a flower that is now dangerously close to extinction. It must have been extraordinary for him to come across this organic oddity, which weighs some twenty to twenty-four pounds and measures thirty-six to forty-two inches in diameter. Resembling a giant piece of pop art placed in the forest by a madcap artist, the ungainly, showy flower cannot survive without a host plant to provide it with water and nutrients, making it a parasite. Raffles was lucky to have found it, since there are only eight days during the entire year when the bud unfurls and the flower reaches its full gargantuan size. After that brief period, it shrivels like a dying alien pod. This flower, *Rafflesia*, is named in honor of its European discoverer, although that credit really belongs to Louis Auguste Deschamps, a French surgeon and naturalist, who discovered the flower in Java in 1797.

"There is nothing more striking in the Malayan forests than the grandeur of the vegetation: the magnitude of the flowers, creepers, and trees, contrasts strikingly with the stunted and, I had almost said, pigmy vegetation of England," Raffles informed the Duchess. "Compared with our forest-trees, your largest oak is a mere dwarf."

On a subsequent trip into the interior of Sumatra, no less exhausting than the first, Lord and Lady Raffles journeyed to Minangkabau, the gold-producing region. It was also one of the sites of an ancient Hindu-Buddhist civilization. Raffles enthusiastically reported that not only had he found the ruins of an ancient city, but the land was surprisingly fertile and the people most hospitable. He had earlier discovered the fantastic Buddhist Borobudur Temple complex in Java. The natives in Sumatra only had one request, Raffles related, namely that the Dutch should be kept out of Padang on the west coast of the island. One can imagine that Raffles was overjoyed when he heard that request. He was only too happy to "enter into a conditional treaty of friendship and alliance with the Sultan of Menangkabu, as the lord-paramount of all the Malay countries, subject of course to the approval of Lord Hastings [Warren Hastings, the powerful governor-general of Bengal and one of the architects of British India]."

During the years he spent in Indonesia and Malaysia, Raffles was obsessed with the Dutch, whom he feared would win control of trade throughout the entire Indonesian archipelago and the Strait of Malacca, shutting out "enlightened" British trade. "The Dutch possess the only passes through which ships must sail into this Archipelago, the Straits of Sunda and of Malacca," Raffles complained, "and the British have not now an inch of ground to stand upon between the Cape of Good Hope and China; nor a single friendly port at which they can water or obtain refreshment. . . .

"At present the authority of the [Company-led] Government of Prince of Wales' Island [Penang] extends no further south than Malacca, and the Dutch would willingly confine that of [Company-led] Bencoolen to the almost inaccessible and rocky shores of the west coast of Sumatra."

Raffles's hatred of the Dutch, whom he characterized in the florid prose of the early nineteenth century as "preposterously wicked," fueled his desire to find a place where free trade would flourish under the British.

"In many respects," Raffles wrote to Lord Minto in 1811, "the commercial policy adopted by the Dutch, with regard to the Eastern Islands, and the Malay states in general, was not only contrary to all principles of natural justice, and unworthy of any enlightened and civilized nation, but characterized by a degree of absurdity for which it is scarcely worth taking the trouble of being so preposterously wicked." He described the infamous death penalty for anyone caught buying nutmeg, mace, cloves, or cinnamon, from anyone other than the Dutch as "outrageously disproportioned to the offense." He was also appalled by Dutch efforts to "destroy and eradicate from a vast range of extensive countries, the most advantageous produce of the land, in order to favour their own petty traffic, and their burning a large proportion of the residue, in order to keep up their monopoly price in Europe on a small proportion of this produce . . ." (Raffles was referring to the Dutch practice of deliberately burning the spices in order to maintain low supplies and high prices.) He concluded that such practices "must be viewed by all liberal-minded and intelligent men, with sentiments of equal contempt and detestation." Raffles vitriol toward the Dutch served as the springboard for the crowning accomplishment of his career—the establishment of Singapore.

The British settlements of Penang and Benkoolen were too remote to serve as way stations between India and China. Consequently, wrote Sophia, Raffles's second wife, in her adoring biography of her husband, Raffles "conceived it of primary importance to obtain a post which should have a commanding geographical position at the southern entrance of the Strait of Malacca, which should be in the track of the China and country traders, which should be capable of affording their protection, and of supplying their wants . . . which might give the means of supporting and defending the commercial intercourse of the Malay states, and which, by its contiguity to the seat of the Dutch power, might afford an opportunity to watch the march of its policy and when necessary, to counteract its influence."

Singapore, sitting at the southern entrance to the Strait of Malacca, offered Raffles such an ideal situation, and he lost little time in putting his ideas into action. On February 29, 1819, he hoisted the British flag there after signing a treaty with a local chieftain and a sultan of Johore on the Malay Peninsula, who was not supported by the Dutch. Even though the Dutch vigorously protested, and the Company also initially objected, Raffles blithely went ahead with this inspired act of imperial land grab. Once again, he relied on his own agenda to extend the influence of Company and Crown, arguing that it wasn't territory ". . . but trade; and a fulcrum whence we may extend our influence politically as circumstances may hereafter require." Incidentally, he also hoped that sailors who went to the new port would have no need "to proceed to the more distant, unhealthy, and expensive port of Batavia." He got his wish— Singapore did indeed supplant Batavia, as we know, becoming one of the world's great trading ports.

The Company, however, did not reward Raffles. After he spent six years in Benkoolen, it shut down the settlement, and all of its money-draining residencies along the southwestern coast of Sumatra, relinquishing these possessions to the Dutch. During his years in Sumatra, four of Raffles's children had died, and years of overwork and illness had broken his health. When he left in 1824, he also lost all his wealth. The ship that was to carry him and Sophia home to England caught fire off Benkoolen. It contained his money and personal property—his extensive natural history collections, rare books, art and artifcacts from Malaysia and Indonesia, along with all of his own manuscripts, documents, and maps. The couple was saved, but everything he owned was lost. The ship also carried a "perfect Noah's ark." Raffles wrote: ". . . there was scarce an unknown animal, bird, beast, or fish, or an interesting plant, which we had not on board: a living tapir, a new species of tiger, splendid pheasants, &c, domesticated for the voyage . . ."

Even Malaysian literature suffered an incalculable loss. Abdullah wrote that when he heard about the fire, his "imagination reeled to think of all the works in Malay and other languages, centuries old, which he [Raffles] collected from many countries, all utterly lost." Raffles and Sophia gamely picked up their lives and took another boat back to London, but he never recovered his health or his money. The man "who spoke in smiles" died two years later at the age of forty-five.

In 1824 the English and Dutch reached an agreement that was to become infamous. It defined the spheres of English and Dutch colonialism in Southeast Asia, and the pepper trade as well, and enlarged Britain's presence in India. By that time, the Dutch East India Company, which had always operated as a quasi-government entity, had been dissolved, and the Dutch government had officially taken its place. The English East India Company was still limping along, but its days, too, were numbered, and the British government had for all intents and purposes replaced it. So the negotiations were between two European countries interested in the profits of Asian trade. Despite centuries of rivalry, war, and hatred, each knew that the time had come to reach an understanding, and Sumatra was sacrificed in order for the agreement to proceed.

Like a piece on a chessboard, the English gave Sumatra to the

Dutch, and Dutch-controlled Malacca, which had been bounced among various European trading powers for hundreds of years, was handed over to the British once again. Singapore became a British free port. Now the British could protect their interests in the Strait of Malacca and secure a protected route to China and its lucrative trade. The British at last had more than an "inch of ground to stand upon Between the Cape of Good Hope and China."

For the Dutch, the 1824 aggreement gave them the Indonesian archipelago. To obtain the vast collection of islands, they had to cede their territorial possessions and factories in India, which stretched along the southwestern Malabar Coast and the eastern Coromandel Coast and into Bengal, and give up any claim to Singapore.

The handover of Sumatra was stated in the dry language of the treaty: "The factory of Fort Marlborough, and all the English Possessions on the Island of Sumatra, are hereby ceded to His Netherland Majesty; and his Britannick Majesty further engages that no British Settlement shall be formed on that Island, nor any Treaty concluded by British Authority, with any Native Prince, Chief, or State therein."

After 140 years in Sumatra, the English were finally leaving. The men who had staked their fortunes on growing nutmeg and clove trees in plantations in Benkoolen were dismayed. These Englishmen argued that the Company had encouraged their activities to offset the Dutch spice monopoly in the far eastern Spice Islands and had repeatedly promised to support and protect the plantations. The spice planters believed that they were "rendering an acceptable service to Great Britain, and were in fact promoting a great national object." Now the Company was pulling out when they had not yet earned an adequate return on their investment. ". . . the Bencoolen planter is as effectually ruined as if every tree in his possession were torn up by the roots," the planters bitterly complained.

What about the people of Sumatra? When the Dutch took over, they reinstituted the forced cultivation of pepper. The people were left to their fate. At the handover ceremonies in 1825, a senior local ruler surveyed the gathering of Dutch and English officials and protested. But there was little that he could do. Sumatra had become a pawn in an imperial land swap between colonial powers. ". . . Against this transfer of my country I protest," the ruler said. "Who is there possessed of authority to hand me and my countrymen, like so many cattle, over to the Dutch or to any other power? If the English are tired of us, let them go away, but I deny their right to hand us over to the Dutch . . . We were never conquered, and I now tell the English and Dutch gentlemen here assembled that, had I the power and the will, I would resist this transfer to the knife. I am however a poor man, have no soldiers to cope with yours and must submit. . . ."

Historians point out that the 1824 treaty was deliberately vague about territorial ambitions. As long as the Dutch limited their interests to the archipelago and kept out the French and other rivals, the British were reluctant to intervene as long as their treasured route to China was protected. In imperial terms, the treaty was a tacit acknowledgment that Indonesia "belonged" to the Dutch while Malaysia was in the British sphere of influence. It forbade Britain to establish settlements in Sumatra, but it did not preclude trade with the island. Under its articles, the Dutch could not charge the British more than double the duty charged to Dutch vessels in Dutch-controlled Indonesian ports, and native rulers in the eastern seas could not sign an exclusive treaty with either the Dutch or the British. All previous treaties were abrogated.

The people of Sumatra were largely unaware of the subterranean currents running through the 1824 agreement that secured the

Dutch and English realms of Asian trade. The Acehnese still believed they would remain independent of the Dutch because of the treaty brokered by Raffles in 1819, which had promised a defensive alliance between Britain and Aceh, protecting Aceh from the Dutch. They were further lulled by a note attached to the 1824 treaty that officially recognized their independence, but it is doubtful that the British would have come to Aceh's defense if the Dutch had attacked Aceh then.

As the nineteenth century progressed, the Dutch became increasingly fearful that Aceh, a strategic gem, could not remain outside of their control. After the Javanese wars of the 1820s, the Dutch moved against Sumatra, subduing Jambi in the 1830s and other regions along the eastern coast in the 1850s. When they had secured most of Sumatra, they finally moved against Aceh in 1873, after a new Anglo-Dutch treaty was signed that explicitly gave the Dutch permission to intervene in Aceh. The Acehnese reached out to Turkey, Britain, and the United States, but their pleas were ignored.

However, the fiercely independent people of northern Sumatra, who since the time of Iskandar Muda had shown remarkable resilience in the face of the European onslaught, would not submit to foreign rule easily. The Acehnese would wage a courageous defense of their land, surprising the Dutch with the strength of their resistance.

The Dutch attacked the seat of power in Banda Aceh in March 1873. Surprisingly, the Dutch soldiers were ill prepared for battle and the force retreated after its commander was killed. Later that year, a larger, better-equipped expedition was launched, and this time the palace of the sultanate was overtaken and the city fell to the Dutch. Rather than being the end of the conflict, however, this proved to be just the beginning of a long war that would eventually claim the lives of ten thousand Dutch and some fifty thousand Acehnese.

After Aceh fell, local rulers elsewhere in northern Sumatra immediately rallied to defend their land, and when those uprisings did not succeed, the war took on the trappings of a religious crusade. The local ulamā, or clergy, organized the resistance. In 1885, Teungku Cik di Tiro, a leader of the resistance, appealed to his fellow Acehnese in Dutch-occupied zones: "Do not let yourself be afraid of the strength of the kafir [infidels], their fine possessions, their equipment, and their good soldiers, in comparison to our strength, our property, our equipment and the Muslim people, for no one is strong, no one is rich, and no one has fine armies but the great God . . . and no one gives victory or defeat than God . . ."

When the tides of the war turned against the Acehnese in the 1890s, the tenor of the argument made by resistance leaders changed to one promoting the glories of life after death, echoing the language used by Islamist extremists today to recruit suicide bombers.

> *. . . to die a shahid [martyr] is nothing. It is like being tickled until we fall and roll over . . .*
> *Then comes a heavenly princess,*
> *Who cradles you in her lap and wipes away the blood,*
> *Her heart all yours . . .*
> *If the heavenly princesses were visible,*
> *Everyone would go to fight the Dutch.*

It took the Dutch some thirty years to conquer Aceh, and in the years that followed the Acehnese remained bitterly opposed to Dutch rule. When the Japanese occupied the island in World War II, the

Acehnese welcomed them. Their hatred for the Dutch overrode their feelings about the Japanese.

Sumatra was the world's leading producer of pepper from the seventeenth to the nineteenth centuries, and the berry exacted an awful price from the people of this island. After WWII, its extensive plantations were largely abandoned and, although pepper is still grown in Indonesia today, Sumatra never regained its prewar eminence in the trade.

Six

The Dutch Terror

IN THE EARLY SEVENTEENTH CENTURY, ANIMOSITY DEEPENED
BETWEEN THE DUTCH AND ENGLISH AFTER TEN ENGLISHMEN
WERE BEHEADED BY THE DUTCH ON THE ISLAND OF AMBOYNA.
ELSEWHERE, THE POLICIES OF VOC GENERAL JAN PIETERSZOON
COEN LED TO THE GENOCIDE OF THE BANDANESE PEOPLE.
COEN SET UP BATAVIA AS THE VOC'S HEADQUARTERS IN ASIA,
WHICH BECAME A GREAT SEAPORT.

•

*"Your Honours should know by experience that trade in Asia must be driven
and maintained under the protection and favour of Your Honours' own
weapons, and that the weapons must be paid for by the profits from the trade;
so that we cannot carry on trade without war nor war without trade,"*
—JAN PIETERSZOON COEN TO THE GENTLEMEN 17, THE DIRECTORS OF THE
DUTCH EAST INDIA COMPANY, FROM BANTAM, JAVA, 1614

"I believe there are nowhere greater thieves."
—ENGLISH PIRATE WILLIAM DAMPIER, 1685,
REFERRING TO DUTCH SEAMEN

Only two years after the English East India Company received its charter from Queen Elizabeth in 1600, the VOC
was established. Soon millions of pounds of pepper began

pouring into Europe, setting the stage for an intense rivalry between the two northern European trading companies that would last some two hundred years. By 1621, the total market for pepper in Europe was about 7.2 million pounds. In Indonesia, the then-new competition between the English and Dutch led to a considerable rise in the purchase price of pepper. They were bidding against each other, and consequently the price for ten Bantam sacks of pepper, about 654 pounds, had jumped fivefold from 1600 to 1620, enriching the rulers of Jambi and Palembang on the east coast of Sumatra. Producers in Aceh, Jambi, Palembang, and Bantam cleared more land to plant pepper gardens to meet the growing demand from Europe, as well as the ever-expanding market in China.

Elsewhere, however, the demand for more spices did not enrich the native inhabitants of Indonesia. In the Banda Islands, the only place in the world where nutmeg trees grew and where the natives were dependent on imported food for survival, the VOC ruthlessly pursued its quest to gain exclusive control of the nutmeg (and mace) trade. Violence had erupted almost as soon as Dutch and English company ships appeared in the far eastern islands.

When the rise in the purchase price of spices threatened the profits of both companies, and politics persuaded the Dutch to maintain good relations with the English, the two rivals were compelled to consider an option loathsome to them—cooperation. In an attempt to keep a lid on the cost of buying spices in Indonesia, the mercantile companies signed a treaty in 1619 that gave the VOC two-thirds of the trade in cloves and nutmegs, with the remainder going to the English East India Company. The pepper trade at Bantam was to be divided equally between the two, eliminating bidding on the spice. Any problems between the companies were to be resolved by the English sovereign and the States-General in Holland.

Each company was also supposed to provide for the defense of their common interests, obliging the English to help pay for Dutch forts—a stipulation that was almost guaranteed to sink the agreement.

The Dutch in Asia did not know about the political forces that shaped the mutual trade agreement. Jan Pieterszoon Coen, the brutal governor-general of the VOC's trade in Asia from 1619 to 1623 and from 1627 to 1629, couldn't believe such a treaty existed. Denouncing it as a gift to the English East India Company, he complained to his bosses in Amsterdam that the English "could not pretend to a single grain of sand of the Moluccas, Ambon or the Banda Islands." He implored: "if you, gentlemen, want great and notable deeds in the honour of God and for the prosperity of our country, so relieve us from the English."

Coen, who studied bookkeeping in his youth, was the antithesis of the tolerant Dutch mercantilist associated with the glory days of Holland in the seventeenth century. Advocating the ruthless enforcement of the VOC's spice monopolies, he once promoted the idea of colonizing the Spice Islands with Dutch colonists who would grow their own food with the help of slave laborers. Even the VOC wondered how native islanders would survive under this scheme, noting that "there is no profit at all in an empty sea, empty countries, and dead people." Rising quickly anyway in the ranks of the company, Coen first sailed to Asia in 1607 at the age of twenty, and only a few years later became the commander of two VOC ships sailing to the far eastern islands. In 1619, when he was thirty-two years old, Coen attained the most powerful position in the VOC's Asian network by being appointed Governor-General. Wielding the power of the VOC, he immediately went about the business of ensuring that the company would have exclusive trade agreements with the inhabitants of the islands.

Violence followed Coen throughout his career, but the murder of

Dutch Admiral Pieter Verhoeven and forty-six of his men by the Bandanese in 1609, undoubtedly helped shape Coen's attitude about the islands—Verhoeven was beheaded. Operating under instructions from the Gentlemen 17, the VOC's directors, Verhoeven had been trying to negotiate an exclusive contract for nutmeg when the attack occurred. His fleet appeared while William Keeling, the captain of the English East India Company's third voyage, was on one of the Banda Islands loading nutmeg. The Dutch immediately suspected that Keeling had instigated the attack by the Bandanese against Verhoeven and his men. The English captain repeatedly declared his innocence and, despite Dutch attempts to prevent him from loading his ships, Keeling didn't leave the islands until he was satisfied with his cargo. Afterward, the Dutch blockaded the island where the killings took place, starving the population. Those who survived signed an exclusive trade contract with the VOC. The Dutch thought the contract extended to all of the Banda Islands, but it did not. In the following years, English ships occasionally appeared, and the people on some of the other islands, notably Ay and Run, turned to them for protection against the seemingly genocidal Dutch.

The Amboyna Massacre

The Dutch and the English both set their sights on the bounty of the far eastern islands, but the Dutch had the better organization and the finances to make first claims. They cleared away the Portuguese and the Spanish, capturing Amboyna from the Portuguese in 1605, and building a fort in east Ternate, once a stronghold of the Spanish, in 1607. The Dutch weren't happy to share the fruits of their efforts with the English ships that occasionally visited.

Almost from its inception, the Anglo-Dutch rivalry was engorged with hatred, but an incident in the early decades of the seventeenth century on a small island in the remote reaches of the South China Sea ensured a long-lasting enmity. Amboyna, an English sea captain wrote in 1621, "sitteth as queen between the isles of Banda and the Moluccas. She is beautified with fruits of several factories, and dearly beloved of the Dutch." Here, where the sea breezes carried the scent of cloves, the Dutch brutally tortured and beheaded ten Englishmen in 1623, an incident known as the Amboyna Massacre.

The Dutch had built a heavily secured fort in the town of Ambon on Amboyna, where they attempted to concentrate the production of cloves. Surrounded by a moat, the fort was festooned with brass ordnance and was a garrison for some two hundred Dutch soldiers and a handful of hired Japanese warriors. A small group of unarmed English traders lived in a house in the town. The Dutch accused them of conspiring to kill the Dutch governor, Herman van Speult, to overthrow the garrison once an English Company ship arrived. Clearly, the English were greatly outnumbered and without arms, but in the tense atmosphere following the agreement of 1619, the conspiracy may have seemed real to van Speult, some historians speculate. The Dutch based their claims on the inquisitiveness of a Japanese warrior who had asked a Dutchman on night patrol a series of questions about the strength of the garrison, which seems fairly innocuous given the setting.

Who knows? Perhaps the man was simply taking a walk and decided to make small talk with the night patrolman. Apparently the Dutch believed that his questions were aimed at obtaining information that would help the English storm the garrison. Rather than making inquiries that may have resolved their suspicions, the Dutch seized the Japanese man, put him to torture, and soon obtained a confession of a conspiracy. Ten Englishmen were then quickly rounded up.

The Dutch also used torture to wring confessions from the unfortunate Englishmen who were arrested. A description of these torments by the surviving Englishman on the island was published in a pamphlet in England, which served for many years as an indelible reminder of Dutch cruelty. Samuel Colson confessed to plotting against the Dutch after he saw what water torture had done to his fellow countryman Edward Collins. The Dutch version of waterboarding involved hoisting a man some two feet off the ground with his arms and legs spread as far apart as possible, fastened to a door post with iron rungs. A cloth draped around his neck and face was pulled out to form a funnel. Then the torturer stepped up on a table and poured water "softly upon his head until the cloth was full, up to the mouth and nostrils, and somewhat higher; so that he could not draw breath, but he must withal suck-in water: which being still continued to bee poured in softly, forced all in inwards parts, came out of his nose, eares, and eyes; and often as it was stifling & choking him, at length took away his breath, & brought him to a swoune or fainting. . . . Then they tooke him quickly down, and make him vomit up the water. Being a little recovered, they triced him up againe, and poured in the water as before . . . till his body was swolne twice or thrice as bigge as before, high cheeks like great bladders, and his eyes staring and strutting out beyond his forehead . . ." If a man refused to confess, his feet, elbows, the palms of his hand, and armpits were burned with lit candles.

Gabriel Towerson, the chief English factor in Amboyna, was beheaded first in late February, 1623. Colson and eight other Englishmen, a Portuguese man named Augustine Perez, and ten Japanese warriors were subsequently executed for conspiring to overthrow the Dutch in Amboyna. Edward Collins and several other Englishmen were pardoned. The trumped-up charges, the confessions obtained through torture, and the executions outraged the English, who had planned to quit the Bandas and the Moluccas anyway, a good two months before the killings took place. They left soon after.

The infamous Amboyna Massacre reverberated for the remainder of the seventeenth century, providing the basis for the enduring hatred between the English and the Dutch, who in Europe fought three wars over trade in the seventeenth century, and a fourth in the eighteenth century that was a disaster for the Dutch. As part of the treaty ending the First Anglo-Dutch War in 1654, relatives of the men who died in Amboyna received £3,615. The events in Amboyna shattered any hopes that the Dutch were inclined to share in the riches of the spice trade.

Jan Pieterszoon Coen wasn't officially governor-general when the Amboyna executions occurred (he had recently left the post and had even promised to send a Dutch ship to Amboyna to bring away the English prior to the accusations of a conspiracy), but the loss of human life probably would not have upset him; his hatred of the English and anyone else who defied the Dutch was well known. In his most notorious act, Coen brought a force of some two thousand men to the Banda Islands in 1621 and slaughtered some thirteen thousand native people. Thousands of other Bandanese subsequently died of starvation or were deported as slaves. Only a few hundred people survived. Afterward, slaves from various parts of Asia were shipped to the islands to harvest nutmeg. Although there were critics in Holland who were outraged by Coen's actions, the VOC did not intervene to stop him.

The Dutch had another strategy to ensure their spice monopoly—laying waste to forests. To prevent outsiders from stealing spices, they cut down spice trees on certain islands to concentrate production on others, an approach that didn't work especially well. According to the pirate William Dampier, a sea captain named "Rofy" related in 1685 that "while he lived with the Dutch, he was sent with other men to cut down the spice trees; and he himself did at several times cut down 700 to 800 trees. Yet although the Dutch take such care to destroy them, there are many uninhabited islands that have plenty of spice trees." Dampier also mentioned a captain of a Dutch ship who told him that "near the island of Banda there is an island where the cloves falling from the trees lie and rot on the ground . . . at times 3 to 4 inches thick under the trees." No matter how many trees they destroyed, the Dutch were never entirely successful in preventing spice piracy. The Dutch monopoly in far eastern spices was also difficult to enforce for another reason: cloves and nutmegs found their way onto English and French ships with the help of corrupt VOC officials. One of the biggest obstacles the Dutch faced during the seventeenth century was the port of Makassar on South Sulawesi.

Defying the Dutch monopoly, the Makassarese sailed to the far eastern Spice Islands and brought nutmegs and cloves back to the port of Makassar, which lies on the southern peninsula of Sulawesi. Consequently, Makassar became a major port for spices and other commodities among European and Chinese traders who wanted to avoid the Dutch. The English set up a factory in the port in 1613, and the Danish, French, Portuguese, and Chinese regularly visited. The traders could buy the spices from the Spice Islands, pepper, cloth from India, and Chinese wares, and they were welcomed in Makassar, which was known for its unusual openness toward foreigners. One of its government officials had a library filled with European books and he was especially keen to learn about Western science.

The VOC often asked Makassarese rulers to restrict trade, to which one ruler famously replied: "God has made the earth and the sea and has divided the earth among men and given the sea in common to all." These were people who didn't believe that the oceans had landlords. Their political and economic acumen made them powerful, and many in eastern Indonesia believed the Makassar kingdom could not be conquered, according to historian Leonard Andaya. But an unlikely alliance between the Dutch and the Bugis people of South Sulawesi, enemies of the Makassar people, would put an end to Makassar rule. Cornelis Speelman, the corrupt VOC commander who later banished the English and other foreign traders from Bantam in Java, led the expedition against Makassar and other major towns along the southwestern coast of the island. Like the Portuguese who enlisted the help of Malaysian rulers to repel an attack on Malacca by Iskandar Muda earlier in the seventeenth century, the Dutch, too, exploited rivalries among native peoples to further their cause.

In late 1666, Speelman sent a fleet of nearly 1,900 Dutch soldiers and sailors, Bugis, and natives from the Spice Islands to destroy the Makassar kingdom. On land they were joined by many more Bugis troops, but they also encountered fierce opposition from an army of some 15,000 Makassarese. Speelman had expected to go to war, although it took more than a year for Makassar to fall. Numerous villages were burned and thousands died.

The Makassarese were a vanquished people. The treaty ending the war gave the VOC control over the trade and foreign affairs of South Sulawesi, while the Bugis ruled internally. Now only the Dutch could trade in Makassar. The Portuguese and the English were immediately expelled and were not allowed to enter or live there again. The VOC reserved the right to trade exclusively in cloth and Chinese wares and it was also exempt from all import and export tolls and duties. Meanwhile, the Makassarese had to pay for damages to VOC property during the war, and no new fortifications could be built without Dutch approval. Finally, the Makassar people could only sail to Bali, the Java coast, Jambi and Palembang in Sumatra, Johor in Malaysia, and Borneo. Any Makassar ship found on the open seas without a Dutch pass risked attack.

Long before the war in Makassar, it was already well established that the Dutch would pursue a spice monopoly by any means. Ironically, their obsession with spices led to one of the most lopsided deals in modern history. In 1666, the same year that the Dutch began their conquest of Makassar, the tiny island of Run, where the Dutch had burned down all of the nutmeg trees, was given to the Dutch by the English. In return, the English got the island of Manhattan.

Put off by the Portuguese forts along the pepper-rich coast of southwest India, the Dutch in the early seventeenth century looked elsewhere to establish a rendezvous, a central location for transshipment of goods to Holland and to Asia. They had first chosen Amboyna as their headquarters but soon realized that it was too far from the nexus of trade in Asia. Malacca was a natural choice, but the Dutch had so far failed to oust the Portuguese. (They finally succeeded in 1641, following a six-year blockade of the Strait of Malacca.) Their interest then turned to the Indonesian archipelago, where pepper could be obtained and where the Straits of Malacca and Sunda were crucial transit points for Asian goods going to Europe and to markets in Asia, especially China. The Dutch had already established a fast route to Indonesia. Unlike other Europeans sailing on the Indian Ocean, they reached Indonesia by setting a course due east along the "roaring forties" after leaving the Cape of Good Hope. When they encountered the southeast trade winds, they set their course north toward the Strait of Sunda.

Until the arrival of Jan Pieterszoon Coen, none of the rulers in Java would grant the Dutch permission to build a fort on their territory. Bantam was the most obvious choice for a fort because it already was a major pepper port, but the Bantamese successfully rebuffed the Dutch. "Permission" would have to be obtained by force of arms, an approach Coen preferred. He found his opportunity in nearby Jakarta, a town situated on a marshy plain at the head of a large bay, well placed to be a center for trade in Asian goods because of its position on the Straits of Malacca and Sunda. Despite some initial jockeying for power between the Dutch and English, who initially showed up with a larger number of ships, Coen finally seized the port in 1619 and destroyed the quarters belonging to the *panegran* (prince), who was sent packing to Bantam. The newly named Batavia was more than ten thousand miles from Holland by way of the Cape of Good Hope.

"All the kings of these lands know full well what the planting of our colony at Jakarta signifies, and what may follow from it, as well as the cleverest and most far-seeing politician in Europe might do," Coen boasted, reveling in his victorious assault and the threat it posed to other Europeans, especially the English. An orderly walled Dutch city, with its tidy rows of houses, canals, and a towering castle known as Casteel Batavia, would be built on the smoldering ruins of old Jakarta. Eventually, nearly all of the VOC's trade in Asia would be funneled through Batavia, a hub system reminiscent of modern-day air travel. Incoming and outgoing Dutch company ships had to stop in Batavia. In the seventeenth century, this port city was unique.

Once considered one of the great seaports of the world, Batavia was a bustling entrepôt frequented by innumerable vessels. A forest of masts filled its bay. The Indiamen of the English East India Company and other ships sailing between Europe and China stopped in Batavia, and it was the main port for Chinese, Indian, and other Asian ships. During its heyday, roughly from the late seventeenth century until 1730, Batavia was known as the "Queen of the East." "The Bay of Batavia is the finest and most secure of any in the world," wrote a French traveler in the 1680s. "Ships ride there without any danger all year round; for that Sea is hardly ever agitated, as well because there are a great number of little Islands that break the waves . . ."

Indeed, Batavia became famous for its sheltered anchorage. VOC Captain John Splinter Stavorinus observed in 1771 that "the road of Batavia is justly esteemed one of the best in the world, as well with regard to the anchoring-ground . . . as with regard to the safety it affords to the ships which anchor in it, and to the number which it can contain. Although the road is open from N.W. to E.N.E. and east, yet ships lie as secure and quiet as if they were landlocked, on account of the numerous islands which lie on that side, and break the force of the waves. Ships, therefore, are never obliged to moor stem and stern here; and the current which runs within the islands is not strong, but without them it is very violent." Stavorinus's informative journals were published in Dutch soon after he died in 1788 at the age of forty-nine. English and French translations quickly followed.

The lure of pepper had brought the Chinese to Java and Sumatra long before the arrival of the Dutch, and they were welcomed in Batavia. Historian Leonard Blussé describes Batavia as a Chinese city built by Chinese migrant laborers who stayed and eventually prospered, often choosing to marry Balinese slave women who were brought to the city. The Dutch needed the Chinese to populate the city because relatively few Dutch wanted to settle in such a faraway place, and in the early years of the city's history Chinese people were abducted in China and brought to Batavia. Over the course of the seventeenth century, the Chinese became an economic force; Batavia, in Blussé's words, was a Chinese colonial town under Dutch protection. Fearing uprisings from the Javanese, the Dutch did not allow them to live in the city.

From the beginning, the Dutch wanted to ensure that Batavia would be the biggest port in Indonesia, and to achieve their goal they resorted to their usual tactics. Only one year after the founding of Batavia, the Dutch blockaded Jambi in eastern Sumatra and Bantam in Java in order to divert Chinese junks to Batavia. Coen also ordered Dutch ships to remove pepper from Chinese junks under the pretext that the Chinese, who often acted as intermediaries in the pepper trade, were in debt to the Dutch.

The unremitting hunger for pepper among the Chinese was one of the engines that drove trade in Batavia. Richly laden Chinese ships brought "coarse commodities" such as porcelain, ironware, textile piece goods, and leaden coins called *picis,* which were traded for large amounts of pepper. In 1694, for example, over two million pounds of pepper were sold to twenty junks that had arrived in Batavia. Indeed, by the end of the seventeenth century the Dutch had pulled out of direct trade with China entirely and allowed the Chinese to trade in the archipelago without safe conduct passes, a rare privilege.

At around the same time, the rather cozy arrangements between the Dutch and the Chinese in urban Batavia began to fray because of Chinese sugar plantations. As the plantations expanded, a large number of the unemployed and undocumented from China poured into Java to work in the mills. The Dutch reacted by imposing quotas on immigration and instituting residency permits. Many undocumented Chinese people were deported to China; a smaller number was banished to the Cape of Good Hope. Meanwhile, Chinese residents inside the city were being pressed by exorbitant taxes and various extortions, in addition to the monthly poll tax that they had paid since Batavia was established.

When the market for Batavian sugar sank due to changes in supplies to Europe in the 1720s, mills were forced to close and desperate workers filled the countryside. By the 1730s, some 50 percent of Batavia's population was Chinese, and the town of some 24,000 was sitting atop a powder keg. In the spring of 1740, VOC authorities lit the fuse with a plan to ship unemployed Chinese people to Ceylon (modern-day Sri Lanka) in order to solve Batavia's "Chinese problem." Rumors spread quickly among the Chinese that the Dutch had no intention of sailing to Ceylon but instead planned to throw workers overboard. Chinese workers in the countryside revolted, attacking sugar mills and breaching the walls of the city. They had expected Batavia's Chinese residents to unite with them, but the VOC quickly put down the revolt. The reaction over the following days was swift and horrible. Thousands of Chinese residences and businesses were plundered. Altogether, some ten thousand Chinese people lost their lives in the 1740 massacre. In the aftermath, the Chinese were no longer allowed to live inside the city.

By the nineteenth century, the town had declined significantly, its high walls destroyed, its canals filled. But its polyglot wealth was still evident among the remaining ornate gates and drawbridges that once graced its numerous canals. An octagon church that held a great organ and teakwood pulpit, and a baronial city hall, among other buildings, were reminders of its former glory when "Europeans would doubtless be dazzled, and inclined to envy his hospitable host, the luxurious Batavian," one observer wrote. Trees with their fragrant blossoms still lined the canals, although the little pavilions where the city's burghers once sat in the evening to enjoy their pipes and beloved beer had disappeared.

Visitors were well aware of the decline in the city's fortunes. Batavia's success as a center for Asian trade in the seventeenth and eighteenth centuries could not shield the city from disease. Like Benkoolen in Sumatra, Batavia proved to be a graveyard. The sugar plantations in the countryside contributed to the problem. As the plantations expanded, fresh water running through the city's canals was diverted for irrigation and more land was cleared of forest, causing silting and stagnant water that became a breeding ground for malaria-carrying mosquitoes. In the late 1770s, Stavorinus described Batavia as a "most unwholesome place of abode, and the mortality greater here, than at any other spot of the Company's possessions . . ."

Thousands of VOC employees died from malaria. Historians estimate that the disease killed about 20 percent of the Dutch population, although the death toll was far higher in some years. In 1768 and 1769, for instance, some 2,400 of 5,490 employees of the company died in the city's hospitals. Situated on a marshy plane, Batavia was "surrounded on all sides by stagnant waters, fens, bogs, and oozy ditches—every street intersected by canals . . . into which every description of filth was thrown," wrote J. N. Reynolds, an American who visited Batavia in the 1830s. He described Batavia, "this boasted mart of the world," as a "garnished sepulcher, . . . teeming with contagion, pestilence and death."

In a relatively short period of time, Indian Ocean ports stretching from India to the Strait of Malacca and the South China Sea became acquainted with Dutch traders in their fast ships. Although the VOC and the English East India Company were established nearly simultaneously, from the beginning the VOC was given far greater powers than its English counterpart.

English sovereigns were content to give the John Company an exclusive charter to sell pepper and other spices; the English government did not have a stake in the Company—sovereigns renewed its charter throughout the Company's existence. By contrast, the Jan Company, as the VOC was called, is often described as a "state within a state." The VOC could negotiate treaties with foreign rulers, hire soldiers, build forts, and arm its ships. It was basically an "armed" company. It also was well financed—the VOC had ten times the capitalization of the English East India Company.

Consequently, the VOC had many more ships than the English East India Company—from 1600 to 1650, for example, the Dutch sent 655 ships to Asia while the English sent only 286, and obviously imported far more pepper. The Dutch took the lead quite early. By 1615 the VOC was importing up to six million pounds of pepper from the East. Pepper accounted for some 60 percent of the VOC's trade in the years 1619 to 1621, and still made up some 50 percent of the value of Dutch trade from Batavia to Europe in 1650. The English East India Company usually lagged far behind during the first half of the seventeenth century, with its annual pepper imports ranging from a low of some 420,000 pounds in 1609 to a high of nearly three million in 1626. The English managed to import more than one million pounds only twelve times in the years between 1603 and 1640.

The VOC was the most successful commercial enterprise of its kind in the seventeenth century, the golden age of Dutch history, when commerce and the arts flourished. This was the age of Rembrandt and Vermeer. Dutch power sprang from its mastery of the seas. A beautiful gold-embossed atlas published in 1630 by Willem Blaeu, one of the most celebrated cartographers of his day, contains depictions of lofty Dutch ships, tricolors unfurled, along the coasts of the New World, Europe, and Asia. In Blaeu's detailed map of Asia, Sumatra is studded with ports. Maps like these hung on the walls of Dutch houses and are seen in some of Vermeer's paintings.

While the VOC profited from trade to Europe, it also benefited substantially from trade to Asia, which was called the country trade. No other European trading company participated in the intra-Asian trade as widely as the VOC did in the seventeenth century. The Dutch joined an already thriving trading network and used their military powers to manipulate it to their own advantage. They understood the vital importance of the intra-Asian trade. "The country trade and the profit from it are the soul of the Company which must be looked after carefully, because if the soul decays, the entire body would be destroyed quickly," the Gentlemen 17, the directors of the VOC, wrote in 1648.

In order to understand the success of the Dutch in Asian trade, one has to begin with India. Indian textiles were the keys that opened the doors to intra-Asia trade, especially the spice trade. Coarse piece-goods as well as exceptional handwoven textiles from India had long been traded for pepper and other spices in Indonesia, and Indian and Arab traders knew the types of cotton cloth that appealed to people living in each of the vast archipelago's major ports. When the Europeans arrived, their textiles could not possibly compete with the amazing variety of heavier calicoes and thinner muslins of India. Available in plain colors, like white or brown, the cotton textiles also were adorned in colorful patterns produced by wood blocks, or were painted. The printed pieces were called chintz and the painted cloths *pintadoes*. The southeast Coromandel Coast was a vital part of the trade, as Hendrik Brouwer, a high-ranking VOC administrator noted in 1612: "The Coromandel Coast is the left arm of the Moluccas, because we have noticed that without the textiles of Coromandel, commerce is dead in the Moluccas." He served in Japan and was Governor-General in Asia from 1632 to 1636, and pioneered the "roaring forties" route across the Indian Ocean to Indonesia.

The Dutch could have bought Indian textiles from Aceh in Sumatra, but the dividend-conscious merchants figured it would be more profitable to purchase these textiles from the source, and that is why the Dutch and the English originally sought factories in the cloth-producing areas of India.

Jan Pieterszoon Coen, the butcher of the Bandas, then based in Bantam, Java, saw the possibilities. He described with unusual clarity the complexities of the intra-Asian trade, envisioning a giant swap market with textiles, spices, and precious metals exchanged in a dizzying symphony of trade. Unlike other Europeans, the Dutch relied heavily on precious metals from Japan to help grease the wheels of trade in Asia, an arrangement that worked well for most of Holland's glorious seventeenth century.

In 1619, Coen wrote to the Gentlemen 17 of his vision. "Guserat textiles must be traded for pepper and gold on the shores of Sumatra; pepper from Bantam for reals and textiles from the coast [of

Coromandel]; Chinese goods and gold for sandalwood, pepper and reals; silver can be got from Japan for Chinese goods; the textiles from the Coromandel coast for spices, other merchandise and pieces of eight; pieces of eight from Arabia for spices and other small goods, making sure that one compensates the other, and that all is done in ships without money from the Netherlands. *Your worships have the principal spices already so what is stopping it? Only a few ships and a little water to work the pumps.* [Italics added.] Are there more ships in the world than in the Netherlands? Is there a lack of water there to prime the pumps? (I mean with this, send enough money, until the marvelous native trade has been reformed)."

Coen omitted a crucial piece of information in his analysis of the intricacies of intra-Asian trade. How would the Dutch pay for the Indian textiles from Gujarat, the first item on his long list, the one that sets in motion all of the other exchanges? The Indians weren't interested in the European goods offered by the Dutch, which perhaps explains his omission. He was well aware that the Indians wanted money, and they wanted it in the form of silver and other precious metals.

Historians estimate that the Dutch shipped cloth from the Coromandel Coast of India to Batavia worth some 22,000 to 44,000 pounds of silver (roughly one to two million guilders) annually from 1620 to 1650. What happened to all of that silver? No one really knows for sure. Silver flowed into Asia like an enormous river (the Spanish silver mines in South America were a major source), but the Dutch were lucky to find additional supplies of precious metals in Asia, especially silver in Japan, which aided their booming intra-Asian business in the seventeenth century. When the Japanese banned the export of silver in the later part of the century, the textile exchange in Asia had already begun to wind down; people in Java and Sumatra, and elsewhere in Southeast Asia, could no longer afford to buy as much cloth, because they were no longer making as much of a profit from growing pepper as they had been earlier in the century.

By the second half of the seventeenth century, the VOC had begun to successfully apply pressure to control prices, forcing spice growers to sell their crops at low contract prices. The long arm of the VOC could be felt throughout the pepper-growing regions of Sumatra and Java. A once-profitable endeavor had now lost its luster, and a Malaysian court chronicle of the late seventeenth century conveys the lamentable predicament of pepper growers: "Let people nowhere in this country plant pepper, as is done in Jambi and Palembang. Perhaps those countries grow pepper for the sake of money, in order to grow wealthy. There is no doubt that in the end they will go to ruin."

When Indian cloth could no longer be traded widely for pepper in Southeast Asia, the VOC and the English East India Company found another item that could be substituted easily—opium grown in India. The narcotic was first traded for pepper along the Malabar Coast of India in 1663, when the Dutch conquered Cochin, and soon after opium began flowing to Indonesia. By 1688 the VOC was exporting some 56,000 pounds of opium from Bengal to the archipelago; twenty years later, the amount had doubled. By the early eighteenth century more than 100,000 pounds were exported during peak years, which rarely satisfied VOC orders of up to 190,000 pounds annually.

Public auctions of opium were held in Batavia, where merchants from Indonesia, Malaysia, and China bought the drug, and the Dutch pursued exclusive contracts to sell opium in Sumatra and Java. After the Dutch conquered Bantam, they made a special effort to make opium widely available in Java, but forbid the sale of the drug in Batavia itself, fearing that slaves in the city would start smoking. Obviously, the Dutch were well aware of the debilitating effects of the drug. Historian Om Prakash writes that opium was smoked everywhere in the Indonesian archipelago, but it was most widely used in Java, Sumatra, and the Malay Peninsula. The predilection for opium among the Malaysians was noted by many European travelers.

"The Mallayans are such admirers of opium that they would mortgage all they hold most valuable to procure it," wrote Charles Lockyer, one of the many Englishmen who engaged in private trade in Asia. In 1711 he described opium addicts who disengaged from their day-to-day lives, caught in the grip of their addiction. "Those that use it to excess are seldom long-lived, which themselves are very sensible of; yet they are no longer satisfied than their cares are diverted by the pleasing effects of it," he noted. "I have been told by an Englishman who accustomed himself to it at Benkoolen; it is a difficult matter to leave it, after once experiencing the exquisite harmony, where with it affects every part of the body. On such a tickling in his blood, such a languishing delight in everything he did, that it justly might be termed a pleasure too great for human nature to support."

The scholar William Marsden commented on opium smoking in his masterwork *The History of Sumatra*. He, too, noted that Malaysians were particularly attached to opium, and estimated that about 120 chests, or about 16,800 pounds, were purchased annually on the west coast of Sumatra. Each sold for about three hundred dollars, although he reported that in times of scarcity a chest could be sold for its weight in silver, and a single chest of about 140 pounds of the drug could fetch up to three thousand dollars. Marsden didn't believe that opium was a problem and described it as a "luxury" in Sumatra. The vicious attacks and furious quarrels attributed to its use were, in his estimation, "idle notions."

In fact, all of the Europeans in the eighteenth century sold the narcotic in Asia because it was another extraordinarily profitable commodity, an integral part of Asian trade. The United States joined the trade at the turn of the nineteenth century when the newly founded country entered the pepper business. Hezekiah Beers Pierrepont, an American merchant, distiller, and major landowner in New York City, knew about opium's importance. He was a pepper trader in his youth. Opium, he wrote in 1796, was the "chief article" bartered for pepper in Penang (off of the west coast of the Malay Peninsula), adding that "consumption among the Mallays is immense." Bengal textile piece goods, iron, old muskets and pistols, among other items, were also traded for pepper, which could be bought at about nine to twelve cents a pound, he noted.

American pepper traders routinely bartered opium for pepper in Indonesia and Malaysia during the nineteenth century. "Nothing is more certain than that opium brings generally 100 percent [profit] when sold to the Malays in Barter, and no reason can be alleged against visiting the Malay Coasts except Danger," wrote merchant Thomas Patrickson to Isaac Hazelhurst in 1789. Hazelhurst owned a shipping company in New York. Patrickson touted the advantages of trading opium for pepper, calculating that 3,000 to 4,000 pounds sterling would buy enough opium in India to acquire an entire cargo of pepper, some 350,000 pounds, from the Malaysians. In turn, the pepper would yield 35,000 pounds sterling, a *1,000 percent* profit on their initial investment.

Opium wasn't the only means of buying pepper. The archipelago had a long history of trade, and coins made of silver, lead, and copper were used to purchase pepper in Indonesia. In 1768 Stavorinus, the VOC captain, for example, sailed from Batavia carrying eight chests with fifty thousand Spanish dollars on board to pay for pepper purchased from the king of Bantam. And it was well known that people in Sumatra liked to wear coins as ornaments. Raffles noticed that in the interior of Sumatra people wore necklaces of coins. He observed that "women and children were decorated with a profusion of silver ornaments, and particularly with strings of dollars and other coins hanging two or three deep round the neck. It was not uncommon to see a child with a hundred dollars round her neck."

When the market for Indian textiles in Southeast Asia declined, a new market opened in Europe for this cloth, which was used for clothing and furnishings. By the late seventeenth century, the export to Europe of piece goods from Bengal, in particular, had soared. The Bengal textiles, a mixture of cotton and silk, were of finer quality than the brightly colored, coarser calicoes from Gujarat and other areas of western India, which were needed for the slave trade in the West Indies. Increasingly, the ledgers of both the VOC and the English East India Company displayed Indian textiles. By 1738 textiles, silk, and cotton accounted for nearly 30 percent of the value of goods exported from Batavia.

By that time tea and coffee, too, had become a staple in the Asia-to-Europe trade. Near the end of the eighteenth century, the English East India Company was importing some fifteen to twenty million pounds of tea from China, a trade that largely eluded the VOC. Millions of pounds of black and green teas, with names like souchong, hyson skin, young hyson, Singlo, Twankay, and Bohea, were packed in chests and loaded onto ships in Canton.

The English East India Company had also taken over the trade in textiles by the last half of the eighteenth century. "The trade in piece goods, which in former times, produced such considerable benefit to the company, is now almost entirely in the hands of the English; at least they are very detrimental to the portion of it that remains with us, by their competition for purchases [in India]," VOC Captain Stavorinus observed in 1770. In the nineteenth century, the English would provide their own textiles to compete with Indian goods in Asia; the advent of machine weaving and spinning in the second half of the eighteenth century allowed the English to sell their textiles at affordable prices for the first time in Asia. Trade in English manufactured goods was still a "new thing" in Asia, noted Pierrepont, the New York-based trader, in 1796.

Textiles and tea became main sources of revenue for the English East India Company in the eighteenth century, although pepper was never omitted from its ledgers. The spice was still an integral part of the intra-Asian trade, especially in China, and millions of pounds were imported to Europe annually. However, by the last half of the eighteenth century the spice that originally inspired ocean travel had been overtaken by other luxuries and temptations in the world's marketplaces.

What contributed to the downfall of the VOC? It is hard to believe that a quasi-military, government-supported company that wielded wide power in Asia in the seventeenth and eighteenth centuries could ever be brought down, but it fell as a result of its own internal dynamics. Part of the reason stemmed from the way it treated its employees. The men employed by the VOC knew that they were risking their lives in the tropics, but they also knew that they could strike it rich in the tropics. Their daily wages were a pittance, but they could buy and sell spices on their own or steal spices from the company's ships and make a fortune. The company, thousands of miles away, could do very little to stop them. "Virtually nobody was able to live on their official pay, let alone save anything for eventual retirement, and pensions were only awarded under very exceptional circumstances before about 1753," wrote historian C. R. Boxer in his groundbreaking book *The Dutch Seaborne Empire*. "The result was that everyone from Governor-General to cabin-boy traded on the side and everyone else knew it." The so-called quasi-legal "private trade," which allowed VOC seamen and merchants to bring home a small amount of goods from the East, was so widely abused that some ships returning to Holland carried more "private goods" than company goods.

Many other opportunities for enrichment existed. Squeezing "extra" commissions from native suppliers, doctoring the books with overvalued goods, using different scales to weigh incoming and outgoing merchandise, and adulterating and pilfering goods destined for VOC warehouses or for voyages to Holland were common ploys.

One enterprising employee in Bengal, India, set up his own company in his wife's name to carry on private trade. Their two nephews, who held important jobs with the VOC in Bengal, were made shareholders of their uncle's company and they negotiated deals to buy private goods on VOC ships at below-market prices using a phony merchant's name. Afterward, they sold the merchandise at a higher price for their uncle's company. If anyone objected, they would claim the private goods for the VOC.

Some notorious cases of graft emerged involving VOC officials who headed factories in India. Disciplinary actions were taken, but business soon returned to its old footing. An investigator estimated that fraud and private trading in India had cost the company as much as 3.8 million guilders from 1678 to 1686.

Fraud was endemic throughout the ranks of the company. Even lowly sailors had ingenious ways of disguising their perfidy aboard VOC ships. "The seamen [the Dutch] who go to the Spice Islands aren't supposed to bring spice back for themselves, except for a small amount for their own use, a pound or two," wrote William Dampier.

"Yet they will meet vessels at sea and sell their cloves—10 to 15 tons out of 100, and yet seemingly carry their complement to Batavia. They will pour water among the remaining part of their cargo, which will swell them to that degree, that the ship's hold will be as full again, as it was before they were sold. This is but one instance of many hundreds of little deceitful arts the Dutch seamen in those parts have among them. . . . I believe there are nowhere greater thieves."

In Batavia, a crucial node for the opium trade, smuggling proved irresistible. In 1676, a year when the harvest was particularly good, company employees smuggled 152,600 pounds of the drug into Batavia, which was several times more than the amount of opium imported by the VOC into the city from India.

At one time corruption was thought to be the main factor that led to the end of the VOC—the initials VOC were once cynically referred to as *Vergaan Onder Corruptie*, collapsed through corruption. Undoubtedly smuggling and stealing, and a thousand other fraudulent insults, caused irreparable damage to the VOC, but modern historians believe that inadequate financing, the continued focus on spices at the expense of new markets such as tea, and the disastrous Fourth Anglo-Dutch War in 1780 also contributed substantially to the VOC's eventual downfall.

The Dutch weren't the only Europeans in Asia who knew how to rip off their employer. Near the end of the eighteenth century, the economist Adam Smith, a leading critic of the English East India Company, wrote that the Company's monopoly relied not only on the price people paid for East India goods and the profits made on its imports, but also on "all the extraordinary waste which the fraud and abuse, inseparable from the management of the affairs of so great a company, must necessarily have occasioned."

Like its Dutch counterpart, the English East India Company also paid its employees a pittance, and consequently fraud and the so-called private trade flourished among everyone working for the Company, from the crews on pepper ships to the highest-ranking factor in India. Some of these men became quite wealthy. Remember Elihu Yale donated his fortune from private trading to found Yale University. He owned four country ships.

The Company could do little to deter private trade. The British, however, had an alternative that was largely unavailable to the men employed by the VOC. Unlike the Dutch, the British could become country traders, men who legitimately traded on their own in Asia, which provided a sort of escape valve for disgruntled English East India Company seamen, who were legion. Desertion was so common among men serving the English and Dutch companies that a standard "form of agreement" for the rendition of deserters had been drawn by the early eighteenth century.

The English East India Company finally gave its employees official sanction to trade in Asian goods, except for pepper and calicoes, in 1667, even though Englishmen had already been trading on their own accounts for decades. As early as 1614, private trade was already well established. That year an English factor in Bantam accused several of his countrymen of "purloining the Company's goods, deceiving private men, insolvent behavior . . . and great wealth they have suddenly gathered together."

Peter Mundy, the Cornish diarist and merchant traveler, encountered an Englishman in Aceh who had a small vessel and was "trading to and Fro in these parts For himselffe." The man from the "Westcountry" was "Friendly and courteously enterteyned by us all in generall," Mundy wrote in 1638. However, the man "privately and ungratefully" sailed away in his boat "carrying with him the Monies off some, and otherwise indebted unto others. Butt itt pleased God that within a Day or two hee was by Foule weather Driven on shoare within a little off this place, his vessel suncke and loste, his goods wett and spoiled, halffe of his company run away and himselffe left to repent of such bad Courses."

During the course of the seventeenth century, English seamen increasingly owned or co-owned boats or were employed by Asian ship owners, and in the eighteenth century they became a potent commercial force. William Dampier was a country trader. They roamed widely over the Indian Ocean, and engaged in a good deal of smuggling. Englishman Roger Wheatley admitted in 1725 that he had been employed by a lady whose husband had been a member of the Council of Batavia to smuggle 150 chests, or about 21,000 pounds, of opium. Independent English traders formed communities in Asian ports and dabbled in Company business and private trade, occasionally serving as pilots on indigenous rulers' ships. By contrast, the VOC would not allow Dutchmen to become country traders.

VOC Captain J. S. Stavorinus was shocked when he saw English ships unloading cargoes of textile piece goods and opium in Batavia in 1769. The VOC prohibited Dutchmen unaffiliated with the company from trading in these items, yet the English could dispose of them, he observed. "These indulgences were . . . extended to all sorts of commodities, both Indian and European, to the great detriment of our own ships' officers and crews, who were not allowed to import their wares; and they who did bring some privileged goods, were forced to sell them at a loss, on account of the glut occasioned by the quantities imported by the English," Stavorinus wrote.

Rampant corruption was one of the reasons the VOC finally collapsed in 1799, ending a two-hundred-year-long rivalry with the English East India Company. The VOC also had been struggling for many years with the ever-increasing costs of running an overseas trading empire and poor management, and had refused to adapt to changes in the market for Asian goods in Europe. Meanwhile, the English East India Company sputtered along until 1833, when it withdrew finally from trade. No longer could a group of Englishmen be given nearly sovereign rights to exclusively buy and sell Asian commodities. However, the Company continued to administer India until it was finally disbanded in 1874.

Pepper Coast
Of
NORTHERN
SUMATRA

Seven

U.S. Pepper Fortunes

THE NORTHWESTERN COAST OF SUMATRA BECAME THE CENTER
OF A VIBRANT PEPPER TRADE WITH THE UNITED STATES IN THE
NINETEENTH CENTURY. SEEMINGLY AMICABLE RELATIONS WITH
THE PEOPLE OF SUMATRA CHANGED IN 1831 WHEN PIRATES
ATTACKED A U.S. PEPPER SHIP, LEADING TO THE FIRST ARMED
U.S. INTERVENTION IN SOUTHEAST ASIA.

•

For the coast of Sumatra now I'm bound,
Pepper for to get if there's any to be found.
From thence for Europe if the Lord spares my life,
And back again to Beverly to get a pretty w[ife].
—PENNED BY A SAILOR ABOARD THE U.S. PEPPER BRIG *Tuskar*, 1841.

If our Government does not send a frigate next season and
destroy Soo-soo, Tangan Tangan, Muckie and South Tallapow, we must bid
adieu to the pepper trade.
—EXCERPT FROM A LETTER WRITTEN IN 1838
BY AN AMERICAN CAPTAIN OFF THE COAST OF SUMATRA,
AND PUBLISHED IN THE *SALEM REGISTER* NEWSPAPER.

"Another class of commercial interloper, who will require
our vigilant attention, is the Americans."
—SIR STAMFORD RAFFLES

At the turn of the nineteenth century, nearly two hundred years had passed since James Lancaster sailed to Aceh to procure pepper on behalf of the nascent English East India Company. Hundreds of millions of pounds of pepper had been produced in Sumatra and transported to Europe and China. From the central highlands of Minangkabau, where streams and rivers carried rafts filled with pepper to the marshy eastern shores of Jambi and Palembang, to the southern Lampongs, northern Aceh, and western Padang, pepper had been cultivated all over the island. By 1800, it appeared that pepper could not be grown anywhere else in Sumatra. Then stories began circulating about a new source of pepper along a small stretch of the perilous reef-filled northwestern coast.

This corner of Sumatra would attract a host of seamen and traders from a recently founded country eager to expand its treasury, opening a new chapter in the history of black pepper. The United States would become a major purveyor of pepper in the nineteenth century, and the source of this pepper was the northwest coast, dubbed the "pepper coast," of Sumatra, some 13,000 miles away. Over the course of the century, 967 U.S. ships sailed to the island.

Many of the two- and three-masted vessels began their journey in the New England port of Salem, Massachusetts, where pepper built the fortunes of America's first millionaires, merchants with names like Crowninshield, Thorndike, Gardner, and Peabody, who in turn invested in the industrialization of New England. (The Gardner Museum in Boston was founded by the daughter-in-law of John Lowell Gardner, a wealthy pepper merchant.) Salem, best remembered today for its witch trials, prospered on the money made from the pepper trade. Ships from Salem and its major rival, Boston, were such frequent visitors to Sumatra that the island's inhabitants thought these New England towns were nations. New York; Beverly, Massachusetts; and Philadelphia played a smaller role in the trade, although many pepper ships discharged their cargo in New York. The Americans brought specie, or silver coin, in the holds of their ships to pay for the peppercorns, as well as opium. The coin proved to be pretty good ballast, and it has been estimated that more than seventeen million silver dollars flowed into Sumatra from the United States in the late eighteenth and early nineteenth centuries.

At the height of its wealth in October of 1825, Salem held a great banquet to celebrate the opening of a new building for the museum of the East India Marine Society. President John Quincy Adams and Boston Mayor Josiah Quincy attended along with many other dignitaries. Some forty-four toasts were made during that long giddy night, and the president particularly praised "the trade to India—no commercial nation has been great without it, may the experience of ages induce us to cherish this rich source of national wealth." In those days "India" was synonymous with the East, and President Adams was surely invoking the pepper coast of northwestern Sumatra when he made that toast. The duties paid on pepper had expanded the U.S. treasury at a critical time in the nation's early history, and Salem was essential to the success of the trade. Surprisingly, most of the Sumatran pepper carried on Salem ships went to European markets, because there wasn't much of a demand for the spice in the United States. Pepper was a thriving import-export business.

The first American seaman to bring back loads of pepper from northwestern Sumatra was Captain Jonathan Carnes, the son of a distinguished privateersman who had fought during the Revolutionary War. Although Carnes wasn't an immediate member of Salem's elite merchant families, he was allied with them through his maternal uncle, Jonathan Peele, a wealthy ship owner. An able navigator, Carnes had been to Benkoolen aboard the *Cadet* in 1788 and the *Grand Sachem* in 1791, a boat owned by one of Salem's most prominent merchants, Elias Hasket Derby.

The fate of the *Cadet* isn't known, and the *Grand Sachem* was wrecked on a reef in the West Indies, but during these voyages to Sumatra Carnes probably heard about newly available pepper in a region north of Benkoolen and Padang, where he had found little of the spice. Carnes somehow made his way back to Salem after these unsuccessful voyages and became master of a newly built schooner called *Rajah*, owned by Ebenezer Beckford and his uncle, Jonathan Peele, and cousin, Willard Peele. Rigged as an agile schooner, the boat had a better chance in unfamiliar shallow waters filled with dangerous reefs where quick maneuvering would be required. It was a secretive voyage; even her small crew of ten men didn't know the ship's destination. The owners and Carnes recognized that they alone were sitting on a veritable pot of gold.

The *Rajah* set sail on a cold New England day in mid-November 1795. The *Salem Gazette* published a list of seagoing ships under the title "District of Salem and Beverly" on November 17, 1795. (Beverly is the port next to Salem.) One entry listed a brig named *Cicero* and nine other vessels. Another noted that thirteen ships were cleared for sailing, including ten schooners, one of which bore the name *Rajah*. The destinations of these vessels varied—Copenhagen, West Indies, Nova Scotia. The *Rajah* was the only one bound for "India." The 120-ton schooner carried a cargo of brandy, gin, iron, and salmon. She arrived in Cape Town in March 1796, and then seemingly vanished. She sailed away and there was no further word about her whereabouts.

Many in Salem believed that the ship had sunk along with its master. But in July 1797, nineteen months after the *Rajah* set sail, the schooner made a seemingly miraculous return to Salem laden with some 150,000 pounds of bulk pepper, the first time such cargo had entered the United States. No one knew where the schooner had been, and Carnes and the Peeles weren't talking. The pepper would earn an incredible profit of *700* percent.

There isn't much that is known about Carnes's activities in north-western Sumatra—no log book survives of the voyage—although he probably visited Soo-soo, a port that was to become a rich source of pepper for the Americans. Somewhere along the coast, the *Rajah* was mistaken for an English vessel by a French privateer from Mauritius. Ten or twelve Frenchmen boarded the schooner and a fierce fight broke out. Carnes's cook lost his arm and a French officer was killed before Carnes showed his American papers, ending the mêlée. Violence certainly did not deter the Americans from the shores of Sumatra; they wanted to make money. After Carnes returned, the *Rajah* was quickly refitted as a brig and slipped out of Salem in 1798, returning fifteen months later with a load of more than 150,000 pounds of bulk pepper. In 1801 Carnes brought back another 150,000 pounds, and it wasn't until the end of that year that Soo-soo's location finally became more precisely known among the merchants of Salem. The Peeles would no longer enjoy a monopoly on Sumatra's pepper. During their brief control of the market, their boats had imported more than 400,000 pounds of pepper.

Carnes returned from his second trip to northwestern Sumatra and gave mementoes of his journey—an elephant's tooth, golden boxes, various shells, pipes, and other items—to the newly established Salem East India Marine Society. These objects inspired the society to begin a "cabinet of curiosities," which was the foundation for the Peabody Essex Museum in Salem.

The British had been to northwestern Sumatra before the Americans arrived, and could have dominated the pepper trade there. However, they bungled opportunities to contain the Americans and thus helped set the stage for them to become extremely successful pepper traders. A group of men from the East India Company first exploited northwestern Sumatra's pepper gardens in the mid-eighteenth century, establishing a firm in Natal, a village several hundred miles north of Benkoolen, for their own private trade. Continually seeking to boost pepper production in Sumatra, the Company supplied loans to the Natal Concern and bought pepper from the firm. Toward the end of the eighteenth century, the head of the firm fortuitously met an enterprising local chief named Libbe Duppoh who ruled in Soo-soo, and struck a deal to buy all the pepper that could be grown in his domain. Duppoh became phenomenally successful, and the area soon was one of the world's major suppliers of pepper. Indeed, when Raffles arrived in Sumatra in 1818, he thought that the Natal Concern would help cure some of the chronic problems of obtaining pepper in the Benkoolen residencies.

Twenty-two years before Raffles appeared in Sumatra, East India Company officials in cash-strapped Benkoolen needed to pay down some of their debts and allowed three American ships to buy some 284 tons of pepper at high prices. When Company officials in London found out, they were furious because the Americans had unloaded more than 500,000 pounds of pepper on the European market, which interfered with the sale of the Company's pepper. ". . . we must express entire disapprobation of the Sale of pepper to neutral vessels as it must of course materially interfere with our Sales of that article for foreign Markets," the London officials wrote to Benkoolen. Eventually, the sale of Benkoolen pepper was prohibited to Americans, a decision that only drove more U.S. ships to Soo-soo.

By the end of Carnes's third voyage, American vessels were flooding the northwestern coast of Sumatra. In the boom years of 1802 and 1803, fifty-two U.S. ships sailed to the coast, carrying away some 78,000 piculs, or more than eleven million pounds, of pepper, an extraordinary haul. Many of these ships belonged to merchants such as George Crowninshield, Joseph Peabody, and Stephen Phillips, who were among the first to follow the Peeles into the pepper trade. The *Belisarius*, an especially fast ship owned by George Crowninshield &

Sons, made two successful voyages to Sumatra in 1800 and 1803, bringing home more than 630,000 pounds of pepper. The firm paid duty of more than $37,000, which would be worth roughly $19 million today. The firm's *America* imported more than 800,000 pounds of pepper in 1802. The duty paid was more than $56,000, or about $28 million in today's dollars.

Many of the relatively small ships that sailed to Sumatra made the 13,000-mile trip to the coast in about four months. They left late in the year in order to arrive in time for the pepper harvest in March. The ships headed southeast across the Atlantic and rounded the Cape of Good Hope, sometimes stopping for provisions in St. Helena, an isolated island in the southern Atlantic Ocean (where Napoleon had died in exile), or in Mauritius before striking out for Sumatra. Detailed logs of the voyages helped captains navigate with surprising ease to Sumatra.

The merchants of Salem knew that these logs would be crucial to the success of the pepper trade. At a meeting in Salem of the East India Marine Society held in November 1801, a committee was chosen to procure "Blank Journals" for the "great object of their institution . . . was the acquiring of nautical knowledge . . ." Each captain would be furnished with a log, which was to be "a regular diary of the winds, weather, remarkable occurrences, during his voyage . . ." The atlas-sized diaries were usually kept by the master of the ship, although a "keeper" was occasionally hired to maintain a chronicle of the voyage. Their pages are filled with nautical notations and weather reports, written in flowing ornate script. A typical journal entry notes that the day "commences with a fine breeze and pleasant weather."

Occasionally the logs of these voyages provide glimpses of daily life aboard the ships, and even about matters that had nothing to do with the business of buying pepper in Sumatra or goods elsewhere in Asia. Benjamin Hodges, a successful Salem merchant who was an early figure in the trade to the East, was the master of the brigantine *William and Henry*, which left Salem in December 1788 on a voyage to China. The log he kept reveals a thoughtful, compassionate man driven at times to melancholy by the tediousness of a long voyage. Along with the usual comments about the weather, Hodges noted in April 1789 that his mood had turned as gloomy as the overcast sky. He complained that the ". . . long passage in which there is such a sameness & the same tedious recurrence to nautical observations that I am, obliged to rally all my little philosophy to drive off the hypochondriac, which hovers about me, for want of more exercise, I often turn to my Lord Boiling broke on Exile though that is more Philosophy in Theory than in Practice."

On the *William and Henry*'s return to Salem in April 1790 from Mauritius, the brigantine encountered a British slave ship, *Philips Stephens*, of Liverpool. Hodges detested slavery and wrote with evident disgust about ". . . a cargo of those (unhappy fellow animals) whose happiness is sacrificed to satisfy the ambition of avarice, men who are proud of living under the light of Christianity and more especially of philosophy. . . . The Captain came on board appeared to be one of those stupid beings of men who never thought or knew whether he was in a right or wrong line . . . in short he appeared a stupid decrepid [sic] devil."

Two years later, Hodges embarked on a journey to Bengal, India, aboard the *Grand Turk*, owned by Elias Hasket Derby, which left Salem in 1792. During this long voyage he noted in the ship's log that the "blue devils" hovered around during a prolonged spell of bad weather.

The darken sky how thick it lowers
Troubled with storms & big with showers

No cheerful gleam of light appears
But nature pours forth all her tears

Long passage dark Gloomy
Weather. Very unpropitious
The Blue Devils hover round.

Americans died during the voyages to Sumatra. Disease claimed some, while others drowned in the surf off the coast, but little is known about their lives. Occasionally a ship's log offers brief accounts of the deceased. The barque *Eliza* left New York for Sumatra in December 1838, and among her crew were Samuel Smith and his son, who was master of the ship and kept its log. After the vessel put in at Analaboo in March 1839, the two men went ashore in a small boat and a Malaysian guide accompanied them into the town. Many ships had already been to the port, they were informed, and no more pepper was available. They would have to sail to other ports to find available pepper. On April 28, 1839, the log reports that Samuel Smith suddenly got sick and died. "He did not talk but very little for about half of an hour before he died. I was obliged to bury him at sea," his son wrote. "That afternoon while he was on shore he drank 4 or 5 cocoas . . . and the last one that he drank he complained of his being very old and said that he had a stomach ache . . ." The ship returned from Sumatra on September 18, 1839, with a full cargo of pepper.

Sometimes U.S. pepper ships could not complete the voyage. The *Sooloo*, owned by Silsbee, Pickman & Stone, left Salem in November 1854 and arrived in Analaboo after 118 days of sailing. The ship was on the coast of Sumatra until mid-May, when she set sail with a full load of pepper. According to the ship's log, the vessel was "rolling heavily and thumping very hard endangering the masts . . .

rendering it almost impossible to stand on the deck to do anything. Before heaving taut the ship's bow swung off to the westward but still hung fast . . . Sounded the pumps and found 3 feet water in the well. . . . Furled all sail and sounded the pumps again, water increased to 5 feet in the well . . ."

Although the crew tried to save the ship, the effort proved futile. Boats came from the shore to take pepper off the *Sooloo* as fast as possible. The last entry of the log stated: "Finished taking pepper out of the between decks the water about 1 foot above the between decks. During the night the ship sunk at her anchors carrying one Malay with her."

Other ships had to be scuttled because they were infested with centipedes, scorpions, cockroaches, and innumerable white ants. Amasa Delano, an American sailor who joined the East India Company, describes putting in at Benkoolen in 1792 and having to sink his ship, the *Endeavour*, because it was overrun with vermin and insects. White ants, in particular, could eat through the timbers of a ship and ruin it in only a few months.

The Beauty of the Tropics

Life aboard ships waiting to be loaded with pepper wasn't entirely dreary. Along with such chores as caulking, refitting the sails, and painting the decks, American seamen did get out and take in the breathtaking, rugged beauty of the tropics, just as Raffles had done during his stay in Sumatra. "Then we went out on the mountain top to gaze at the view and it was one of the most beautiful scenes that I have ever beheld," wrote Gorham P. Low, a seaman from Gloucester, Massachusetts, who sailed to the pepper coast for the first time in 1834. He had climbed to a dwelling on the top of a mountain to attend to a sick boy. "From that high peak the land and sea looked very different from anything I had ever seen before," Low wrote. "The shore line from the sea seemed to be nearly straight but from here we could see it in all its sinuosities in both directions for many miles. It was like looking down from another world." Low's first impressions of Sumatra were over-whelmingly positive, and he was especially struck by the dig-nity of the people and by some of their customs, such as filing the ends of their teeth square and dying them black. He sailed to several ports on that first voyage because there were so many American ships along that coast that it was difficult to find pepper, and the competition made the spice expensive. In fact, his ship had to leave the coast because the price of pepper, $6.50 per picul, was too high. Low spent twenty years at sea, and became a wealthy businessman who served on the Massachusetts State Legislature.

Another American described the beauty of Soo-soo as something almost otherworldly. "Could an American of the north have been conveyed suddenly from his home and placed where we stood as we stepped from the boat, he would have been in ecstasy, if he had any susceptibility to the beauty of nature," wrote a chaplain in 1838. "The stream was almost embowered by the leaves of the palm, graceful and fan-like, curving over their half circle of gorgeous foli-age in their place, and blending with the tall trunks of the cocoa-nut tree, spreading its top like an umbrella upon a pole, but Asiatic and picturesque beyond description in its effect; while the bay-tree, and the banana, and the forest giant, and their lesser and more graceful associates, with the tall and luxurious bamboo everywhere softening the scene, surrounded us."

The extensive reefs lying off the pepper coast of northwestern Sumatra were charted by numerous captains who plied these tropical waters. The most important landmark as the ships neared Sumatra was what the Americans called Hog Island, about ninety miles southwest of Soo-soo. The most-frequented pepper ports—Analaboo, Qualah Batoo, Soo-soo, Tally-Pow, and Muckie—lay south of Banda Aceh, but the ports were not controlled by the sultan. Each was ruled by a chief, or "rajah" (and sometimes by more than one chief), and the Americans had to strike up individual relationships in each port in order to procure their pepper. Usually, they had to make arrangements with someone called the *Dattoo,* who set up contracts on behalf of the chiefs in each port.

Nathaniel Bowditch was a brilliant navigator and mathematician and one of the most important figures in the Salem pepper trade. In November 1802, when he was twenty-nine, Bowditch sailed on the *Putnam* to Sumatra. He was the master and part owner of the ship, and kept a log of its voyage (now in the Phillips Library of the Peabody Essex Museum in Salem). In its last pages, Bowditch wrote an influential essay on the pepper trade along the northwest coast of Sumatra, offering an intelligent guide to how Americans should conduct their business with the Dattoo and with each other. He explicitly states that the Dattoo is a free agent who makes arrangements according to his own best interests. If only American captains had paid more attention to Bowditch's words.

"On arrival at any of these ports you contact with the Dattoo for the pepper and fix the price," Bowditch explained. "If more than one vessel is at the port, the pepper which comes daily to the scales is shared between them, as they agree, else they take it day and day alternatively. Sometimes the Dattoo contracts to load one vessel before any other is allowed to take any, and he holds to this agreement as long as he finds it for his interest to do so and no longer, for a handsome present or an increase in price will prevent the pepper from being brought in for several days, and the person who made the agreement must either quit the port or else add an additional price."

Bowditch noted that the price of pepper in 1803 ranged from ten to eleven dollars per picul, and in previous years had been as low as eight dollars, "but the demand for it had risen the price considerably, there being near thirty sail of American vessels on the coast." He carefully described how pepper was weighed using American scales and weights, and was sold by the picul, equal to $133\frac{1}{3}$ pounds. Dollars were the accepted coin, and the Malaysians did not take halves or quarters. American captains, he added, shouldn't have any trouble making contacts since some natives spoke English fairly well.

The ports supplying pepper to the Americans were clustered along a seventy-five-mile stretch of coastline. Soo-soo and Muckie were the most important, and each exported 18,000 piculs [about 2.4 million pounds] of pepper in 1803, according to Bowditch's calculations. These ports did not produce pepper prior to the turn of the nineteenth century. Depending on the harvest and on how many American ships were in Sumatra, U.S. vessels would wander from port to port seeking a deal. Several American ships would inevitably end up in the same port, especially during boom years. Courtesy demanded that the captains wait their turn for the pepper, as Bowditch had recommended, but these men weren't always willing to wait.

When a certain American captain was outbid for pepper by a rival in 1839, the losing captain sent a threatening letter to the local chief in the village of Bakungan threatening to sink his *prahus* (Indonesian boats) if he gave any pepper to his rival. A similar situation occurred two years later when a captain fired a gun at a prahu bringing pepper to a rival American ship.

Disputes between American captains had been occurring since the beginning of the U.S. pepper trade. George Nicols, a Salem seaman and merchant who sailed to the Far East, Sumatra, and Europe, was the master and supercargo of the *Active*, which set out from Salem to Sumatra in December 1801. (The supercargo managed all of the commercial transactions of a merchant ship's voyage.) When the ship arrived in the port of Muckie, the *America* was already there. Nicols went ashore and discovered "great numbers of Malays, all well armed." He soon negotiated to buy a cargo of pepper, but after fixing the price he learned that the pepper could not be delivered until the *America* was fully loaded. The *America* was three times as large as the *Active* and she wasn't even half full, Nicols claimed, so he declined to wait unless the "governor" could give him a time when the *Active* would begin receiving pepper. "It was finally agreed that I should begin to receive in a week, whether the *America* was loaded or not."

When the captain of the *America,* Jeremiah Briggs, heard about this arrangement he "objected strongly" and insisted on completing the loading of his ship. "I now used every argument in my power to induce Captain Briggs to come to some amicable terms, but all my efforts were fruitless," Nicols wrote. The stakes had to have been very high for these compatriots to be bickering over pepper in a small port in Sumatra. It was understood that American captains were not supposed to undermine one another, but in this case Nicols was determined to get his share even though his boat wasn't the first to arrive in the port.

Understandably, Briggs did everything he could to prevent pepper from being loaded onto the other ship. One day, as one of Briggs's crew was picking up bags of pepper on shore, a Malaysian man drew his creese. The American ran, and when the native man couldn't catch him, he turned on one of Nicols's men and immediately a group of nearby Malaysians drew their weapons. The natives were talked down, but even though both Briggs's and Nicols's men were targets, the violence caused Briggs to quit the port with only about two-thirds of his cargo of pepper. Nicols stayed on. He claimed to have threatened the rajah with firing his ship's guns upon the town to ensure the safe loading of his ship. The rest of his cargo was filled quickly.

By the time the Americans arrived in Sumatra, the reputation of Malaysians as pirates was already firmly established. The Strait of Malacca was, and still is, notoriously dangerous. Innumerable small harbors and beachheads along both sides of the Strait provided hideouts for pirates. In the days of sail, their nimble prahus easily overtook large, heavily loaded ships, and reports of plundered Chinese junks appear at least as early as the thirteenth century. Navigating the Strait unmolested was something of a trick, and it was always best to travel on a ship with many cannons.

Throughout the maritime world, it was widely known that Malaysian prahus should not be allowed to approach a ship at night. Hezekiah Beers Pierrepont, the wealthy New York merchant who sailed to Sumatra and Canton in his youth and observed the opium trade, noted in 1796 that each of the numerous "proas" in the Strait of Malacca carried up to fifty Malaysians armed with cutlasses and long spears, or lances, and firearms. Surprisingly, the pirates were heavily involved in the pepper trade, Pierrepont pointed out in a letter. "They carry on a considerable trade and are generally provided with . . . pepper . . . but are always . . . eager to commit piracy on whomsoever they can find weaker than themselves, or can overpower by surprise or stratagems. When going to an attack . . . their practice is to board and they never fail to put every sail to death. . . . The danger from them is greater when at anchor, or in a calm, or at night."

In the nineteenth century, piracy continued unabated, despite longtime efforts by the European trading companies to defeat it. American ships were also plundered. The American ship *Marquis de Somereulas*, named after a Cuban official, was attacked in 1806 while loading pepper along one of the branches of the River Jamba in eastern Jambi, and its carpenter was killed. The *Marquis* returned to Salem in March 19, 1807. William Story, the ship's master, told the *Salem Register* that the men who attacked his ship were not associated with the sultan, and he had traded in Jambi previously and had seen no reason to suspect treachery among the hundreds of Malaysians who had been on his ship.

Twelve years later *The Asiatic Journal,* the newspaper of the East India Company, published a brief news story about pirates that "swarm on our coast." The item reported that the British ship *Hunter* had recently fought off a fierce attack by a number of Malaysian prahus, while an American schooner called *Duckling* met a worse fate. Malaysian pirates captured the American ship, stole twenty thousand silver dollars, and sank her. Twelve officers and crew escaped by boat.

There were other incidents involving American ships in the Strait of Malacca, but amazingly no U.S. vessel was attacked on the northwest coast of Sumatra for the first thirty years of the pepper trade, when some four hundred voyages were made by U.S. vessels to the pepper coast. The absence of violence doesn't mean that the trade had gone smoothly. The native inhabitants of Sumatra had already learned over some two hundred years that foreigners from the West were not altogether trustworthy. They regarded Americans with apprehension, and for good reason.

Along the coast of northwestern Sumatra, U.S. ships could not dock in port because of the tumultuous surf, and therefore pepper had to be weighed and packed into bags on shore, placed in prahus, and rowed to waiting ships. The weights, based on the picul, were supposed to be the equivalent of 133⅓ pounds. But the number was fudged by both sides. The American weight was about 136 pounds and the Malaysian 130. Usually a compromise was reached, and the American and Malaysian weights would alternate days.

Natives would add sand and other material to the pepper, and the Americans would put mercury or other substances into their hollow-beam scales, to add pounds to the scale. It was widely known that the Americans would use a set of false weights to obtain more pepper than they had paid for. Americans carry "complete sets of false weights thus often times getting five Piculs of pepper by paying but for one . . ." observed American midshipman Levi Lincoln in the 1830s.

A British writer in the 1840s acknowledged that the practice was initiated by American and English shipmasters. "Who introduced false weights?" he wrote. "Who brought to the coast 56 lb. weights with a screw in the bottom which opened for the insertion of from ten to fifteen pounds of lead, after their correctness had been tried by the native in comparison with his own weights? . . . I challenge contradiction, when I assert, that English and American shipmasters have for thirty years been addicted to these dishonest practices . . ."

. . .

Perhaps it was just a matter of time before the people of northwestern Sumatra turned against the Americans, but the seemingly amicable relations took a terrible turn in 1831 when the first U.S. ship was attacked by pirates along the northwest pepper coast. Ironically, the pepper ship embroiled in the upheaval was called the *Friendship*, owned by the wealthy firm of Silsbee, Pickman & Stone. She was under the veteran command of Captain Charles Moses Endicott when she set out with a crew of seventeen sailors and officers for Sumatra's pepper coast in 1830. At the time, the supply of pepper along the coast greatly exceeded demand, and prices reached new lows of thirteen cents per pound amid a six-year-long economic slump in the pepper market.

According to Endicott's account of the incident, the ship was anchored three-quarters of a mile off Qualah Battoo on the morning of February 7, 1831, when he and an officer and four crewmen went ashore to assist in weighing and dispatching the pepper. Endicott had been promised that he would be furnished with one hundred to two hundred bags a day, enabling his ship to be completely loaded in forty days. He left strict instructions that in his absence no more than two Malaysians were to be permitted on board at the same time, and no boats should be allowed to approach the ship at night, the usual precautions taken by foreign ships lying along the pepper coast.

However, while Endicott and some of his men were onshore, the *Friendship* was approached by a prahu and a group of armed Malaysians were allowed on board. The chief officer had scoffed at the precautions and boasted that he could "clear the decks with a hundred such fellows with a single handspike." He lost his life. The Malaysians attacked the crew, killing three Americans and wounding three others, and took over the ship. The remaining unharmed crew jumped overboard. On shore, meanwhile, Endicott and his men saw that the ship was in trouble and quickly got into their own boat. A large group of Malaysians who were nearby brandished their creeses and pursued them from the banks of a river. The Americans narrowly escaped with the help of one Malaysian man, whom the Americans called Po Adams. They rowed to Muckie, a port about twenty-five miles up the coast. In Muckie, an exhausted Endicott met the captains of three other American pepper ships who rallied to his side. Their vessels sailed to Qualah Battoo with Endicott and retook the *Friendship* in early February.

Captain Endicott discovered that his ship had been thoroughly stripped of almost everything, except her pepper. The twelve chests of opium and thousands of dollars' worth of silver specie that she was carrying were gone. (Endicott would later declare that the *Friendship* was seized by drug addicts desperate for opium.) Spare sails and rigging, charts, chronometers, and other nautical instruments, as well as the bedding, cabin furniture, pistols, and other armaments, were gone. Along with the pepper, only the ship's provisions of beef, pork, and bread were spared.

Assisted by the other vessels, the *Friendship* was refitted and Endicott sailed to Tallapow, another pepper port, where he was followed through the streets by great crowds "exulting and hooting . . . 'Who great man now, Malay or American?' 'How many man American dead?' 'How many man Malay dead.'" With the help of Po Adams, Endicott recovered his sextant and one of his chronometers, which enabled him to navigate his ship.

Rumors about the *Friendship* had already begun circulating even before she arrived back in Salem on June 16, 1831, thanks to another ship that had arrived earlier in Boston. When the *Friendship* finally came into port, she caused a sensation. Crowds overwhelmed the ship. "The curiosity of some visitors was so great that they would not be satisfied until they knew the exact spot where every man stood who was either killed or wounded," Endicott wrote. "Even the casing of the cabin, so much cut up in the search for money or other valuables, was an object of the greatest interest."

Concerned that the pepper trade in Sumatra was threatened with immediate extinction, the merchants of Salem and Nathaniel Silsbee, a United States senator who was one of the owners of the *Friendship*, sought government action. Such pressure, however, was hardly necessary. The story of the ship's capture was widely reported in the press, and the administration of President Andrew Jackson was itching for action. Even before receiving Silsbee's appeal, Navy Secretary Levi Woodbury had ordered "every necessary preparation be made . . . to demand immediate redress for the outrage committed."

Thus began the first armed, officially sanctioned, U.S. intervention in Southeast Asia.

The recently commissioned U.S. frigate *Potomac*, one of the finest warships of its day, was about to embark on another assignment when President Jackson decided to send the ship to Sumatra instead. John Downes, the commander of the *Potomac*, was an experienced hand who had served in the War of 1812, and he was given orders to gather information about the murder of Americans at Qualah Battoo. If he found that Endicott's account was true, then he was to demand restitution of the plundered property or an indemnity from the rajah or other authorities. If he didn't get a response, he was authorized to seize the murderers and send them back to the United States for trial or take harsher measures. In other words, Downes was supposed to gather information first and then act.

The *Potomac* set sail from New York in August 1831, with five hundred officers and sailors, and a contingent of marines. She carried some fifty mounted guns and other artillery on her gun and spar decks. After stopping in Rio de Janeiro for three weeks, the ship proceeded to Cape Town, where Commander Downes and his officers dined with British army and navy officials who claimed to know about the East Indies.

The Americans also made pleasant excursions to the countryside to drink wine. Sometime during this layover, Commodore Downes decided that the rajahs of Qualah Battoo were guilty as charged, and there would be no need to spend time gathering information in Sumatra itself. Perhaps the British had finally convinced him that he could not possibly seek restitution. What we know about this decision comes from J. N. Reynolds, who visited Batavia in the 1830s and was horrified by the decline of the port city. He was Downes's personal secretary during the voyage to Sumatra and published a book about the *Potomac*. According to Reynolds, the information "already obtained" in Cape Town, "seemed to leave no doubt, that neither the character of the people on the coast of Sumatra, particularly at Quallah-Battoo, nor the government under which they nominally lived, and under whose sanction piracies had frequently been committed on commerce, promised the least hopes of success from a mere formal demand of restitution, unless that demand was accompanied, at the same time, by a force sufficient to carry it into effect."

The *Potomac* arrived off the coast of Sumatra on February 5, 1832, disguised as a large merchant ship. Downes already had a fairly good idea of the layout of the five forts in the village of Qualah Battoo from a chart that Endicott had drawn, but he wanted more accurate information and that day sent ashore two officers in civilian clothes who were to act as captain and supercargo anxious to procure a supply of pepper. They were accompanied by several lieutenants dressed as sailors who would scout the village. This bit of playacting was foiled when a large number of creese-bearing Malaysian men gathered as the Americans neared the shore and scared them away. Reynolds noted that the "physical force of the Malays" further convinced Downes of the "correctness of the plans he had previously matured . . ."

Plans were immediately made for a nighttime surprise landing, and the "spirit of enterprise pervaded the whole ships's company," according to Reynolds. Navy regulations prohibited Downes from leaving the *Potomac* and he entrusted the attack to Lieutenant Irving Shubrick. Before his men left, Downes told them that their first objective was to surround the forts and "intercept the flights of the rajahs," and on no account were they to fire upon the Malaysians unless they were attacked first. Did Downes actually think that the inhabitants of Qualah Battoo would not try to defend themselves when their forts were surrounded?

At two o'clock in the morning, 282 men armed with pistols, boarding pikes, and muskets were dispatched to their boats. A six-pound gun, which the men called Betsey Baker, was placed on a launch and towed astern. It was a still, moonless night and not a word was spoken as the boats made their way toward the shore. The men landed about a mile north of the settlement and separated into four divisions, reaching the village at daybreak. The first attack occurred at the northernmost fort. After breaking down a heavy gate, the Americans entered, killing the fort's chief and most of his men. The fighting was fierce. ". . . such was the desperation with which these fellows resisted us, that [in the northernmost fort] . . . 13 out of its 14 defenders were destroyed: 12 while defending themselves, the 13th in the act of escaping after the before mentioned were dead! The other got out of the fort safely, it is presumed," wrote midshipman Levi Lincoln, who was the son of a Massachusetts governor.

The mother of one of the fort's chiefs and other fearless Sumatran women lost their lives in the assault. One woman delivered a "severe blow" with a saber, nearly severing the hand of one of the American men. A sailor near the wounded man shot the woman to death. Still another woman fought with the "spirit of a desperado," according to Francis Warriner, the Potomac's chaplain.

After the first fort fell, a second was easily taken and its inhabitants put to death, allowing more men to join the assault on the largest fort, which stood directly in front of the town. From the launcher, the Betsey Baker pounded the fort as parts of two divisions began to force the gate open. Fire broke out along the outer walls and soon the inner compartments of the fort were engulfed by flames. The inhabitants were caught between the crossfire from the boats and the two divisions, and they didn't stop fighting until the fort was practically in ashes and nearly all had been killed. Yet another fort was taken before Shubrick decided it was time to call off his men.

The entire assault had lasted less than two and a half hours. Two American men had been killed and eleven wounded. The number of native men, women, and children killed ranged from about sixty, according to an account by the people of Qualah Battoo, to at least 150, according to Shubrick's estimate.

The next morning, American flags were flying over the forts. Most of the town had been reduced to ashes. Commodore Downes warned the people of Qualah Battoo how "reckless and inconsiderate they must be ever again to provoke" the naval power of his country, and pointed out that it was not a policy of his government "to make conquest and form establishments in foreign ports." Accordingly, Downes immediately "restored" the town to its people.

After Downes left Qualah Battoo, he sailed east to Java, China, and South America, and didn't return to the United States until May 1834. Meanwhile, a long, bombastic poem called "The Battle of Qualah Battoo" was published as a broadside at the request of some of the crew members of the *Potomac*. A brief excerpt describes the shining heroism of Downes and the Americans in Sumatra.

> *"All around us in ambush these savages lay—*
>   *And the bullets like hail-stones were scattered abroad;*
> *But still on their forts we continued to play,*
>   *To conquer our object—Potomac's the word.*
>
> *Exposed to their fires, the Potomacs undaunted*
>   *Beneath their rude ramparts stood firmly and brave*
> *Resolved that the stripes and the stars of* Columbia
>   *Ere long on their ramparts in triumph should wave."*

Fortunately, the poem wasn't the last word on the battle. The *New York Evening Post* soon published a story by an anonymous crewman on the *Potomac* that conveyed an entirely different view of the attack. Rather than shining heroism, it described wanton killing and looting by undisciplined sailors. "The marines entered the second fort at bayonet charge, and put all to death except three women who supplicated for mercy," the crewman wrote. "There were several women killed who had the hardihood to take up arms when they saw their husbands fall at their feet—indeed it was impossible to distinguish the sex, they dress so much alike. Having possession of the forts they [the Americans] proceeded to fire them and the town, and to destroy everything of value that was left (for I assure you that some of the boys brought plunder on board)."

This account was later confirmed by Francis Warriner, the *Potomac*'s chaplain, who reported that the sailors broke ranks and were difficult to control. They killed indiscriminately, and "cared little about death." When a sailor was questioned just as he was about to kill a woman, the man replied: "It matters not, for if there were no women, there would be no Malays." Many of the sailors carried away gold scabbards, earrings and rings, anklets and bracelets, and small quantities of gold and silver coin. Other spoils included a Chinese gong, a Koran, and pieces of rich gold cloth. Ducks and other animals were also seized, but the men had to return to the ship before they could feast.

Although the *Evening Post*'s report stirred the House of Representatives to ask President Jackson for copies of Downes's orders, lawmakers soon moved on to other matters. The nation's newspapers, however, didn't ignore the issues raised by Downes's actions, which are still as valid today as they were some 180 years ago. Historian David F. Long notes that the debate raged in the pages of the Washington–based *Globe*, which supported the Jackson administration, and its rival, the *National Intelligencer*. In an editorial in 1833, the *Globe* claimed that "The Malays have been regarded as pirates by all the European nations, and have constantly acted as such. . . . No regular government of either the East or West will take exception to the punishment inflicted by the frigate *Potomac* on this horde of barbarians."

The *National Intelligencer* retorted: "If some of the Malays are pirates, we must be allowed to say . . . others of them are unoffending people. The institutions of government of that country are older than those in the United States by a thousand years. Some at least of those who live on the sea coast are represented as an enterprising and commercial people, who live under a fundamental government; and have made progress in arts and civilization. . . . There are pirates on the coast, it is true; for a piracy was committed on the *Friendship*. So there are pirates on the coast of China. But would any Power of Europe think of ravaging the village of that country with fire and sword because a piracy had been committed on one of its ships?"

Meanwhile, other newspapers criticized Downes's decision to attack Qualah Battoo before seeking information from its inhabitants about the capture of the *Friendship*. Some also questioned whether the president could go to war without the approval of Congress; a debate that occurred some 130 years before the Vietnam War. The *Salem Gazette* opined that "Neither the President of the United States nor the Captain of a Frigate has power to make or proclaim war."

Despite public pronouncements that Downes had done his job, President Jackson and Navy Secretary Woodbury were not happy. A confidential letter Woodbury wrote to Downes during the height of the controversy in July 1833 questioned Downes's actions. "The President regrets that you were not able [,] before attacking the Malays at Qualah Battoo, to obtain . . . fuller information of the particulars of their outrage on the *Friendship*, and of the character and political relations of the aggressors. . . ." Downes was asked to provide a full accounting of the incident to President Jackson "since it may hereafter become material."

Downes defended his actions, but his reply must not have been satisfactory. When he returned to the United States, he wasn't treated like a conquering hero and was not given another overseas appointment. He never again commanded a U.S. warship and ended his career as a lighthouse inspector.

Downes's admonition to the people of Sumatra didn't mean very much; the senseless destruction of Qualah Battoo did not prevent piracy along the Sumatran pepper coast. A little more than a year after the *Potomac* left Indonesia, attempts were made to overtake two American ships along the pepper coast, although the pirates were unsuccessful. And in 1838, an incident occurred in another port along the northwest coast, prompting the American government to intervene again in Southeast Asia. That year pirates captured the *Eclipse*, a Salem ship owned by Joseph Peabody. Captain Charles F. Wilkins and a young man named William F. Babbage of Salem lost their lives in a plot involving local chiefs at Muckie and nearby Soo-soo and Qualah Battoo.

The first mate and four crewmen were weighing pepper on shore when the pirates attacked the ship. They stole some $26,000 in silver and two chests of opium, along with two trunks of the captain's best apparel, some gold watches, spyglasses, muskets, and other items. The remainder of the crew escaped aboard a French barque. Later a local chief helped the first mate recover the *Eclipse*, which had already been abandoned by the pirates. The incident triggered the usual calls for revenge. "If our Government does not send a frigate next season and destroy Soo-soo, Tangan Tangan, Muckie and South Tallapow, we must bid adieu to the pepper trade," wrote a captain who had helped recover the *Eclipse*. "If we do not have a frigate out next year, the Malays are growing so insolent that they will be for taking all the vessels where there is the least chance of success," he added.

Once again an American warship was dispatched to the shores of northwest Sumatra. This time Commodore George C. Read was sent to negotiate, and he must have known about the controversy enveloping Downes because he didn't bombard the coast until he had spoken to the chiefs of all three settlements and sent ultimatums demanding restitution. He commanded the U.S. frigate *Columbia*, which was accompanied by a corvette, a smaller warship, called the *John Adams*. Although there was little or no resistance, the Americans went ashore and set fire to Qualah Battoo and Muckie. Captain Wyman of the *John Adams*, who led the expedition against Muckie, reported to Read on Jan. 1, 1839:

"In execution of your order to me for the entire destruction of the town of Muckie, I this day landed on the beach at the head of the harbor, and about one hundred and fifty yards from the town, with six divisions of small arms, men, and marines, consisting of three hundred and twenty men, detailed for the service from the squadron under your command.

"Upon getting on shore, the different divisions were, together with the marines, immediately formed by their respective commanding officers, when all moved forward for Muckie, which was entered about half-past twelve, in the afternoon; and by two o'clock the town was in our possession. Five forts were taken without opposition, and the guns found therein, to the number of twenty-one, spiked and thrown over the parapet into the ditch—the forts set fire to and entirely demolished. The town, at the same time, was set on fire in numerous places, which was entirely consumed, together with all the property in and near the place—consisting of proas, coasting craft, and boats of various sizes and descriptions, and the rigging, yards. &c., &c., found on shore, belonging thereto, were destroyed in the general conflagration; and upon embarking, nothing remained visible to the eye but the ashes covering the smoking ruins, upon the site on which the town of Muckie and the forts once stood."

From the mizzen top of the *Columbia*, Fitch W. Taylor, a chaplain to the squadron, viewed the devastation. "The town now exhibited one scene of extended and extending ruins. The light and dry bamboo buildings burned like stubble; and the better houses added intensity and continuance to the devouring element. . . . The dark columns of smoke rolled high in the rarefied air, and the long and seared leaf of the cocoa-nut, and the crimped foliage of other thickly embowering trees, added to the general mass of fuel; while the spiral sheet of fire wound up the stem and shot through the branches and overtopped the highest trees. The very heat seemed to reach me in the mizzen-top, while the loud cracking of the green foliage, and the splitting of the tall and thick bamboo, in the general roar and loud cracking of a vast and extending conflagration, came distinctly and clear to the ear."

Only one American was killed or wounded. Unlike Downes, Read was treated well on his return and was rewarded with the command of the African Squadron.

Although there were other piracies in the following years, no other American pepper ship was ever again seized by Malaysians along the pepper coast of northwest Sumatra and no U.S. warship ever again destroyed villages there. Fast American clipper ships began stopping in Padang along Sumatra's west coast (to the south of the pepper coast) when the coffee trade took off in the 1850s.

Around this time the pepper trade had begun to wane in Salem, caused in part by another downturn in prices for the spice. Consequently, by the middle of the nineteenth century, Salem lost its leading position in the pepper trade to its greatest rival, Boston, which boasted a much larger port and had far better access to the burgeoning trade in the interior of the country after the opening of the Erie Canal in 1825. The last bulk cargo of pepper entered Salem in November 1846. By that time, many of Salem's leading pepper merchants had moved to Boston; the last to relocate was Silsbee, Pickman & Stone in 1865, which had made some 105 voyages to the pepper coast.

A change in business practices, along with the advent of the clipper trade in 1850s, helped end the U.S. pepper trade to Sumatra. "Clipper competition was facilitated by the new type of business in the Far East," wrote James W. Gould, whose treatise on the U.S. pepper trade in Sumatra is still one of the best sources available. "The establishment of American business houses there eliminated the previous advantages of the private contacts and knowledge which had sustained so much of the old trades. The pepper trade was probably the most specialized and technical of the old India trades. After 1853, any American merchant could buy pepper from the American firms like Paine, Strickler & Co. in Batavia or Revely & Co. in Penang."

The American pepper trade in Sumatra also declined because of the industrialization of New England and the opening of the western United States for settlement. Pepper was still bought and sold after the debut of the clipper ships, but the spice increasingly came from the island's east coast, where Dutch warships could guard the cargo. Indeed, American ships could now pick up their cargo in Singapore, Penang (off the west coast of the Malay Peninsula), or Batavia, and forgo the treacherous reefs and the worry about pirates.

The last U.S. pepper ship put in at New York in 1867, and the last U.S. ship in the nineteenth century to bring coffee back from Sumatra was in 1873, a fateful year in Sumatran history. In the following years, the people of Sumatra abandoned their pepper gardens along the northwestern coast, fleeing in the wake of the Dutch invasion. Qualah Battoo was the last pepper port to bow to the Dutch, and it fell in 1881. The vines along the pepper coast had already suffered from years of neglect and never again produced pepper.

Eight

An Infinite Number of Seals

HUNGRY MEN ABOARD PEPPER SHIPS BOUND FOR ASIA
CRAVED FRESH FOOD. THE BIRDS ON THE MASCARENE
ISLANDS IN THE INDIAN OCEAN, MAURITIUS, RÉUNION, AND
RODRIGUES, WERE ESPECIALLY VULNERABLE, AND THE DODO
QUICKLY BECAME EXTINCT. SHIPWRECKED FRENCH
SEAMAN FRANÇOIS LEGUAT DESCRIBED RODRIGUES AS
AN ISLAND FILLED WITH GIANT TORTOISES AND THE
MARVELOUS SOLITAIRE, A BIRD.

•

*. . . birds that are the size of ducks and do not fly because they have
no feathers on their wings . . . and we killed them in any number
we wished, and they brayed like donkeys.*
—AN ANONYMOUS SAILOR IN VASCO DA GAMA'S SMALL FLEET
ALONG THE COAST OF SOUTHERN AFRICA

*On the third of August the general went in his pinnace, and other boats
with him, to kill whales, for all the bay is full of them.*
—A DESCRIPTION OF WATERS AROUND ROBBEN ISLAND, SOUTH AFRICA,
DURING THE 1604 VOYAGE OF HENRY MIDDLETON FOR THE
ENGLISH EAST INDIA COMPANY

Europrean ships destined for Asia during the age of discovery faced many obstacles, but perhaps the most overwhelming one was supplying food. How do you ensure that hundreds of men receive an adequate diet during voyages that could last up to nine months and were entirely dependent on the winds? In other words, how do you stretch a supply line thousands of miles without the benefit of modern technology?

Although the pepper ships left the English Downs and the Dutch Texel Roads with fresh provisions, the food soon ran out, especially in the early days of ocean travel. Thus the search for pepper was invariably accompanied by the search for fresh meat. Luckily, the pristine lands and waters that the Europeans encountered on the way to India and the East Indies provided a genuine feast.

Few animals escaped the notice of the hungry men bound for Asia. Penguins and whales, seals and tortoises, fish and birds, whatever waddled, swam, crawled, or flew, were slaughtered for their meat. At times, some of the animals, who were totally unaccustomed to humans, were taken by hand. On the island of Mauritius, a man named Pieter Willem Verhoeven (not the admiral of the same name who was killed in 1609) observed in 1611 that birds "similar in size to swans" were found "in large numbers though the Dutch have been catching them and eating them daily, and not only these birds, but many other kinds, such as wild pigeons and parrots, which they beat with sticks and catch . . ." The large birds Verhoeven described probably were dodos, which quickly became extinct as a result of European incursions onto their island habitat.

On Ascension, an isolated island near St. Helena, the Cornish diarist and traveler Peter Mundy described killing a hundred birds "with sticks and hands." The men on his voyage also caught 130 to 140 goats, hogs, "hidds," and pigs. European pepper ships often stopped to obtain fresh water and food on this island in the vast southern Atlantic Ocean. "It [Ascension] is uninhabited, and perfectly sterile, being almost nothing but a bare rock," wrote VOC Captain J. S. Stavorinus in 1771. "It, however, affords fresh water, though the watering-place is difficult to access," he noted. "The beach abounds in turtles, who lay their eggs in the sand, in order to be hatched by the heat of the sun. The Danes frequently visit this island, for the sake of procuring a supply of turtles."

The nearly limitless supply of animals was intoxicating. A sort of exuberance underlies the descriptions of wanton killing along the pepper route. After da Gama's fleet made landfall in southern Africa in November 1497, the sailors found a colony of three thousand seals and fired on them with cannon, killing penguins, too, "as many as was our will," according to an anonymous account. More than one hundred years later, Peter Mundy described the taste of penguins as "somewhat fishey." The "fowle," he noted, "are easily taken, not being able to flye nor runne, only bite a little to noe purpose . . ."

European lands and waters had been steadily stripped of animal life over hundreds of years. By the sixteenth century, fishing stocks had declined sharply off the coast of England. But in the age of discovery, ships sailed in waters teeming with life. The rich menagerie impressed the merchants and captains of the pepper ships, who recorded their observations in their journals. An especially detailed account is given in the second voyage of the East India Company, which set off from the Downs in southeastern England on April 2, 1604, with a fair wind and full crew under the command of Henry Middleton. He had been the *Susan*'s captain on the Company's first voyage, led by Lancaster.

Although the market for pepper was glutted and plague had struck London, the small fleet of four ships—the same vessels engaged in Lancaster's voyage—set out for the East Indies. Less than a year had passed since the last of Lancaster's fleet had arrived in London, but he had left a group of merchants in Bantam with goods and money, including some three thousand bags of pepper. There was just too much at stake for the Company's investors to forego a second voyage.

The Company sent orders for Middleton to load two of his ships with goods in Bantam and send them back to London, while he would take the remaining two ships to Amboyna and the Banda Islands to buy cloves and nutmegs, the first expedition by the Company to the far eastern islands. The money sent out with the fleet was not to be used to buy pepper with which "theis partes of Christendome were already glutted," but was to be invested in Chinese raw silk, or "suchlike commodities."

Middleton was told by the Company not to stop in Table Bay, the tip of South Africa, because of the "danger of that place," but if necessary to seek refreshment on his return along the coast of Madagascar. However, after only a few months on the high seas, scurvy had already struck Middleton's crew. They beseeched him to save their lives by putting in at Table Bay. Outside his own cabin door, Middleton saw a "swarme of lame and weake, diseased cripples," and beholding this "lamentable sight" he decided to grant their request, according to a factor on one of the ships who kept a journal of the voyage.

Due to strong winds, the ships waited four days to make anchor at Table Bay. On July 18, 1604, Middleton finally went ashore with some of his crew to set up tents, where they met people who owned a large number of oxen and sheep. The Englishmen traded their small pieces of iron for twelve sheep, but trading stopped abruptly when the natives saw that the foreigners intended to set up tents. Although the Englishmen tried "all means possible" to buy more animals, the natives quickly pulled down their own tents and immediately left with their cattle. Some of his men urged Middleton to overtake the retreating natives and grab their animals, which could be easily done, but he refrained, believing that "they would returne againe, seeing we offered them no wrong."

The next day, the sick men were put ashore to rest. On July 20, the boats were sent to Penguin Island (modern-day Robben Island, the site of an infamous prison where Nelson Mandela spent eighteen of his twenty-seven years in jail) "where wee found such infinite number of seals that was admirable to behold." It is here that the anonymous merchant records his awe at the abundance of seals and other wildlife. "All of the seashore lyes overspread with them [seals], some sleeping, some traveling into the island and some to the seaward; besides all the rockes, which lie a prettie distance off, so full as they can hold; thousands at a time going and as many comming out. There bee many of them as bigge as any beare, and as terrible to behold. And up towards the middle of the island there be infinite numbers of fowles called pengwines, pelicans, and cormerants." The theme of "infinite numbers" echoes throughout the early days of the spice race. In this instance, it appears that the men simply observed the animals and did not kill them.

A few days later, Middleton and his men went out in several boats to "kill whales; for all the bay is full of them." Here they plunged their harping irons into a young whale, and eventually hauled her closer to wound her with spears. The young whale's mother, however, "would not depart from the little one, although it had received many wounds." The mother remained by her wounded calf and fought all of the boats, striking them with her powerful tail and swimming underneath to overturn them. Middleton's boat had to be abandoned because the whale split all of its timbers and boards. It took three days for the ship's carpenters to repair the damage. "It was verie good sport to stand and looke on, but verie dangerous to them in the boats," wrote the anonymous merchant on the voyage.

It took all day to kill the young whale, and the mother whale never left until she was sure her calf was dead. The men had killed the whale for oil, "for in all the shipps we had great lacke." But the young whale scarcely yielded four gallons because it was so "young and leane."

By the latter part of the eighteenth century, European ships had better provisions, but the crew still craved fresh food. When VOC Captain J. S. Stavorinus embarked for Batavia on June 10, 1768, his ship was provisioned for a nine-month journey. On board were 147 seamen, twenty-seven soldiers, and a passenger who was a mechanic. Due to changing winds, however, the ship didn't actually clear the English Channel until the beginning of August. After sighting Madeira, Stavorinus reports that "we began to see many flying fish [*Exocoetus volitans*] and we frequently made a good breakfast, upon such as had fallen upon the ship, during the night, as they frequently do . . ." As the ship approached the equator, "the more fish we had about the ship, of which we caught large quantities; dorados, albacores, and likewise bonitos, sharks, and others; which afforded a most welcome and agreeable refreshment to the seamen." Stavorinus particularly liked dorado, or "john-doree," describing it as "the most delicious seafish that is caught. It is long and flat, and covered with very small scales. It is from four to eight feet in length; but I seldom saw any caught that exceeded six feet, and ten or twelve pounds in weight. . . . Although the dorado is the finest fish that is caught at sea, it is yet somewhat dry eating. The tail roasted is very good, and tastes much like a roasted cod's-tail."

When the weather was calm, the men also went after shark, which they pursued more for sport than for eating, although the tail "sometimes affords a meal to the sailor; but it must always be first trodden upon, or otherwise bruised, till a light foam exudes from it." Sharks were commonly caught by a large hook, fastened to a double or triple brasswire of four or five feet attached to a long and strong cord. A slab of pork or beef served as bait. The animals had to be hauled on board and killed by repeated blows on the head with handspikes or iron "crows." Stavorinus reported that the men managed to kill a pilotfish (*Gasterosteus doctor*) that accompanies sharks, and found that it was "very nice eating, and not so dry as other seafish."

Occasionally, the men went ashore, where they hunted land animals for sport. During a layover in Bengal in northeast India, Stavorinus and two friends took a boat up the Ganges to tour the country and go hunting. They sailed a fair way up the river and found a small village surrounded by thick woods, crowded with monkeys. "These animals were about the size of a spaniel, with long tails, which, when they ran, they turned upwards. The body was covered with hair, of a grey colour, and the fore part of the head was black," Stavorinus related. "As soon as we had fired one shot, they all ran up the high trees, and some of them threw their young ones, which they held between their fore paws, into the bushes below; and whatever pains we bestowed in looking for them, we could not find them. The large ones sprang with an inconceivable quickness, from branch to branch, and from tree to tree. We shot some of them, and when the others saw these fall, they set up a most horrid cry."

Stavorinus may have suspected that this exhibition would upset the Bengalese, who asked the Dutchmen to stop killing the animals. ". . . for their superstitious belief in the transmigration of souls after death, makes them think that these creatures, in particular, are the receptacles of human souls." Before leaving Bengal, the Dutchmen met a man in the ruins of a stone building. Venerated as a saint, he was naked and his long tangled hair was strewn with ashes and dirt.

Stavorinus observed that he wore a brass ring about the thickness of a quill and three inches in diameter, "which was passed through the substance of the glans of the penis, though in such a manner, that the urethra remained unhurt." While the Dutchmen were with him, a woman hoping to become pregnant came by "to kiss this disgusting mortal, on the part which was supposed to possess the prolific virtue required." Linked to the brass ring were three iron rings, which Stavorinus guessed weighed about two and a half pounds. "When he walked, he let the whole hang loose, without seeming to be in the least incommoded." Stavorinus noted that there were many of these "sanctified beggars" wandering about the country, who torture their "bodies so unmercifully, for the love of religion . . ."

Not surprisingly, animals living on islands in the Indian Ocean where pepper traders stopped on their way to Asia were especially vulnerable to the depredations caused by hungry men seeking fresh food. The dodo, the quintessential symbol of extinction, lived on one of these islands. By 1690 these odd-looking flightless birds with their huge heads and beaks were no longer seen on Mauritius, succumbing to men and the pigs, monkeys, dogs, cats, rats, and other animals introduced deliberately or accidentally on the island.

In the 1630s, the Cornish traveler Peter Mundy described two dodos in Surat, India, where a mogul emperor kept a zoo, providing one of the few eyewitness accounts of the living bird. He wrote: "Dodoes, a strange kinde of fowle, twice as bigg as a Goose, that can neither flye nor swymm, being Gloven footed; a wonder how it should come thither [Mauritius], there being none such in any part of the world yet to be found. I saw two of them in Surat house that were from thence [Mauritius]."

Based on recollection of the birds in Surat, Mundy also described dodos as being "covered with Downe, having little hanguing wings like short sleeves, altogether unuseffull to Fly withal, or any way with them to helpe themselves. Neither Can they swymme butt as other land Fowle Doe [when] on Necessity Forced into the water, being Cloven Footed as they are."

Mauritius, along with Réunion and remote Rodrigues, are three volcanic islands known as the Mascarenes, named after the Portuguese explorer Pedro Mascaregnas who is said to have discovered Réunion in the early sixteenth century, although Arab sailors probably preceded him. Lying some five hundred to nine hundred miles east of Madagascar, these islands were in the path of European ships going to and coming from Asia. Mauritius, the only one of the islands to offer good, deep harbors, was the first to be settled, in 1638 by the Dutch. The French subsequently annexed Réunion and gradually built a settlement, while tiny Rodrigues was uninhabited until the eighteenth century because it was surrounded by reefs and could not be approached easily.

All three islands once hosted abundant wildlife. In the words of Alfred North-Coombes, the eminent historian of Mauritius, when "ships began to call and man came to stay, hogs and dogs, cats and rats, sailors and settlers began a frenzy of destruction that wiped out these harmless animals within a few decades."

Today, we can appreciate the extraordinary wildlife that once existed on Rodrigues thanks largely to a French traveler named François Leguat, who spent two years on the island near the end of the seventeenth century. Amazingly, his daring journey didn't begin until he was a middle-aged man and nearly bankrupt.

In 1685 Louis XIV reneged on his promise to tolerate French Protestants and revoked the Edict of Nantes. Facing persecution, thousands of non-Catholics were forced to leave France, and among them was Leguat, who went to Holland in 1689. By that time he was fifty-two years old and newly impoverished, because Protestants leaving France had to forfeit all of their property. Dejected and rootless, he heard about a scheme to establish an ideal French Huguenot republic on the island of Réunion, which was then believed to have been abandoned by the French. The chance to start a new life with his fellow Huguenots appealed to Leguat, and he enlisted, despite the fact that he was considered well past his prime. He felt as if he had nothing to lose. "After having been forc'd to leave my Native Country," he wrote, "with so many thousands of my Brethren, to abandon my small Inheritance, and to forsake for ever, according to all outward appearance, those Persons that were dear to me, without finding in the New Country . . . that sufficient Relief which my present necessity demanded, I gave my self up entirely to Providence . . . and at an Age already advanc'd beyond its Prime, I thought I wou'd endeavor to live in a Place where I might be free from the common and frequent Dangers to which I was expose'd. I had nothing to lose . . ."

Leguat and nine young compatriots left the Texel in July 1690 aboard the *Hirondelle*, a small frigate under the command of a man named Antoine Valleau. The frigate subsequently joined a convoy of twenty-four English and Dutch ships that sailed north of Scotland to avoid a French squadron in the English Channel. When his ship reached the Cape of Good Hope, it was not clear whether French warships had visited Réunion or had gone to India without stopping at the island. Whether Valleau set sail from the Cape for Réunion or Rodrigues isn't known, but a cyclone hit the frigate after it left the Cape and he lost his bearings. Dutch-controlled Mauritius, not Réunion, was first sighted by him in early April 1691, and Valleau set the frigate's course for Rodrigues.

The *Hirondelle* arrived at Rodrigues and Leguat and seven other men decided to remain there. Valleau sailed away and never returned. Left on their own in an island paradise, the men had little trouble surviving—there were many sources of fresh spring water, rivers crowded with eels, thousands of huge tortoises on the land, numerous shellfish along the shore, enormous sea turtles, large, easy-to-catch flightless birds, and an edible palm that yielded a tasty juice, or "palm-wine." They built huts and settled in as castaways on the pristine island. Although food and water was plentiful, the isolation became unbearable and two years after they arrived, they began to make plans to leave the island.

The resourceful men built a boat and were able to set it afloat. After a difficult voyage to Mauritius, some 406 miles to the west, their suffering did not end. The Dutch there threw them into prison, where they stayed for three years. In 1696 the Frenchmen were sent to Batavia, where they remained for one year. When they were finally allowed to leave, only three of the castaways were still alive, Leguat and two of his companions. They finally arrived in Holland in 1698. Ten years later, Leguat published his incredible story, *A New Voyage to the East-Indies,* in French, English, and Dutch. Leguat himself lived a remarkably long time after his ordeal, and died at the age of 97 in 1735.

Leguat's description of the wildlife on Rodrigues was almost immediately questioned, especially his account of the solitarie, a bird he obviously adored. "The Females are wonderfully beautiful, some fair, some brown; I call them fair, because they are of the colour of fair Hair: They have a sort of Peak like a Widow's cap upon their Breasts, which is of a dun color. . . . They walk with so much Stateliness and good Grace, that one cannot help admiring and loving them . . .

"Tho' these Birds will sometimes very familiarly come up near enough to one, when we do not run after them, yet they will never grow Tame: As soon as they are caught they shed Tears without Crying, and (obstinately) refuse all manner of Sustenance till they die." His affection for the bird did not deter him from making a meal of the animal. He reports that its flesh tasted "admirably well, especially while they are young . . ."

By the time other visitors came to Rodrigues, most notably to view the transit of Venus (when the planet passes between the Earth and Sun) in 1761, the solitaire was gone, casting further suspicion on Leguat's descriptions of the bird. A little over one hundred years later, bones were finally discovered on Rodrigues that confirmed Leguat's story, especially an unusually small, round bony mass under the feathers of the wings in both male and female solitaires.

Leguat's account is filled with many other interesting observations, but perhaps the most memorable is a description of the startling number of tortoises on Rodrigues, which provoked much skepticism. ". . . such a plenty of Land-Turtles in this Isle, that sometimes you see two or three thousands of them in a Flock, so that you may go above a hundred paces on their Backs; or, to speak more properly on their *Carapaces*, without setting foot to the Ground," wrote Leguat.

The giant tortoises of the Indian Ocean once thrived on all the Mascarene Islands, but by the time Leguat was in Rodrigues these animals were already becoming less abundant on Mauritius and Réunion. Prized for their healthful oil as well as tasty meat, the tortoises weighed more than a hundred pounds. "This Flesh is very wholsom, and tastes something like Mutton but 'tis more delicate: The Fat is extreamly white, and never Congeals nor rises in your stomach, eat as much as you will of it," wrote Leguat. "We all unanimously agreed, 'twas better than the best Butter in Europe. To anoint one's self with this Oil, is an excellent remedy for Surfeits, Colds, Cramps and several Distempers. The Liver of this Animal is extraordinarily delicate, 'tis so Delicious that one may say of it, it always carries its own Sauce with it, dress it how you will."

Once the French lifted a ban on the removal of reptiles from Rodrigues in 1735, the destruction of tortoises and sea turtles on the island accelerated, and by the end of the century the tortoises had been destroyed. In one killing spree, about thirty thousand tortoises from the island were killed for fresh meat during an eighteen-month period. Tortoises on Mauritius, Réunion, and the nearby Seychelles were slaughtered similarly. It took only a few decades to drive the giant land tortoises on Rodrigues into extinction.

The only giant tortoises that survive today in the Indian Ocean live on the Aldabra atoll. Lying about 250 miles north of Madagascar, Aldabra comprises a small group of three islands surrounding an enormous central lagoon. Writer David Doubilet took a motor boat into the nearly untouched atoll in 1995. "Channels like witches' hands reach into the green cauldron of Aldabra," he writes in *National Geographic* magazine. "A crust of land surrounds a lagoon so large that Manhattan could float in it like a bathtub toy."

In 1874 Aldabra was going to be exploited for its mangrove timber. Fortunately, a number of notable men rallied to save the tortoises on the atoll, among them Charles Darwin. By that time, there was some concern that the animals might become extinct. A party landing on Aldabra in 1878 took three days to find one animal. In the 1960s, the atoll's fauna and flora was again in peril after the British announced plans to build an air base with a nine-thousand-foot-long runway. An outcry from scientists and conservationists caused the plans to be shelved, and in 1982 Aldabra was named a world heritage site by UNESCO.

Today, about a hundred thousand tortoises survive there, compared with a few thousand tortoises that live on the Galapagos Islands in the Pacific Ocean. It is amazing that any of the giant land tortoises survive. Their delicious meat and valuable oil, coupled with their inability to escape their captors, made them easy targets for hungry seamen during the age of discovery and beyond. Live animals were packed onto ships like stacked crates.

Herman Melville wrote an unforgettable account of the giant tortoises of the Galapagos Islands in *The Encantadas or Enchanted Isles*, a series of ten short "sketches" published in the 1850s. He describes the islands as "heaps of cinders" unparalleled in their desolation and melancholy. In the sketch titled "Two Sides to a Tortoise," Melville characterizes the "spectre-tortoise," whose breastplate of a "faint yellowish or golden tinge" helps brighten the unmitigated gloom of the islands. In the sketch, a group of men go ashore and bring back three "huge antediluvian-looking tortoises" that require a great deal of effort to haul on board. ". . . behold these really wondrous tortoises—none of your schoolboy mud-turtles—but black as widower's weeds, heavy as chests of plate, with vast shells medallioned and orbed like shields, and dented and blistered like shields that have breasted a battle, shaggy, too here and there, with dark green moss, and slimy with spray of the sea. These mystic creatures suddenly translated by night from unutterable solitudes to our peopled deck, affected me in a manner not easy to unfold. . . .

"The great feeling inspired by these creatures was that of age:— dateless, indefinite endurance."

The three "ponderous strangers" drag themselves around the deck of the ship and refuse to go around obstacles. Melville marveled at their intransigence but was haunted by their slow-motion nudging and trudging. Their "crowning curse," he wrote, "is their drudging impulse to straightforwardness in a belittered world." Despite his admiration, the next evening, "strange to say, I sat down with my shipmates, and made a merry repast from tortoise steaks and tortoise stews; and supper over, out knife, and helped convert the three mighty concave shells into three fanciful soup-tureens, and polished the three flat yellowish calipees into three gorgeous salvers."

Tens of thousands of giant tortoises met a similar fate.

Nine

Medicinal Pepper

THE ANCIENT ALLURE OF PEPPER AS A MEDICINE IS
ATTRACTING ATTENTION TODAY. SCIENTISTS IN THE WEST
ARE INTRIGUED BY PEPPER'S ABILITY TO QUELL
INFLAMMATION. EXPERIMENTS SUGGEST THE SPICE COULD
HAVE A ROLE IN COMBATING CANCER. BETEL, ONE OF
PEPPER'S SIBLINGS, APPEARS TO BE A PROMISING TREATMENT
FOR THE PARASITIC DISEASE LEISHMANIASIS.

•

*Piper nigrum L. (Piperacea) has insecticidal properties and could potentially
be utilized as an alternative to synthetic insecticides.*
—JOURNAL OF AGRICULTURAL AND FOOD CHEMISTRY

*Traditional plant remedies, particularly those used in traditional
Chinese medicine and Indian Ayurvedic medicine have, in many cases,
been observed to yield positive results.*
—PLANTA MEDICA

*"Many physiological effects of black pepper, its extracts or its major active
principle, piperine, have been reported in recent decades."*
—KRISHNAPURA SRINIVASAN, DEPARTMENT OF BIOCHEMISTRY
AND NUTRITION, CENTRAL FOOD TECHNOLOGY RESEARCH INSTITUTE,
MYSORE, INDIA

The healthful properties attributed to pepper some four hundred years ago—its ability to soothe the lungs, vanquish fevers, ease a variety of aches and pains, and even reduce the size of tumors—is gaining traction today. Thanks to the growing interest in natural products in the West, a small renaissance in the study of pepper as a medicine is under way. The spice and its *Piper* siblings still inspire our curiosity and enterprise, and perhaps one day a derivative of black pepper will become an important medicine for the treatment of cancer or other diseases.

Scientists in the United States, Britain, and Italy are now testing pepper's potency as an anti-inflammatory and antimicrobial agent; an anticancer therapy; a preservative; an insecticide; an antioxidant; an analgesic; and a treatment for vitiligo, a skin pigmentation disorder. A small number of studies in scientific journals even suggest that pepper could improve mood and slim the waistline. In Japan, researchers are evaluating whether inhaling the aroma of black pepper oil, which is used in the fragrance industry and is not pungent, can improve swallowing by stimulating parts of the brain in elderly people who have suffered strokes. They hope to prevent aspiration pneumonia, a common cause of death in these patients. The Japanese are also evaluating whether the smell of pepper oil can stimulate other parts of the brain to help people quit smoking.

And in China, where pepper has long been used as a folk remedy for the treatment of epilepsy, chemicals derived from the spice are now incorporated into medicines to treat epileptic seizures in children.

By far, though, the property that is drawing the most scrutiny is pepper's tendency to act as a sort of booster, or biological enabler, of medicines. In this role, the spice helps make medicines more "bioavailable" by increasing the amount of the drugs in the bloodstream and helping them to remain longer in the body. The liver and the intestine often throw up barriers that prevent medicines from doing their job. The usual culprits are metabolic enzymes that chew up medicinal compounds before they can be absorbed in the body, rendering them less useful. In the mid-1980s, a team in India discovered that piperine, a compound that is abundant in black pepper and which gives the spice its famous kick, inhibited the activity of certain enzymes in the liver and intestine. This finding sparked an interest in piperine's propensity to make medicines more effective.

Since then a number of clinical studies have shown that piperine boosts the levels of phenytoin for epilepsy, propranolol for high blood pressure, theophylline for asthma, rifampin for tuberculosis, and nevirapine for HIV infection, among other medications. The ability of black pepper to make drugs more bioavailable may be the main reason why an herbal mixture called *trikatu* is so widely prescribed along with other treatments in Ayurvedic medicine, a system that aims to prevent disease and promote well-being. By enhancing the effects of these other medicines, trikatu would serve as a sort of all-purpose medicinal amplifier.

More than three hundred citations for scientific papers related to black pepper are in PubMed, the huge database maintained by the National Library of Medicine in the United States. The scientific work on black pepper is proving that it possesses properties that have long been exploited in Ayurvedic medicine. This system of healing has not been embraced in the West, although other alternative or complementary medicines from Asia are becoming more popular in Western countries. The British attempted to rid India of Ayurvedic medicine altogether, when, in 1835, they banned teaching the system in India. More recently, in 2000, the House of Lords issued a report saying that there wasn't evidence to support Ayurvedic's role in the diagnosis and treatment of disease. A review of studies involving some 166 plant species—from sage leaves, cinnamon, and fenu-greek to nutmeg, dandelion, and white sandalwood—utilized in Ayurvedic medicine presents a different picture. The survey by Sarah Khan and Michael Balick, an ethnobotanist at the Institute of Economic Botany at the New York Botanical Garden, reveals that 43 percent of the plants had undergone testing in at least one human clinical trial and 62 percent had been evaluated in studies in animals. Although the authors acknowledge that many of the studies lack the appropriate rigor associated with the "gold-standard" of clinical testing in the West, such as adequate sample size and controls, their review suggests which plant species might be suitable for larger and better-controlled clinical trials. They conclude that the studies in the scientific and medical literature dispel "the all-too-commonly held notion that no clinical or other evidence exists to support the use of plants used in traditional medical systems."

Spices were frequently mentioned in ancient Ayurvedic texts, and some seven hundred drugs derived from pepper, turmeric, ginger, cinnamon, and other spices were described by a physician named Sushruta the Second in about 500 B.C. It isn't surprising that people who were surrounded by spice plants found extensive uses for them. In ancient times, black pepper was a remedy for constipation, diarrhea, earache, heart disease, hernia, indigestion, liver problems, and joint pain, among other ailments. In India today, the pepper mixture trikatu is relied on to treat a wide variety of illnesses, in combination with other herbal preparations. The mixture contains black pepper, long pepper, and ginger in equal proportions, and is part of most prescriptions in traditional Ayurvedic medicine. Many are taken as pills or powders and are often consumed with honey to make them more palatable. In South Asia pepper is also widely employed in a broad array of folk remedies, especially as a treatment for diarrhea. Most medicines in the West, too, are derived from plants. Willow bark was the original source of aspirin, and the latest treatment for malaria, artemisinin, is a compound found in a shrub applied in traditional Chinese medicine.

Among spices, turmeric, a spice in yellow mustard and Indian curry, called *haldi* in Hindi and *jiang huang* in Chinese, has been given the most attention by Western scientists because of its potential as a treatment for Alzheimer's, cancer, and other diseases. But scientists have not neglected black pepper, which shares some of turmeric's properties.

Black pepper contains many compounds, but piperine is the most abundant. First identified in 1820 by a Dutch chemist named Hans Christian Orstedt, piperine is considered an alkaloid. (Long pepper, *Piper longum,* also contains piperine.) Alkaloids are common in nature—some 10 to 20 percent of plants contain this type of chemical, according to Van Nostrand's *Scientific Encyclopedia.* Caffeine, heroin, and nicotine are also alkaloids, however there is no evidence that piperine is addictive. Most alkaloids contain the element nitrogen embedded in rings of carbons. Stronger pepper is packed with more piperine, the reason that pepper grown in Malaysia and Indonesia is more pungent than pepper grown in Brazil.

The ability of piperine to boost the effectiveness of a particular treatment for cancer is the focus of a research project underway at Fox Chase Cancer Center in Maryland led by urologic surgeon Robert Uzzo and scientist Vladimir Kolenko. They are evaluating whether the compound can make a medicine for treating advanced prostate cancer more effective and easier to tolerate. Piperine inhibits a liver enzyme that is responsible for the degradation of a drug called docetaxel, which combats various kinds of tumors. Docetaxel, itself a natural product derived from the Pacific yew tree, is a medicine approved by the U.S. Food and Drug Administration to treat men with cancers resistant to the hormones that are the usual first line of treatment. However, the drug only increases the survival of patients by two to four months and has the usual side effects associated with chemotherapy, such as vomiting, hair loss, and nausea. Docetaxel has to be administered intravenously three times a week, because the liver will destroy the drug in its pill form. Patients would be much more comfortable if the drug could be administered orally. Could the addition of piperine make this possible? If the pepper compound inhibits the liver enzyme, can it increase the amount of time the anticancer agent remains in the bloodstream? Would tumor cells be exposed to the agent for a longer period of time than is otherwise possible, enhancing the effectiveness of the chemotherapy? The physician researchers want to find the answers to these questions.

Piperine may also enhance the activity of a natural product called curcumin, the active ingredient in the spice turmeric, that is the ongoing subject of clinical studies at MD Anderson Cancer Center in Houston and elsewhere. Like pepper, turmeric is an ancient spice that is widely used in traditional medicine in India, where it is most renowned for its capacity to fight inflammation. It was this property that led Bharat B. Aggarwal, chief of the Cytokine Research Section at MD Anderson and a former scientist at the biotechnology company Genentech, to explore the feasibility of using curcumin as an anticancer agent.

Some investigators believe that piperine has the capacity to quell inflammation, which would make it an appealing compound to incorporate into treatments for a wide variety of diseases. The idea that inflammation is tied to cancer stems in part from the discovery of a substance called tumor necrosis factor, a powerful protein linked to inflammation that also appears to play an important role in driving the growth of tumors. (Aggarwal and his colleagues at Genentech purified tumor necrosis factor in the 1980s.) This protein is also produced in people with various autoimmune diseases, such as psoriatic arthritis and inflammatory bowel disease, and medicines designed to neutralize it are taken by millions of people worldwide.

The destructiveness of the protein becomes clearer through its relationship to a molecule called nuclear factor kappa beta (NF Kappa B). Tumor necrosis factor activates this molecule, which has been linked to immune and inflammatory processes, cell growth, and many other biological processes. Normal cells have lower levels of NF Kappa B than tumor cells. The interesting observation here is that curcumin and piperine have each been shown to suppress the activity of NF Kappa B. More than eight hundred compounds are also known to inhibit the molecule, though, so further research is needed to figure out if the specific activity of the spice chemicals will have any meaningful effect in the clinic.

Most intriguing are the possibilities of using piperine to improve the bioavailability of curcumin, and combining the two spice ingredients to generate a more powerful response. In a small laboratory study published in 2009 by researchers at the University of Michigan, each compound by itself and in combination inhibited the renewal, or generation, of certain stem cells in the breast that may be the source of cancer cells. Additionally, they found that the compounds did not harm normal tissue, at least in the laboratory setting. Indeed, piperine has been shown in a series of other laboratory studies to inhibit colon cancer in rats induced by a known carcinogen and to protect against DNA damage in animals with induced lung cancer.

Already the Internet is serving up a large dollop of news about pepper's anticancer properties. "Pepper's hot stuff because it contains pungent piperine, which goes into search-and-destroy mode when breast stem cells are trying to turn cancerous," boasts a Web site bearing the headshots of "Dr. Oz" and "Dr. Mike." "Pass the Pepper," shouts a headline from the *National Post* in Canada, in an article that includes information about piperine's ability to increase the bioavailability of curcumin and to help with weight control, at least according to research on mice.

For anyone inspired to eat a lot of black pepper based on all of these findings and reports, there doesn't appear to be much risk. In animal studies, rats and mice fed up to one hundred times more black pepper than is normally consumed in the Indian diet did not suffer any ill consequences; their gastrointestinal tracts did just fine. Rather than cause distress, some researchers believe that piperine in very high doses may promote digestion and protect the lining of the stomach and intestine.

While black pepper may be associated with promising areas of medical research, it isn't a panacea. Modern research is usurping the long-held notion that pepper is an excellent preservative. Krishnapura Srinivasan, who has studied the physiological effects of piperine for more than thirty years, says that pepper has "limited application" as a preservative, especially in comparison to other spices such as turmeric and garlic. Pepper also appears to fall short in another potentially exciting application, as an antioxidant that squelches rogue oxygen molecules contributing to cancer, hardening of the arteries, and other diseases. Curcumin is effective, but piperine is not.

However, black pepper may have a less exalted role in natural insect repellents. A study published in 2008 by scientists at the University of Florida and the U.S. Department of Agriculture reported that repellents containing compounds called piperidines, which are closely related to piperine, warded off mosquitoes more than three times longer than DEET, the active ingredient in most insect sprays.

DEET was discovered in 1953, and scientists still do not know how it prevents insects from biting. Volunteers in the 2008 study comparing the two wore arm patches laced with the piperidine compounds and bravely held their arms in a chamber filled with about five hundred mosquitoes. The DEET kept the insects away for an average of almost eighteen days, while some of the piperidines were effective for up to seventy-three days. One of the scientists who led the research says that the new compounds have the advantage of being unsticky and unsmelly (surprising for compounds related to piperine) compared to most of today's insect repellents.

Black pepper is not the only member of the *Piper* family of plants that is being investigated by scientists. The intriguing effects of pepper's close relative, *Piper betle,* the foundation of habit-forming betel chewing in Asia, have not gone unnoticed in the laboratory. Ever since Europeans first set foot in Asia, they have observed that betel seemed to promote good health. One of the many travelers to comment on betel's apparently life-enhancing properties was Tomé Pires, the Portuguese ambassador to China in the sixteenth century, who wrote: "It greatly helps digestion, comforts the brain, strengthens the teeth, so that men here who eat it usually have all their teeth, without any missing, even at eighty years of age. Those who eat it have good health and if they do not eat it one day their breath is unbearable."

Like black pepper (*Piper nigrum*), betel is used in Ayurvedic medicine for constipation, headaches, ringworm, conjunctivitis, and other conditions. We know that it also produces a sense of well-being and increases alertness. In India today, preparations of betel quid, which may combine sliced areca nut, lime, aniseed, clove, coriander, cardamom, or other ingredients with betel leaves, are still offered on ceremonial occasions, such as marriages and religious festivals. As in the days when Europeans first traveled to Asia, it is still considered impolite not to offer a guest a chew. India isn't the only country where betel is chewed—millions of people in China, Malaysia, Indonesia, and other countries also partake. The leaf is probably the most widely exploited *Piper* sibling, second only to black pepper itself. In fact, some six hundred million people are estimated to consume betel daily. The controversial association of betel leaf with mouth cancer is mainly due to other ingredients, such as areca nuts and tobacco, which are combined with betel to make quid. While in most parts of Asia the betel leaf is essential for making paan, people in the Chinese city of Xiangtan in Hunan Province like to chew only the husk of fresh areca nut, which they call "binglang," the basis for a 1.18-billion-dollar industry. Blackened gums and stained teeth are the hallmarks of crunching the nut.

The interest in natural products has cast a new light on betel, and the spotlight is shining on betel's antimicrobial properties, which probably explain why the leaf seems to preserve one's teeth, as Tomé Pires observed nearly five hundred years ago. Indeed, a study from the department of oral biology at the University of Malaya in Kuala Lumpur, Malaysia, reported that extracts from *Piper betle* and *Psidium guajava* (guava) suppressed the growth of bacteria that contribute to dental plaque.

Other researchers are evaluating an entirely different property of betel, its capacity to inhibit an enzyme called xanthine oxidase. The enzyme is critical to the production of uric acid in the body. High levels of the acid may lead to gout and kidney stones. The drug allopurinol, which inhibits the enzyme, is a treatment. But the drug has serious side effects, such as kidney failure, allergic reactions, and impaired functioning of the liver. Alternatives are being investigated by a research group in Japan. The characteristics of the chemicals found among the plants in the *Piper* family inspired the group to screen black pepper and its siblings for activity against xanthine oxidase. Among all the plant extracts tested, betel was the most potent inhibitor of the enzyme. They subsequently identified a chemical in betel called hydroxychavicol, which appeared to be responsible for shutting down the enzyme.

Most important are reports in the scientific literature suggesting that betel may combat the parasite that causes a disease called leishmaniasis, which is transmitted through the bite of a tiny sand fly. As many as two million people in the world are currently infected, and every year another one to two million new cases occur, according to the World Health Organization. Few countries are unaffected. There are two forms of the disease, cutaneous and visceral. The manifestations of the cutaneous form are skin sores that can last for years before healing on their own. The sores can be disfiguring if they occur on the face, and some of these volcano-like eruptions are painful.

The visceral, more severe form of the disease affects the internal organs and can be fatal. More than 90 percent of people infected with visceral leishmaniasis live in India, Bangladesh, Nepal, Sudan, and Brazil, according the U.S. Center for Disease Control and Prevention in Atlanta. Current therapies for the visceral form of the disease aren't very effective and have a variety of side effects. Drug resistance is also increasing. So there is a real need to develop new drugs to fight leishmaniasis, and several laboratories in India report that extracts from betel kill leishmania parasites in a laboratory setting.

Scientists are just beginning to explore betel's potential utility as a medicine. While there is no guarantee that these early observations will eventually be turned into therapies, there is hope that its great potential will bring healing to millions.

Epilogue

The roster of countries that produce pepper today hasn't changed much since Europeans first crossed the Indian Ocean to find the spice. It is, after all, a tropical plant with a penchant for a particular type of soil and climate, and it cannot be easily transplanted, as the Portuguese learned when they tried to cultivate the plant in Brazil during the seventeenth century. It took nearly three hundred years for that particular experiment to work, and it was the Japanese who first introduced large-scale pepper plantations into Brazil in 1933. After World War II, pepper was introduced in Africa, and its production expanded in Southeast Asia, particularly in Vietnam and parts of southern China.

Today Vietnam has emerged as the leading pepper grower, contributing about 30 percent of worldwide production, followed by India, Brazil, China, Indonesia, and Malaysia. Black pepper is an integral part of food consumed everywhere, and some 640 million pounds are harvested each year in the world. The highest quality pepper—Malabar garbled and Tellicherry extra bold—is grown in

India, which exports the most pepper to the United States. Traders bet on the market prices of pepper in India, where the spice is traded on a commodity exchange in Kochi. Pepper is the world's biggest selling spice, and its profitability depends on the vagaries of weather and soil. Demand fluctuates slightly but generally remains fairly steady year to year.

The biggest problem facing pepper growers today is foot rot disease, caused by a fungus with the scientific name of *Phytophthora*. The fungus has spread throughout the world's pepper-growing regions since it was first detected in Indonesia in the late nineteenth century. The invading fungus quickly wilts the green leaves of pepper vines and strangles the roots of the plant, and it has destroyed many small-scale homestead pepper farms in Kerala in India, along with farms in many other pepper-growing areas. In Vietnam the devastating disease is called *quick wilt* or *quick death*. Efforts to keep crops free of this dreaded disease have led to the extensive use of fungicides. An intensive search is underway for hybrid strains that can resist the fungus and reduce the use of fungicides.

Surveying the wreckage of colonization and subjugation in Latin America, the writer Eduardo Galeano observes that "places privileged by nature have been cursed by history." His words could easily apply to black pepper in Asia. The spice that lured the West to Asia gave birth to the modern age of global trade, with all of its attendant miseries. The brutal and racist men who plied the Indian Ocean in search of pepper or in defense of pepper, from Vasco da Gama in the sixteenth century, to the infamous Jan Pieterszoon Coen and Cornelis Speelman in the seventeenth century, and to John Downes in the nineteenth century, reflected to some extent the prevailing beliefs of their day. But there were men who sailed to Asia who did try to understand other cultures, who were revolted by violence, and who felt inspired by the sheer natural beauty of the places they visited. Their voices, too, deserve to be heard above the din of conquest and imperialism, slavery and genocide. There was the Cornish traveler Peter Mundy, who described in almost adoring terms a pepper garden in India. There was William Keeling, the English East India Company captain who spent a delirious day being fêted in the clear-flowing waters of Aceh. There was the adventurer William Dampier, who was disgusted by the way in which an English administrator of the Benkoolen pepper settlement treated Malaysians. There was the American seaman Levi Lincoln, who unflinchingly reported how the Americans cheated the pepper-weighing scales in western Sumatra. Even Stamford Raffles, the ever-political, ever-calculating servant of the English East India Company, the model of the Company man, reformed the racist laws in the Benkoolen settlement. There were also Europeans who adopted Asia as their homeland, who went native, like Judith of Malacca, the shipwrecked English maidservant who Peter Mundy mentioned in his journals.

Certainly the history of pepper cannot be detached from the rise in the seventeenth century of two great Western mercantile companies, the Dutch and English East India companies. Their rabid, almost never-ending quest for supremacy in Asia over a period of some two hundred years was ferocious, even though in Europe the English and the Dutch were sometimes allied with each other against the Spanish or the French. Occasionally peace prevailed when politics obliged the English and the Dutch to work together in Asia to dispel a common enemy. Over the course of its existence, the VOC employed hundreds of thousands of men and was a vital engine for the economy of the Netherlands, especially during the golden seventeenth century of Dutch history. The company paid large dividends, making its shareholders rich, but the demands of supporting and arming such a far-flung, fundamentally corrupt organization finally brought the VOC down. The VOC was millions of guilders in debt when it went bankrupt in 1799.

The English East India Company had to adopt the tactics of its Dutch rival in order to thrive, and in the eighteenth century it became a military and political entity to protect its interests in Asia, especially in India. The Company generally left the spice trade to the Dutch and concentrated its efforts in India and China. Its powers began to wane in the late eighteenth century when the movement toward free and open trade took precedence over monopoly trade. The Company withdrew from trade in the East in 1833, but it remained infamously tied to British imperialism in India. The same held true for the VOC, although the Dutch company was always seen as an arm of government. After the company was disbanded, the Dutch government inherited the VOC's holdings, eventually becoming the overseer of the Dutch East Indies, which it ruled until 1949. Both companies left an indelible and horrific mark on the lands and peoples they conquered.

Black pepper, the spice that was the primary reason the northern Europeans established their trading companies, lives on today as a commodity, a common seasoning, and as a potentially valuable medicine in the West. Its history, though, as Voltaire observed more than two hundred years ago, is soaked in blood.

ACKNOWLEDGMENTS

In a book like this, I mined the work of historians who have written about the age of discovery, when Europeans sailed to Asia. C. R. Boxer, Anthony Reid, John Bastin, Holden Furber, and M. A. P. Meilink-Roelofsz are among the pioneers in this field, and their books and articles were my constant companions. Many books about the Dutch East India Company have been published; among the best are those by Femme S. Gaastra. In order to understand the East India Company, I turned mainly to John Keay. But most of all, I owe gratitude to those men and women who died long ago and left diaries and journals about their travels, especially Peter Mundy, J. S. Stavorinus, William Dampier, Thomas Best, and the sailors and merchants aboard the Indiamen who left the Downs in southeastern England, and whose words were published by the Hakluyt Society.

I am grateful to many people who offered support and encouragement along the way. Many thanks to David Oshinsky and Anna Shapiro, who took the time to read and comment on the manuscript, and to Mark Pendergrast, for suggesting an epilogue with information about plant diseases that affect pepper today. I am grateful to Krishnapura Srinivasan, one of the world's experts on pepper's chemical properties, who reviewed the chapter on medicinal pepper and patiently answered my seemingly endless questions.

Sybille Millard, an extraordinary photo researcher, helped gather the illustrations, photos, and maps and negotiated far better prices than I ever could. She was enormously helpful. I also want to thank Larry W. Bowman, who collects antiquarian books and other material about the Indian Ocean, for leading me to the Aldabra tortoises.

I had the pleasure of working in various libraries throughout the years it took me to research this book. The Wertheim Study at the New York Public Library provided a haven, and I want to thank the librarians at the Phillips Library at the Peabody Essex Museum in Salem, Massachusetts, who welcomed me and steered me to the logbooks of U.S. pepper ships of the nineteenth century. Thanks also to the librarians at the New York Academy of Medicine Library, Bobst Library at New York University, and the LuEsther T. Mertz Library of the New York Botanical Garden (NYBL), in the Bronx. I am grateful to Stephen Tabor of the Huntington Library in San Marino, California, for obtaining the illustration from Linschoten's *Itinerario* and to Marie Long of NYBL for sorting out the provenance of Garcia da Orta's drawing of a peppercorn.

This book was written at the Writer's Room in New York City, where I finally found a place where I could settle down and write. My employer, NYU School of Medicine, allowed me to work part-time to write this book, and I want to especially thank my colleagues Lynn Odell and Thomas Ranieri for their support. Finally, my agent, Joanne Wang, provided crucial support throughout the entire process of researching and writing this book. She never lost faith in me, and I was fortunate to have her by my side.

NOTES

One: Meet the Pipers

1. *"Pepper is the bride around which everyone dances."* Jacob Hustaert's quote is cited in George D. Winius and Marcus P. M. Vink's *The Merchant-Warrior Pacified* (Oxford University Press, 1991) p. 35.

2. *"The virtue of all peppers . . . is to heat, to move a man to make water, to digest, to draw to, to drive away by resolution, and to scour away those things that darken the eyesight."* This quote from Dioscorides is from *A New Herball,* by William Turner, three volumes (1551–1568), volume two, edited by George T. L. Chapman, Frank McCombie, Anne Wesencraft (Cambridge University Press, 1995) p. 507–508. Turner, known as the father of English botany, was born around 1508.

3. *". . . conconction, to discuss wind, to do good against the cold affects of the stomack, and yet not to heat the liver or the blood, wherein consisteth as singular propertie of this medicine."* *A Short Discourse on Three Kinds of Peppers in Common Use,* William Bailey, 1588. New York Academy of Medicine, Rare Books. Bailey relied on the work of Galen, a renowned Roman physician, for his description of pepper's healing powers.

3. "... *wholesome for the brain.*" *A Rich Store-house or Treasury for the Diseased*: Wherein, are many approved medicines for diverse and sundry diseases, which have long been hidden, and not come to light before this time. ... By A. T. Rebus. London, printed for Thomas Purfoot, and Raph [sic] Bower, 1596. New York Academy of Medicine, Rare Books.

3. ... *another published a year later recommended the spice alone or combined with other substances for conditions ranging from headaches and gas to leprous facial sores and tumors.* William Langham's *The Garden of Health* (London: 1597), a popular herbal treatise. Langham described sixty-four medical uses for pepper.

4. *a Pfeffersack (pepper sack) was a common expression that referred to a merchant who made handsome profits from the pepper trade.* Cambridge World History of Food, editors Kenneth F. Kiple and Kriemhild Coneè Ornelas (Cambridge University Press, 2000) p. 436.

4. *But for most people, pepper was too expensive—in 1439, a pound of pepper was roughly equal to more than two days' wages in England.* This calculation by John Munro, an economic historian, is cited in Paul Freedman's *Out of the East: Spices and the Medieval Imagination* (Yale University Press, 2008) p. 127. Pepper wasn't the most expensive luxury good. By comparison, velvet would have cost between two and three hundred days' wages in 1439.

5. *Voltaire wrote that after the year 1500 there was no pepper obtained in Calicut that was "not dyed red with blood."* Calicut, an important pepper port along the southwest coast of India, was where Vasco da Gama first made landfall in south Asia in 1498, and it played a prominent role in the pepper trade in the following centuries.

6. "*Pepper is the seed of the fruit of a tree that groweth in the south side of the hill Caucasus in the strong heat of the sun.*" Bartholomew, a thirteenth-century encylopedist, is quoted in Lorna J. Sass's *To the King's Taste* (St. Martin's/Marek, 1975) p. 24.

7. *Garcia da Orta, who lived in Goa* ... One of the pioneers of tropical medicine, da Orta was the first European to catalogue South Asian medicinal herbs and to describe cholera. He described three kinds of pepper: black, white, and long, and mistakenly believed that white pepper

and black pepper were different climbing plants. He appreciated the trade value of the spice and knew that the greatest quantities of black pepper were found in Malabar and Sumatra. His book, *Conversations on the Simples, Drugs and the Medicinal Substances of India,* was abridged and annotated by a leading European botanist named Charles Lécluse, who published it in Antwerp in 1567. The abridged version was translated into many languages without acknowledgment of da Orta's authorship. Da Orta was born in Portugal around 1501, after his Jewish parents were forced to flee the Inquisition in Spain and convert to Christianity. He settled in Goa in 1538. Although he wasn't hounded by the Inquisition in Goa, he was tried postmortem as a "crypto Jew" and his bones were exhumed and burned. A year after his death, his sister was burned at the stake.

8. *"Att the Foote of these trees they sett the pepper plant . . ." The Travels of Peter Mundy,* Vol. III, Part I (The Hakluyt Society, 1919) and reprinted in 1967 by Kraus Reprint Limited, p. 79.

12. *"The betel nut is cut in four pieces and wraped up (one each in an Arek leaf), which they spread with a soft paste made of lime or Plaifter and then chew it altogether. . . ."* William Dampier, *Voyage Around the World,* Vol. I, 1685, p. 318. This edition of his book is from the Rare Books and Manuscript Division of the New York Public Library. Dampier's book is available on Google Books.

12. *". . . everyone knows what the Betel-Leaves and Arequa Nuts are . . ." The Voyage of François Leguat of Bresse to Rodriguez, Mauritius, Java, and the Cape of Good Hope,* edited and annotated by Captain Pasfield Oliver (The Hakluyt Society, 1891) p. 229.

12. *" . . . when ladies go out in Jakarta, they are invariably attended by four or more female slaves, one of whom bears the betel-box."* J. S. Stavorinus *Voyages to the East Indies,* translated by S. H. Wilcocke, 1798 (reprinted by Dawsons of Pall Mall, London, 1969) Vol. I, p. 322.

12. *"makes their spittle of a crimson colour . . ."* Ibid., p. 317.

12. *"longer than the most inveterate tobacco chewer over his plug."* Gorham P. Low, *The Sea Made Men: The Story of a Gloucester Lad,* edited by Elizabeth L. Alling (Fleming H. Revell Company, 1937) p. 192.

14. *"I do not recognize them, for which I feel the greatest sorrow in the world."*

Lardicci, Francesca, editor, *A Synoptic Edition of the Log of Columbus's First Voyage* (Brepols, 1999) p. 58. Columbus's original journals have been lost. The accounts of his four voyages are based mainly on a biography written by his second son, Fernando Colón, who had access to his father's papers, and on the *History of the Indies* by Spanish historian Bartolomé de Las Casas, who knew Columbus's family and had consulted their archives. Las Casas also made a handwritten copy of Columbus's log of the first voyage, although it isn't considered to be complete. Undoubtedly, the Spanish monarchs Isabella and Ferdinand did not want their enemies to profit from Columbus's discoveries.

Two : The King of Spices

17. *"Pepper is small in quantity and great in virtue."* Plato's quote is cited in Waverly Root's *Food: An Authoritative and Visual History and Dictionary of the Foods of the World* (Simon and Schuster, 1980) p. 341.

17. *"The King of Portugal, Lord of Spices, has set . . . prices just as he pleases, for pepper, which, at any cost, no matter how dear, will not long go unsold to the Germans."* Cited in Wolfgang Schivelbusch's engaging book *Tastes of Paradise: A Social History of Spices, Stimulants, and Intoxicants* (Pantheon, 1992) p. 12.

18. *Pepper's worth had not escaped the Goth. His army finally left Rome laden with thousands of pounds of gold and silver, thousands of silk tunics and scarlet-dyed skins, and three thousand pounds of pepper.* This information is attributed to Gibbon, who wrote that Alaric the Goth lifted the siege "on the immediate payment of five thousand pounds of gold, of thirty thousand pounds of silver, of four thousand robes of silk, of three thousand pieces of fine scarlet cloth, and of three thousand pounds weight of pepper." See "Spices and Silk: Aspects of World Trade in the First Seven Centuries of the Christian Era," by Michael Loewe, *Journal of the Royal Asiatic Society of Great Britain and Ireland*, No. 2, (1971), p. 175.

19. *"Apicius showed it [pepper] employed, ground or whole, black or white, in almost every recipe . . ."* Innes Miller, *The Spice Trade of the Roman Empire, 29 BC to AD 641,* (Clarendon Press, 1969) p. 83. See also Sally Grainger's article "The Myth of Apicius," in the journal

Gastronomica, Spring 2007, for a diverting discussion of the epicure as greedy and obsessed.

19. *For the Feast of St. Edward in 1264, Master William, a saucier, prepared a sauce that incorporated 15 pounds of cinnamon, 12.5 pounds of cumin, and 20 pounds (320 ounces) of pepper.* See Pamela Nightingale, *A Medieval Mercantile Community: The Grocers' Company and the Politics and Trade of London*, 1000–1485 (Yale University Press, 1995) p. 74.

20. *Two hundreds years later, Duke Karl of Bourgogne, considered one of the wealthiest men in Europe, ordered 380* pounds *of pepper for his wedding dinner in 1468. The Cambridge World History of Food*, Vol. 2, edited by Kenneth F. Kiple and Kriemhild Coneè Ornelas (Cambridge University Press, 2000) p. 436.

21. *"No less than Palmyra and Petra, the city [Venice] owed everything to its preeminence in Oriental trade—a term that was virtually synonymous with spices—and was proud to proclaim it."* John Keay, *The Spice Route: A History*, (London: John Murray, 2005) p. 139.

21. *"History has shown that the hunger for spices was capable of mobilizing forces very much as the present-day need for energy sources has done."* Schivelbusch, *Tastes of Paradise: A Social History of Spices, Stimulants, and Intoxicants*, p. 9.

22. *"Throughout the middle ages the Garden was believed, somehow, to have survived the flood . . ." The Garden of Eden: The Botanic Garden and the Re-Creation of Paradise* (Yale University Press, 1982) p. 9.

22. *"In the thirteenth century, cinnamon, ginger, and other spices were believed to float down the Nile from Paradise. Fishermen cast their nets into the river to gather this aromatic bounty."* Ibid, p. 30.

23. *"fantasies of absurd plentitude"* Paul Freedman, *Out of the East: Spices and the Medieval Imagination* (Yale University Press, 2008) p. 137.

23. *"After our departure from Batavia [modern-day Jakarta] wee arrived att Suratt the 23th October last. And going ashore to the villadg called Swalley, wee sawe there manie people that perished of hunger; and whereas heretofore where were in that towne 260 famillyes, ther was not remaininge alive above 10 or 11 famillyes." The Travels of Peter Mundy in Europe and Asia, 1608–1667,* Vol. II (The Hakluyt Society, 1919; reprinted in 1967 by Kraus Reprint Limited) p. 344.

24. *. . . that helped allay the Queen's fears that an English trading company would anger the Spanish.* See Heidi Brayman Hackel and Peter C. Mancall, "Richard Hakluyt the Younger's Notes for the East India Company in 1601: A Transcription of Huntington Library Manuscript EL 2360," *The Huntington Library Quarterly,* Vol. 67, No. 3 (2004), pp. 423–436, 2004.

24. *"in an age wherein God hath raised so general a desire in the youth of this realm to discover all parts of the face of the earth."* Quote from Richard Hakluyt cited in Russell Shorto's *The Island at the Center of the World: The Epic History of Dutch Manhattan and the Forgotten Colony that shaped America,* (New York: Doubleday, 2004) p. 20.

26. *In 1418, an irate English grocer reported that he had been defrauded by a man who gave him tin spoons and stones rather than silver spoons, silver, and jewels in exchange for twelve pounds of pepper.* Anecdote related in Aubrey Joseph Rees, *The Grocery Trade: Its History and Romance* (Duckworth and Company, Ltd, 1910) p. 94.

26. *When Isabella married Charles I of Spain . . . in 1524, her brother, John III of Portugal, paid part of her dowry in pepper.* Cited in Waverley Root, *Food: An Authoritative and Visual History and Dictionary of the Foods of the World* (Simon and Schuster, 1980) p. 338.

27. *In the eighteenth century, the largest quantity of nutmeg sold by the VOC in Holland was only 280,964 pounds.* Figure cited in *Voyages to the East Indies,* by J. S. Stavorinus, translated by S. H. Wilcocke, 1798 (reprinted by Dawsons of Pall Mall, London, 1969) Vol. I, p. 334.

27. *"If the present misunderstandings between the two nations should ferment to an open war it would thought by the vulgar, but a war for pepper which they think to be [a] slight thing, because each family spends but a little [on] it. . . ."* Quote is from *The British in West Sumatra (1685– 1825): A selection of documents, mainly from the East India Company records preserved in the India Office Library, Commonwealth Relations Office, London,* with an introduction and notes by John Bastin (Kuala Lumpur: University of Malaya Press, 1965) p. xi.

28. *Around 1515 Portugal made about one million cruzados from the trade in spices, equal to all of its ecclesiastical revenues and double the value of*

its trade in gold and metals. Figures cited in *Spices in the India Ocean World,* edited by M. N. Pearson (Ashgate Variorum, 1996) p. xxvi.

29. *Under the Sung Dynasty (960 to 1127) the trade in pepper expanded and the spice was often brought as tribute from visiting Southeast Asian embassies.* Historian Yung-Ho Ts'ao enumerates the trade embassies carrying pepper as tribute and describes the pepper trade in China in the subsequent centuries in his article "Pepper Trade in East Asia" (T'oung Pao [Netherlands], 1982) 68 (4–5): 221–247.

30. *"At the end of the five days' journey lies the splendid city of Zaiton [modern-day Quanzhou]. . . ."* Marco Polo: *The Travels,* translated and with an introduction by Ronald Latham (Penguin Books, 1958) p. 237.

30. *". . . anyone seeing such a multitude would believe"* Ibid., pp. 216–217.

31. *"When the period of the tenth moon arrives, the pepper ripens; [and] it is collected, dried in the sun, and sold. . . ."* Ma Huan, *The Overall Survey of the Ocean's Shores* (published for the Hakluyt Society by Cambridge University Press, 1970) p. 143.

32. *The Chinese implemented an extraordinary campaign to obtain the wood for their massive ships by planting more than fifty million trees in the Nanking area in 1391.* From Jacque Gernet, *A History of Chinese Civilization* (Cambridge University Press, 1982) p. 399.

32. *Andrea Corsali reported in 1515 that there was "as great profit in taking spices to China as in taking them to Portugal."* Quoted in M. A. P. Meilink-Roelofsz's masterwork *Asian Trade and European Influence in the Indonesian Archipelago Between 1500 and About 1630* (The Hague: Martinus Nijhoff, 1962) p. 62.

33. *". . . the houses in the town make a good appearance, are built with stone, and ranged in streets, much like our small sea-ports in England."* Charles Lockyer, *"An Account of the Trade in India:* containing rules for good government in trade, . . . with descriptions of Fort St. George, . . . Calicut, . . . To which is added, an account of the management of the Dutch and their affairs in India," London 1711, chapter III, pp. 74–75.

Three : Drugs and Souls

38. *Boast no more about the subtle Greek* . . . Luís Vaz De Camões, *The Lusíads,* translated by Landeg White, Oxford University Press, 1997, p. 3.

38. *"Between the town and the king's palace there is nothing but houses and there is no place in all India . . ."* François Pyrard, *The Voyage of,* translated by Albert Gray (The Hakluyt Society, 1887; reprinted in the U.S.A. by Burt Franklin, 1964) p. 366.

38. *". . . bad order and discipline in the ships; for there was no piety or devotion, but plenty of oaths and blasphemy, disobedience to officers, mutiny and carelessness, and every day quarrelling, assault, thefts, and the like vices."* Ibid., p. 5.

39. *". . . wore their hair long and had no beards except around their mouths. They landed wearing cuirass, helmet and vizor, and carrying a certain weapon (sword) attached to a spear. Once every two years they returned with 20 to 25 ships."* Quote cited in Carney T. Fisher, "Portuguese as Seen by the Historians of the Qing Court," in *Vasco da Gama and the Linking of Europe and Asia,* A. R. Disney and E. Booth, editors (Oxford University Press, 2000) p. 308.

39. *"The entire land wished him ill."* See Felipe Fernandez-Armesto, "The Indian Ocean in World History," in *Vasco da Gama and the Linking of Europe and Asia,* p. 13.

40. *"And what I want from your land is gold and silver and coral and scarlet [cloth],"* See Sanjay Subrahmanyam, *The Career and Legend of Vasco da Gama* (Cambridge University Press, 1997) p. 144.

43. *A Portuguese writer named Figueiredo Falcao, who had access to official records, wrote in 1612 that some thirty-five Indiamen were wrecked in the years 1580 to 1610. Other observers have estimated that between 1550 and 1650, some 130 Portuguese ships were lost either through shipwrecks or enemy attacks.* See C. R. Boxer, *The Tragic History of the Sea* (University of Minnesota Press, 2001) pp. 24–25.

43. *. . . between 1601 and 1620 the English sent out eighty-one Indiamen, the best ships of their time, and only thirty-five of the ships returned to England, a dismal record.* Kenneth R. Andrews, *Trade, Plunder and Settlement: Maritime Enterprise and the genesis of the British Empire, 1480–1630* (Cambridge University Press, 1984).

44. *The sixteenth day our general departed Bantam and came aboard to proceed on his voyage to the Malucos; this night died Henry Dewbry of the flux . . . The seventeenth day died of the flux William Lewed, John Jenkens, and Samuel Porter. The Voyages of James Lancaster to the East Indies,* edited by Clements R. Markham (The Hakluyt Society, 1877) p. 19.

45. *Nearly 16 percent of the Jesuits' annual income in the seventeenth century was derived from Eastern spices . . .* See Dauril Alden, *The Making of an Enterprise: The Society of Jesus in Portugal, Its Empire and Beyond, 1540–1750* (Stanford University Press, 1996) p. 529.

46. *At the end of his reign, the Ming emperor Zhu Di, an ardent supporter of oceanic trade, suffered a series of calamities that led him to suspend future voyages of the Treasure Fleet.* One of the best accounts of the time when China was a great maritime power can be found in Louise Levathes's *When China Ruled the Seas* (Oxford University Press, 1994).

47. *In practice, many of the Portuguese ships were delayed because of administrative problems, the prolonged wait for a full cargo of pepper, or lack of cash to buy pepper ahead of time.* See C. R. Boxer, *The Tragic History of the Sea* (University of Minnesota Press, 2001) p. 8.

47. *"The Portuguese, as at other places in India, are a degenerate race of people, well stocked with cunning and deceit; instead of that courage and magnanimity their own writings are so full of,"* Charles Lockyer, "An account of the trade in India: containing rules for good government in trade, . . . with descriptions of Fort St. George, . . . Calicut, . . . To which is added, an account of the management of the Dutch and their affairs in India," London 1711, chapter III, p. 75.

48. *". . . being grown rich in trade, they fell to all manner of looseness and debauchery; the usual concomitant of wealth, and as commonly the forerunner of ruin."* Dampier also had heard that in Malacca the Portuguese made use of native women, *"such as they liked they took without control."* William Dampier, *A New Voyage Around the World,* Vol. II, 1685, p. 160. Rare Books and Manuscript Division of the New York Public Library.

48. *"they as little restrained their lust in other places; for the breed of them is scattered all over India."* Ibid, p. 160.

48. *The voyages were so unpopular that in 1623 it was reported that sailors had to abducted and kept in irons until an India-bound ship had sailed.* See Boxer, *The Tragic History of the Sea*, p. 10.

48. *François Pyrard described a fleet of four carracks, each carrying about a thousand soldiers, sailors, and passengers, which departed Lisbon in 1609. When the ships arrived in Goa, only three hundred men were alive on each of the ships.* Figures cited in Niels Steensgaard's "The Return Cargoes of the Carreira in the 16th and 17th Century," in *Spices in the Indian Ocean World*, edited by M. N. Pearson (Ashgate Publishing Co., 1996).

49. *Between 1629 and 1634, only 2,495 of 5,228 soldiers who left Lisbon survived the trip to Goa.* M. N. Pearson, "The People and Politics of Portuguese India During the Sixteenth and Seventeenth Centuries," in *The Organization of Interoceanic Trade in European Expansion, 1450–1800*, edited by Pieter Emmer and Femme Gaastra (Ashgate Publishing, 1996) p. 31.

49. *"The country abounds with timber and is fruitful in other respects; the air is wholesome, the heat moderate, and every thing else, as agreeable to European constitutions as can be expected in a climate within 2 deg. 30 min. of the equator."* Charles Lockyer, "An account of the trade in India: containing rules for good government in trade, . . . with descriptions of Fort St. George, . . . Calicut, . . . To which is added, an account of the management of the Dutch and their affairs in India," London 1711, chapter III, p. 67.

50. *"This city of Malacca is the richest seaport with the greatest number of wholesale merchants and abundance of shipping and trade that can be found in the whole world,"* gushed Duarte Barbosa, a Portuguese sea captain, in 1517. Cited in Jonathan Cave's *Naning in Melaka* (Malaysia Branch of the Royal Asiatic Society, 1989) p. 6.

51. *"And the Franks engaged the men of Malaka in battle, and they fired their cannon from their ships so that the cannon balls came like rain . . ."* Quote cited in John Bastin and Robin W. Winks, *Malaysia Selected Historical Readings* (Oxford University Press) 1966, p. 36.

52. *"The walls of the fortress are of great width; as for the keep, where they are*

usually built, you will find few of five storeys like this. The artillery, both large and small, fires on all sides," wrote Tomé Pires in *The Suma Oriental of Tomé Pires* (Laurier Books Ltd., 1990), p. 34.

52. *"Everyone was startled . . . when they heard the noise, their surprise all the greater because never in their lives had they heard such a sound or seen how the power of gunpowder can lift bits or rock as big as houses."* *The Hikayat Abdullah,* Abdullah Bin Abdul Kadir, annotated translation by A. H. Hill (Oxford University Press, 1970) p. 63.

53. *"Look there, how the seas of the Orient, . . . "* Luís Vaz De Camões *The Lusiads,* translated by Landeg White, Oxford University Press, 1997, p. 223.

53. *Cloves, saffron, pepper and other aromatic spices were said to have been presented in gold and silver caskets to a bishop in Rome in the fourth century.* Robin A. Donkin, *Between East and West: The Moluccas and the Traffic in Spice Up to the Arrival of Europeans* (American Philosophical Society, Philadelphia) 2003, p. 112.

55. *Portuguese was for many years the dominant language in many of the maritime ports of Asia, and vestiges of Portuguese could still be heard in Malacca and along the Malabar Coast in the twentieth century . . .* See A. J. R. Russell-Wood's *The Portuguese Empire, 1415–1808: A World on the Move* (Johns Hopkins University Press, 1998).

56. *". . . eager to barter for all sorts of merchandise brought from Europe, India, and the Islands of the Moluccas . . ."* *China in the Sixteenth Century: The Journals of Matteo Ricci, 1583–1510,* translated by Louis J. Gallagher (Random House, 1953) p. 129.

56. *On the rare occasions when vessels bound for Goa from Lisbon carried women, there were no more than twenty.* See C. R. Boxer, *Women in Iberian Expansion Overseas, 1415–1815* (Oxford University Press, 1975) p. 67.

57. *"old servant who built a pinnace in the Somers Islands, and is known to be very skilful, and willing to go and live in India for seven years with his two sons."* Great Britain. Public Record Office Calendar of State Papers, 1618–1621 (London: Longman, Brown, Green).

58. *". . . an Englishwoman Married to a Portugall Mestizo of some quallity,*

are well to live, and have beetweene them one pretty boy." The Travels of Peter Mundy, Vol. III, Part I (The Hakluyt Society, 1919; reprinted in 1967 by Kraus Reprint Limited) p. 141.

58. *Margaret Reymers who dressed in men's clothes and enlisted as a soldier . . .* J. S. Stavorinus, *Voyages to the East Indies,* translated by S. H. Wilcocke, 1798, and reprinted by Dawsons of Pall Mall, London, 1969, Vol. I, p. 195–197.

59. *Another woman who disguised herself as a man was named Dona Maria Ursula de Abreu e Lencastre.* See C. R. Boxer, *Women in Iberian Expansion Overseas, 1415–1815* (Oxford University Press, New York, 1975) p. 80.

62. *". . . two silk garments made, one for formal visits, and the other for ordinary wear . . ."* Quote from Ricci's journal is cited in John D. Young's *East-West Synthesis: Matteo Ricci and Confucianism* (University of Hong Kong, 1980) p.16.

63. *". . . had all the Marks of Distinction . . . which . . . Envoys of the court . . . have in this Empire; our Countrymen were not a little surprised when they saw him . . ."* Excerpt from a letter written by Jesuit Father de Premare to Father De La Chaize, confessor to his majesty King Louis XIV, Canton, Feb. 17, 1699. Jesuits. Edifying and curious letters of some missioners, 1707, p. 107. Rare Book Division, The New York Public Library. Manuscripts and Archives Division. Astor, Lenox, and Tiden Foundations.

64. *A French Jesuit named Father Pelisson, who was based in Canton, describes a cruel persecution that he had learned about from a Spanish Jesuit named John Anthony Arendo . . .* Father Pelisson's letter to Father De La Chazie, December 9, 1700. Jesuit Letters from the missions. Travels of the Jesuits. 1743, p 19. The New York Public Library. Manuscripts and Archives Division. Astor, Lenox, and Tilden Foundations.

Four : Golden Elephants

69. *"The Situation of the Port of Achen is admirable, the Anchorage excellent, and a healthful Air along the Coast."* Excerpt from a letter written by Jesuit Father de Prémare to Father De La Chaize, confessor to his

NOTES

majesty King Louis XIV, Canton, Feb. 17, 1699. Jesuits. Edifying and curious letters of some missioners, 1707, p. 96. The New York Public Library. Manuscripts and Archives Division. Astor, Lenox, and Tilden Foundations.

71. *"At first appeared to me like the landscapes framed by the Imagination of some painter or Poet . . ." Letter by de Prémare,* p. 98.

72. *". . . lieth well to answere to the trade of all Bengala, Java, and the Moluccas, and all China . . . to the decrease and diminishing of all Portuguals trade, and their great forces in the Indies." The Voyages of James Lancaster to the East Indies,* edited by Clements R. Markham (The Hakluyt Society, 1877) p. 82.

72. *"garden of pleasure." The Voyages and Works of John Davis* (The Hakluyt Society, 1877) p. 146.

72. *"pleasing and fertile . . . Of pepper they have exceeding plentie, Gardens of a mile square."* Ibid., p. 146.

72. *"plentie of Gold and Copper Mines, divers kinds of Gummes, Balmes, and many kinds of Drugges [spices], and Indico."* Ibid., p. 147.

72. *"The Ayre is temperate and wholsome, having everie morning a fruitfull dew, or small raine."* Ibid., p. 147.

72. *"built in a wood, so that wee could not see a house till we were upon it. Neither could wee goe into any place . . ."* Ibid., p. 147.

73. *Cornelis Houteman's infamous first voyage* is described in Giles Morton's engaging book *Nathaniel's Nutmeg* (Penguin, 1999), paperback edition, pp. 58 to 65.

73. *" foure Barks riding in the Bay, three of Arabia, and one of Pegu (Burma), that came to lade Pepper." The Voyages and Works of John Davis* (The Hakluyt Society, 1877) p. 140.

74. *"the Queene, of her Basha's, and how she could hold warres with so great a King as the Spaniard?"* Ibid., p. 143.

75. *"by reason of their gold mines, and the frequent resort of strangers, they are richer, and live in greater plenty."* William Dampier. A collection of voyages: in four volumes: containing Captain William Dampier's *Voyages Around the World . . .* London, 1729, p. 129 (Sabin Americana. Gale, Gengate Learning. New York University. Gale document number CY3803300281).

75. *"consists of 7 or 8000 houses and in it there are always a great many merchant-strangers, viz. English, Dutch, Danes, Portuguese, Chinese, Guzarats, etc. The houses of this city are generally larger than those I saw at Mindinao, and better furnished with household goods."* Ibid., p. 129.

76. *"like hops from a planted root, and windeth about a stake set by it until it grow to a great bushie tree."* The Voyages and Works of John Davis (The Hakluyt Society, 1877) p. 146.

77. *. . . total quantity of pepper shipped to Europe reached a peak of some fourteen million pounds in the 1670s, nearly double the amount from earlier decades.* These estimates are from Anthony Reid's essay "Humans and Forests in Pre-colonial Southeast Asia" in *Nature and the Orient: The Environmental History of South and Southeast Asia,* edited by Richard H. Grove, Vinita Damodaran, Satpal Sangwan (Oxford University Press, 1998) p. 116.

78. *". . . there is much pepper, and it is better than that from India or Malabar, so much that yearly one should be able to load four or five thousand quintals of pepper, Portuguese weight."* Jan Huyghen van Linschoten's *Itinerario,* quoted in Julie Berger Hochstrasser, *Still Life and Trade in the Dutch Golden Age* (Yale University Press, 2007) p. 102.

79. *"hundred six and fortie buts of wine, an hundred threescore and sixteene jarres of oyle, twelve barrels of oyle, and five and fiftie hogsheads and fats [vats] of meale, which was a great helpe to us in the whole voyage after. . . ."* The Voyages of Sir James Lancaster (Hakluyt Society, 1940) p.78, from the account in *Purchas His Pilgrimes,* originally published in 1625. Richard Hakluyt published logs, journals, and many other historic and geographic records of ocean voyages in the age of discovery, and after he died in 1616 all of the unpublished material went to Reverend Samuel Purchas, who was most likely given the material by Sir Thomas Smythe, the first governor of the East India Company. Unfortunately, Purchas drastically abridged the voluminous materials and was said to have been careless with them. Nevertheless, he published an enormous amount of material; the 1905 reprint is twenty volumes. The original manuscripts of Lancaster's journals were lost, and the anonymous account in *Purchas* was probably written by a merchant on the *Dragon.*

79. *"certain bottles of the juice of limons [lemons] and gave three spoonfuls each morning* to each man on the ship." Ibid., p. 79.

80. *"good things of his creation," are dispersed "into the most remote places of the universal world . . ."* Ibid., p. 94.

82. *"The biggest of these elephants was about thirteen or fourteen feet high. . . ."* Ibid., p. 91.

82. *"as strong as any of our aquavita: a little will serve to bring one asleep."* Ibid., p. 93.

82. *"and these women were richly attired and adorned with bracelets and jewels . . ."* Ibid., p. 93.

84. *"If there be anything here in my kingdom may pleasure thee, I would be glad to gratifie thy goodwill."* Ibid., p. 109.

85. *" . . . a good store of gold, in dust and small graines, which they wash out of the sands of rivers, after the great flouds of raine that fall from the mountaines, from whence it is brought."* Ibid., p. 113.

87. *" . . . [the Dutch] will so watch their times as they will hurt us either by affording to our people bad pepper better cheap, to beat down the price of our better pepper . . . or by some other device as by experience we daily find."* Quote cited in K.N. Chaudhuri, *The English East India Company: The study of an Early Joint-Stock Company, 1600–1640,* (reprinted by Routledge/Thoemmes, 1999) p. 155.

87. *In 1606 a Portuguese carrack returning with a cargo of peppercorns from Cochin, India, went down near Lisbon. . . .* See Filipe Castro, "The Pepper Wreck, and early 17th-century Portuguese Indiaman at the mouth of the Tagus River, Portugal," *The International Journal of Nautical Archaeology* (2003) 32.1:6–23.

88. *Iskandar Muda made Aceh even more powerful than his grandfather.* One of the best and most comprehensive descriptions of the golden age of Aceh is found in Anthony Reid's *An Indonesian Frontier: Acehnese and Other Histories of Sumatra* (Singapore University Press, 2005) pp. 94–136, and in his masterwork *Southeast Asia in the Age of Commerce,* Volume One, *The Lands Below the Winds* (Yale University Press, 1988) and Volume Two, *Expansion and Crisis* (Yale, 1993), which also provide a wonderful overview of entrepôts in Southeast Asia.

89. *Iskandar Muda was said to have one hundred bahars of gold. . . .* Anthony Reid, *Southeast Asia in the Age of Commerce,* Volume One, p. 98. The bahar varied widely in Asia, and especially in Southeast Asia, where one bahar equaled 369 pounds in Bantam, Java, and 560 in Benkoolen in West Sumatra. In Achin, one bahar equaled about 412 pounds, according to Furber's *Rival Empires of Trade.* Thus, 100 bahars would be about 41,200 pounds. Other sources state that the bahar in Achin was equal to 395 pounds.

89. *"nothing but the ships covered the sea . . ."* C. R. Boxer, "The Acehnese Attack on Malacca in 1629, as described in contemporary Portuguese sources" in *Malayan and Indonesia Studies,* edited by John Bastin and R. Roolvink (Clarendon, 1964) pp. 105–121.

90. *"They [the Acehnese] left the whole of their fleet bottled up in the river with many cannons great and small, . . ."* Ibid., p. 119. Excerpt from a letter by the Portuguese Captain-General of Malacca, António Pinto da Fonseca, to the governors of India.

90. *"These maimed and dismembred people wee saw some about the towne . . ."* *The Travels of Peter Mundy,* Vol. III, Part II (The Hakluyt Society, 1919; reprinted in 1967 by Karaus Reprint Limited) p. 330.

90. *"sundry sorts off exquisite torments, viz., divers cutt in peeces; . . ."* Ibid., p. 331.

92. *". . . Then came a squadron of Elephantts with certain things like little low turretts on their backes, . . ."* *The Travels of Peter Mundy,* Vol. III, Part I (The Hakluyt Society, 1919; reprinted in 1967) p. 121–123.

93. *"Doing their uttermost to hurt each other and Drive backe by shooving . . ."* Ibid., p. 127.

94. *". . . full of strength and sleight, seeming therein to have a kind of discourse, and was indeed the most pleasing fight twixt beasts I ever saw."* *The East India Company Journals of Captain William Keeling and Master Thomas Bonner, 1615–1617,* edited by Michael Strachan and Boies Penrose (University of Minnesota Press, 1972) p. 136.

94. *". . . which made a very excellent and fierce fight. Their fearcenes such that hardly 60 to 80 men coulde parte them, fastening ropes to their hind legs to drawe them asunder."* *The Voyage of Thomas Best,* edited by Sir William Foster (The Hakluyt Society, 1934) p. 52.

94. *". . . which likewise made very greate fight; and so continued till it was darke, that wee coulde not see longer."* Ibid., p. 52.

94. *"bankett of at least 40 dishes, with such plenty of hott drincks as might have suffized a druncken armye."* Ibid., p. 52.

96. *"They are here, as at Mindanao, very superstitious in washing and cleansing themselves from defilements, . . ."* William Dampier, quoted in Anthony Reid's *Southeast Asia in the Age of Commerce, Volume One,* p. 50.

96. *"They came to a place wher they washed themselves; the King sitting upon a seatt in the midst of the river, . . ."* "The Standish-Croft Journal" in *The Voyage of Thomas Best,* edited by Sir William Foster (The Hakluyt Society, 1934) p. 158.

97. *"I . . . attended him to the spring of the river about 5 or 6 mile from the towne where we dyned w[i]th him & and his nobilitie sitting above the waist in water, the cleerest and coolest I ever saw or felt."* The East India Company Journals of Captain William Keeling and Master Thomas Bonner, 1615–1617, edited by Michael Strachan and Boies Penrose (University of Minnesota Press, 1971) p. 137.

97. *"I sent to the King and bought 300 bayars of his pepper from Pryaman . . ."* Ibid., p. 138.

97. *"I came aboard the* Dragon *as well to prepare the* Peppercorne *to her speedy lading [of] pepper as for my health, now too impaired by a long flux [dysentery],"* Ibid., p. 138.

98. *It has been estimated that each raft reaching downstream ports in Jambi could carry 150 piculs [about 19,950 pounds], and that forty thousand to fifty thousand bags of pepper were taken annually from the Jambi highlands.* Figures cited in Barbara Watson Andaya's *To Live as Brothers: Southeast Sumatra in the Seventeenth and Eighteenth Centuries* (University of Hawaii Press, 1993) p. 49.

Five : The British Invade

101. *"Of those productions of Sumatra, which are regarded as articles of commerce, the most important and most abundant is pepper."* William Marsden, *The History of Sumatra* (Oxford University Press, 1966) p. 129.

101. *"This [Benkulen] is without exception the most wretched place I ever*

beheld." Lady Raffles, *Memoir of the Life and Public Services of Sir Thomas Stamford Raffles, F.R.S. &c.* (London: 1830) p. 293.

102. *"how long we may be able to keep our station . . ."* Quoted in K. N. Chaudhuri and Jonathan I. Israel, "The English and Dutch East India Companies and the Glorious Revolution of 1688–9," in *The Anglo-Dutch Moment: Essays on the Glorious Revolution and its World Impact,* edited by Jonathan I. Israel (Cambridge University Press, 1991) p. 416.

102. *. . . the Dutch could not dislodge the English from the Malabar Coast.* The VOC's attempts to take over the pepper trade in India have been described by many historians, including John Bastin, "The Changing Balance of the Southeast Asian Pepper Trade," in *Essays on Indonesian and Malayan History;* George D. Winius and Marcus P. M. Vink, *The Merchant-Warrior Pacified;* and Holden Furber, *Rival Empires of Trade in the Orient 1600–1800.*

102. *Pepper is "the bride around which everyone dances on this coast and she has many lovers, namely the English, Danish, Portuguese and Surat traders, etc.,"* See George D. Winius and Marcus P. M. Vink, *The Merchant-Warrior Pacified* (Oxford University Press, 1991) p. 68.

103. *By 1672, a particularly robust year for pepper, the English East India Company was enjoying a huge increase in its pepper imports, shipping more than seven million pounds of the spice from Indonesia to Europe compared to only some 465,000 pounds from the Malabar Coast.* From tables compiled by K. N. Chaudhuri and Jonathan I. Israel, "The English and Dutch East India Companies and the Glorious Revolution of 1688–9," in *The Anglo-Dutch Moment,* edited by Jonathan I. Israel (Cambridge University Press, 1991) pp. 414–415.

105. *" 'Tis said the Dutch have more Forces coming and if they land their men, undoubtedly Bantam is theirs."* From "A True Account of the Burning and sad condition of Bantam in the East-Indies," a letter published in March 1681 by the English East India Company, p. 2.

106. *"This force serves nominally to defend the person of the king from all hostile attempts; but, in fact, to have him always in the Company's power,"* *Voyages to the East Indies,* by J. S. Stavorinus, translated by S. H. Wilcocke, 1798 (reprinted by Dawsons of Pall Mall, London, 1969) Vol. 1, p. 62.

108. *Their dismissal from Bantam did teach the English a valuable lesson—if they wanted to establish another factory in Indonesia, they had best build a real fortification.* This idea is drawn from Anthony Farrington's essay "Bengkulu: An Anglo-Chinese partnership" in *The Worlds of the East India Company*, edited by H. V. Bowen, Margarette Lincoln, and Nigel Rigby (Boydell Press, 2002) pp. 111–117.

108. *Elihu Yale,* a black pepper trader, led the ill-fated negotiations for a fort in Priaman and donated the fortune he earned on his private trading account to establish Yale University. See James W. Gould, "America's Pepperpot 1784–1873," Essex Institute Historical Collections, XCII (1956), pp 83–89.

110. *"It was a fatall and never enough to be repented errour of our President and Council of Fort St George [Madras] . . ."* John Bastin, *The British in West Sumatra (1685–1825)* (University of Malaya Press, 1965) p. viii. Historian John Bastin, one of the leading scholars on the British in Southeast Asia, published a wide selection of documents related to the Benkoolen residency from the voluminous records of the East India Company. His book is an invaluable resource for anyone interested in the Company's disastrous settlement in Sumatra.

111. *". . . many of the pepper gardens in ruins, the people restless, and in many cases unwilling to commence cultivation,"* William Marsden, *The History of Sumatra*, p. 452.

112. *". . . Wee are by Sicknesse all become uncapable of helping one another & ye great Number of people that came over not above thirty men [are] well,"* John Bastin, *The British in West Sumatra (1685–1825)*, p. 12.

112. *"Our people dayly die & now we are in worse Condition then ever, . . ."* Ibid., p. 13.

112. *"We are sorry to hear ye Sickly Condition you are in though are little better or Rather worse our Selves."* Ibid., p. 15.

112. *"At our first Settlement here, you Promised at all time to Stand by & assist us, when ever any Occasion required it."* Ibid., p. 16.

113. *". . . 74 dozen and a half of wine [mostly claret], 24 dozen and half of Burton Ale and pale beer, 2 pipes [each 105 gallons] and 42 gallons of Madeira wine, 6 Flasks of Shiraz [a Persian wine], and 164 gallons of Goa [toddy] . . ."* See A. G. Harfield, *Bencoolen: A History of the*

NOTES

Honourable East India Company's Garrison on the West Coast (Barton-on-Sea: A&J Partnership, 1995) pp. 69–70.

113. *"so much Insolence and Cruelty with respect to those under him, and Rashness in his management of the Malayan Neighbourhood, that I soon grew weary of him . . ."* Cited in Bastin, *The British in West Sumatra,* p. xxii.

114. *"I treat them as a wise man should his wife, am very complaisant in trifles, but immoveable in matters of importance."* Ibid., 43.

114. *Collett's day in Benkoolen started with a good breakfast of bread and butter and Bhoea tea, a popular black tea from China, at about seven o'clock.* Ibid., p. 44.

115. *". . . families in upstream villages planted pepper and maintained the pepper gardens. Men cleared the jungle forests for the gardens, and women planted and harvested, as well as sold pepper in local markets.* See Barbara Andaya Watson, "Women and Economic Change: The Pepper Trade in Pre-Modern Southeast Asia," *Journal of the Economic and Social History of the Orient* (Brill, 1995). This fascinating article describes how the pepper trade affected the traditional agricultural role of women in Sumatra.

116. *". . . bind their subjects to plant 2,000 pepper vines annually, and to give their assistance to the English officials to see that the terms were enforced."* See John Bastin, *The Native Policies of Sir Stamford Raffles in Java and Sumatra* (Clarendon Press, 1957) p. 75.

116. *". . . the scarcity of rice such as was never known here before has forced People to quit their Habitations . . ."* See Bastin, *British in West Sumatra,* p. 62.

117. *". . . encreasing the investment of pepper is the material point in view for the interest of the Company,"* Ibid., p. 69.

117. *"The People of Manna and Laye [Lais] Residencies have really been remiss [in cultivating pepper], and as the mallays are a stubborn, ignorant people, it is very Difficult task to make them sensible of their Interest."* Ibid., p. 64.

118. *"natural indolence of the natives,"* Marsden, p. 131.

118. *"In the northern countries of the island, where people are numerous and their ports good,"* Marsden, p. 130.

118. *The British did attempt to attract the Chinese to Benkoolen, . . .* See Far-rington, "Bengkulu: An Anglo-Chinese Partnership" for a brief dis-cussion of the English East India Company's efforts to establish Benkoolen as an alternative to Batavia.

119. *"This country being very thinly inhabited"* Bastin, *British in West Su-matra* p 67.

119. *Pierre Poivre* was part of a group of French Enlightenment botanists in the mid-eighteenth century who advocated forest conservation and other measures. He spent part of his career on Mauritius, which was a center for early conservation activities. See Richard Grove's *Green Im-perialism: Colonial Expansion, Tropical Island Edens, and the Origins of Environmentalism, 1600–1860* (Cambridge University Press, 1995).

120. *"It will be pretty obvious that the population is for the time as effectually enslaved to the local Resident as the Africans of the West [Indies] . . ."* Raffles, as quoted in John Bastin, *British in West Sumatra*, p. 155.

121. *"Of the desolating effects of this system I can hardly convey to your Honble. Court anything like an adequate idea,"* Ibid., p. 155.

122. *Raffles abolished slavery in West Sumatra and set up a system of "free" pepper cultivation, although natives who didn't grow pepper still had to pay an annual tribute of two dollars, a huge sum of money, or they had to deliver fifty pounds of pepper to Company storehouses.* Ibid., p. xxx, and see Bastin's *The Native Policies of Sir Stamford Raffles in Java and Sumatra* for Raffles's efforts to change the pepper plantation system in Sumatra.

122. *"Mallayans, at work or play are never dressed till their naked daggers are in their girdles . . ."* Charles Lockyer, *"An Account of the Trade in India*: containing rules for good government in trade, . . . with de-scriptions of Fort St. George, . . . Calicut, . . . To which is added, an account of the management of the Dutch and their affairs in India." London 1711. Eighteenth Century Collections Online (ECCO), Gale, New York University, Gale Document Number CW106401529.

122. *"What saves him is the large proportion in his make-up of humanitar-ian principle,"* Emily Hahn, *Raffles of Singapore* (Doubleday, 1946) p. 13.

124. *"Now as to Mr. Raffles's physical features I noticed that he was of medium build, neither tall nor short, neither fat nor thin,"* The Hikayat Abdullah, Abdullah Bin Abdul Kadir, annotated translation by A. H. Hill (Oxford University Press, 1970) p. 75.

125. *"creatures of the sky, the land and the sea; of the uplands, the lowlands and the forest; things which fly or crawl; things which grow and germinate in the soil; all these could be turned into ready cash,"* Abdullah Bin Abdu Kadir, *The Hikayat Abdullah*, p. 76.

126. *"abounding in precious metals."* The Asiatic Journal, London, [Monday], February 01, 1819; p. 215, Issue 38, Empire, 19th Century UK Periodicals, Gale, Cengage Learning, Gale Document Number CC1903193162.

126. *"Sumatra should undoubtedly be under the influence of one European power alone and this power is of course the English."* Cited in Bastin, *Essays in Indonesian and Malayan History,* Singapore, 1961, p. 164.

127. *"our view opened up on one of the finest countries I have ever beheld . . ."* Lady Raffles, *Memoir of the Life and Public Services of Sir Thomas Stamford Raffles* (London: F.R.S. &c., 1830) p. 318.

128. *"Neither on this nor on the preceding day was there a vestige of population or cultivation; nature was throughout allowed to reign undisturbed; and from the traces of elephants in every direction, they alone of the animal kingdome seemed to have explored the recesses of the forest."* Ibid., p. 317.

128. *"The most important discovery throughout our journey was made at this place; this was a gigantic flower, of which I can hardly attempt to give any thing like a just description."* Ibid., p. 316.

129. *Rafflesia.* See *Rafflesia of the World*, by Jamili Nais, (Kota Kinbalu: Sabah, Malaysia; in association with Natural History Publications: Borneo), 2001, for beautiful pictures and a wealth of details about the world's largest flower.

129. *"Compared with our forest-trees, your largest oak is a mere dwarf."* Lady Raffles, *Memoir of the Life and Public Services of Sir Thomas Stamford Raffles*, p. 317.

130. *". . . enter into a conditional treaty of friendship and alliance with the*

Sultan of Menangkabu, as the lord-paramount of all the Malay countries, . . ." Ibid., 388.

130. *"The Dutch possess the only passes through which ships must sail into this Archipelago, the Straits of Sunda and of Malacca . . . and the British have not now an inch of ground to stand upon between the Cape of Good Hope and China; nor a single friendly port at which they can water or obtain refreshment. . . ."* Ibid., p. 306.

131. *"In many respects . . . the commercial policy adapted by the Dutch, with regard to the Eastern Islands, . . ."* Ibid., p. 75 (from a letter written in 1811 by Sir Raffles to Lord Minto).

131. *"conceived it of primary importance to obtain a post which should have a commanding geographical position at the southern entrance of the Strait of Malacca, . . ."* Ibid., p 375.

133. *". . . imagination reeled to think of all the works in Malay and other languages, centuries old, which he [Raffles] collected from many countries, all utterly lost."* The Hikayat Abdullah, Abdullah Bin Abdul Kadir, annotated translation by A. H. Hill (Oxford University Press, 1970) p. 195.

134. *"rendering an acceptable service to Great Britain, and were in fact promoting a great national object."* "Spice Planters," The Asiatic Journal, (London, English), Thursday, July 01, 1824; p. 92, Issue 103, Empire, from 19th Century UK Periodicals, Gale, Cengage Learning, Gale Document Number CC1903144628.

134. *"The factory of Fort Marlborough, and all the English Possessions on the Island of Sumatra, are hereby ceded to His Netherland Majesty; . . ."* Bastin, The British in West Sumatra, p. 190.

134. *". . . the Bencoolen planter is as effectually ruined as if every tree in his possession were torn up by the roots."* Ibid.

135. *". . . Against this transfer of my country I protest. . . ."* A. G. Harfield, p. 499.

Six: The Dutch Terror

137. *"Do not let yourself be afraid of the strength of the kafir [infidels], . . ."* Anthony Reid, Heaven's Will and Man's Fault, p.13 (Flinders University of South Australia, 1975).

137. *". . . to die a shahid [martyr] is nothing. It is like being tickled until we fall and roll over . . ."* Ibid., p. 16, excerpted from the verse epic *Hikayat Perang Sabil,* translated by James Siegel from "The Rope of God."

139. *"Your Honours should know by experience that trade in Asia must be driven and maintained under the protection and favour of Your Honours' own weapons, . . ."* Coen quoted in C. R. Boxer's *The Dutch Seaborne Empire 1600–1800* (Hutchinson & Co., 1965) p. 96.

139. *"I believe there are nowhere greater thieves."* William Dampier, *A New Voyage Around the World,* 1698, Volume I, p. 317, New York Public Library, Rare Books and Manuscript Division.

140. *By 1621, the total market for pepper in Europe was about 7.2 million pounds.* See C. H. H. Wake, "The Changing Patterns of Europe's Pepper and Spice Imports, ca. 1400–1700," *Journal of European Economic History,* Vol. 8, 1979, p. 390.

141. *Each company was supposed to provide for the defense of their common interests, obliging the English to help pay for Dutch forts, a stipulation that was almost guaranteed to sink the agreement.* Historian Vincent C. Loth examines the 1619 treaty in "Armed Incidents and Unpaid Bills: Anglo-Dutch Rivalry in the Banda Islands in the Seventeenth Century," *Modern Asian Studies,* Vol. 29, No. 4 (Oct., 1995), pp. 705–740, http://www.jstor.org/stable/312802

141. *"could not pretend to a single grain of sand of the Moluccas, Ambon or the Banda Islands."* Coen's infamous quote is published in Femme S. Gaastra's *The Dutch East India Company* (Walberg Press, 2003) p. 40, and appears in many other secondary sources.

141. *"if you, gentlemen, want great and notable deeds in the honour of God and for the prosperity of our country, so relieve us from the English."* Ibid, p. 43.

141. *". . . there is no profit at all in an empty sea, empty countries, and dead people."* Quote cited in Holden Furber, *Rival Empires of Trade in the Orient, 1600–1800* (University of Minnesota Press, 1976) p. 48.

142. *The Dutch immediately suspected that Keeling had instigated the attack against the Bandanese . . .* Vincent Loth's "Armed Incidents and Unpaid Bills," p. 711.

143. *"sitteth as queen between the isles of Banda and the Moluccas. She*

is beautified with fruits of several factories, and dearly beloved of the Dutch." This quote is attributed to a man named Captain Fitzherbert in *The Voyage of Sir Henry Middleton to Bantam and the Maluco Islands,* edited by Bolton Corney (The Hakluyt Society, 1855) p. vi.

144. *"softly upon his head until the cloth was full, up to the mouth and nostrils, and somewhat higher; . . ."* This quote from a widely circulated pamphlet about the killings in Amboyna titled "A True Relation of the Unjust, Cruell, and Barbarous Proceedings Against the English at Amboyna in the East-Indies by the Neatherlandish Governour and Councel there," helped fuel outrage over the executions in Ambon. London, 1624, Early English Books Online (EEBO) ProQuest LLC. http://eebo.chadwyck.com.

145. *The executions outraged the English, who had planned to quit the Bandas and the Moluccas . . . before the killings took place. They left soon after.* D. K. Bassett, "The 'Amboyna Massacre' of 1623," *Journal of Southeast Asian History,* Vol. 1, No. 2 (Sept., 1960), Cambridge University Press, http://www.jstor.org/stable/20067299. Even today, the underlying reasons for the executions aren't clear. This intriguing article describes how, in the years leading up to 1623, the English East India Company was not optimistic about its business prospects in the Spice Islands and finally decided to leave only one month before the Englishmen were beheaded by the Dutch. David Kenneth Bassett, who was one of the leading historians on European trade in Southeast Asia in the seventeenth and eighteenth centuries, argued that Dutch Governor Van Speult, a "humane and reasonable man," did have reason to believe that the English were conspiring to overthrow the garrison in Ambon, no matter how implausible.

145. *. . . relatives of the men who died in Amboyna received £3,615 . . .* Furber, *Rival Empires of Trade in the Orient,* p. 49.

146. *. . . slaves from various parts of Asia were shipped to the islands to harvest nutmeg.* Historian Markus Vink points out that, unlike the Atlantic slave trade, the Dutch and other Europeans in Asia relied on already well-established systems of slavery. Until the 1660s, the Dutch obtained slaves mainly from India; afterward most slaves

were from Southeast Asia, particularly after the fall of Makassar in South Sulawesi. Thousands of slaves from Bali and South Sulawesi were taken to Batavia by Asian vessels between 1653 and 1682. See Markus Vink, " 'The World's Oldest Trade'. Dutch Slavery and Slave Trade in the India Ocean in the Seventeenth Century," *Journal of World History*, Vol. 14, No. 2, pp. 131–77, University of Hawaii Press. http://www.jstor.org/stable/20079204

146. *". . . while he lived with the Dutch, he was sent with other men to cut down the spice trees; and he himself did at several times cut down 700 to 800 trees."* William Dampier, *A New Voyage Around the World*, 1698, Vol. 1, p. 317, New York Public Library, Rare Books and Manuscripts Division.

147. *"God has made the earth and the sea and has divided the earth among men and given the sea in common to all."* See Leonard Y. Andaya, *The Heritage of Arung Palakka: A history of South Sulawesi (Celebes) in the Seventeenth Century*, (The Hague: Martinus Nijhoff, 1981) p. 46. See also Anthony Reid, "Pluralism and progress in seventeenth-century Makassar," pp. 55–73, in *Authority and Enterprise Among the Peoples of South Sulawesi*, edited by Roger Tol, Kees van Dijk, and Greg Acciaioli, (Leiden: KITLV Press, 2000).

149. *"All the kings of these lands know full well what the planting of our colony at Jakarta signifies . . ."* Coen's threatening quote is published in C. R. Boxer's *The Dutch Seaborne Empire 1600–1800*, p. 189, among other secondary sources.

150. *"The Bay of Batavia is the finest and most secure of any in the world." The Voyage of François Leguat of Bresse to Rodriguez, Mauritius, Java, and the Cape of Good Hope,* Edited and Annotated by Captain Pasfield Oliver (The Hakluyt Society, 1891) p. 226.

150. *"the road of Batavia is justly esteemed one of the best in the world, as well with regard to the anchoring-ground . . ." Voyages to the East Indies,* by J. S. Stavorinus, translated by S. H. Wilcocke, 1798 (reprinted by Dawsons of Pall Mall, London; 1969) Vol. I, p. 211.

151. *Over the course of the seventeenth century, the Chinese became an economic force; Batavia . . . was a Chinese colonial town under Dutch protection.* Historian Leonard Blussé has written extensively about

the far-reaching impact of the Chinese in Batavia and on the events leading to the massacre of 1740, including "Batavia, 1619–1740: The Rise and Fall of a Chinese Colonial Town," *Journal of Southeast Asian Studies*, Vol. 12, No. 1, "Batavia, 1619–1740: The Rise and Fall of a Chinese Colonial Town," (March, 1981), pp. 159–178 (Cambridge University Press) URL: http://www.jstor.org./stable/20070419, and *Strange Company: Chinese Settlers, Mestizo Women and the Dutch in VOC Batavia* (Foris Publications, 1986).

151. *"Only one year after the founding of Batavia, the Dutch blockaded Jambi in eastern Sumatra and Bantam in Java in order to divert Chinese junks to Batavia."* Historian M. A. P. Meilink-Roelofsz's masterly *Asian Trade and European Influence in the Indonesian Archipelago Between 1500 and About 1630* (The Hague: Martinus Nijhoff, 1962) is one of the seminal books on European trade in Asia during the age of discovery. See pp. 253–261 for a description of how the Dutch intervened in the pepper trade in Bantam and eastern Sumatra.

152. *"In 1694 . . . over two million pounds of pepper were sold to twenty junks that had arrived in Batavia."* Figure cited in Leonard Blussé's *Strange Company*, p. 126.

152. *"Indeed, by the end of the seventeenth century the Dutch had pulled out of direct trade with China entirely . . .* Leonard Blussé, "No Boats to China. The Dutch East India Company and the Changing Pattern of the China Sea Trade, 1635–1690," *Modern Asian Studies*, Vol. 30, No. 1 (Feb. 1996), pp. 51–76, Cambridge University Press, URL: http://www.jstor.org/stable/312901

152. *Many undocumented Chinese people were deported to China; a smaller number was banished to the Cape of Good Hope.* See Kerry Ward, *Networks of Empire: Forced Migration in the Dutch East India Company* (Cambridge University Press, 2009) p. 99.

153. *"Europeans would doubtless be dazzled, and inclined to envy his hospitable host, the luxurious Batavian."* Jeremiah N. Reynolds, *Voyage of the United State Frigate* Potomac . . . *in 1831, 1832, 1833, and 1834* (Harper & Brothers, 1835), p. 299.

153. *" . . . most unwholesome place of abode, and the mortality greater here, than at any other spot of the Company's possessions . . ."* J. S.

Stavorinus, *Voyages to the East Indies,* translated by S. H. Wilcocke, 1798, (reprinted by Dawsons of Pall Mall, London, 1969) Vol. III, p. 398–399.

154. *"The VOC had many more ships than the English East India Company— from 1600 to 1650, . . . the Dutch sent 655 ships to Asia while the English sent only 286 . . .* From J. R. Bruijn and Femme S. Gaastra's *Ships, Sailors and Spices: East India Companies and their Shipping in the Sixteenth, Seventeenth, and Eighteenth Centuries* (Amsterdam: NEHA, 1993).

155. *"The English managed to import more than one million pounds only twelve times in the years between 1603 and 1640."* From a table compiled by K. N. Chaudhuri, *The English East India Company* (Routledge) p. 148.

155. *"The country trade and the profit from it are the soul of the Company which must be looked after carefully . . ."* Cited in Om Prakash, "The Portuguese and the Dutch in Asian Maritime Trade: a comparative analysis" in *Merchants, Companies and Trade: Europe and Asia in the Early Modern Era,* edited by Sushil Chaudhury and Michel Morineau (Cambridge University Press, 1999) p 182.

156. *"The Coromandel Coast is the left arm of the Moluccas . . ."* Hendrik Brouwer's famous quote is published in George D. Winius and Marcus P. M. Vink's *The Merchant-Warrior Pacified* (Oxford University Press, 1991) p. 12, among other secondary sources.

156. *"Guserat textiles must be traded for pepper and gold on the shores of Sumatra; pepper from Banten for reals and textiles from the coast [of Coromandel]; . . ."* Dutch historian Femme S. Gaastra published the full text of Coen's 1619 letter in *The Dutch East India Company* (Walberg Press, 2003) p. 121. Excerpts from this letter are published in many other secondary sources about Dutch trade in Asia.

157. *Historians estimate that the Dutch shipped cloth from the Coromandel coast of India to Batavia worth some 22,000 to 44,000 pounds of silver (roughly one to two million guilders) annually from 1620 to 1650.* Figure cited in "Economic and Social Change, c. 1400–1800," by Anthony Reid, in *The Cambridge History of Southeast Asia,* Volume One, edited by Nicholas Tarling (Cambridge University Press, 1992) page 471.

157. *"When the Japanese banned the export of silver in the later part of the century, business began to wane."* Om Prakash, "The Portuguese and the Dutch in Asian Maritime Trade: a comparative analysis" in *Merchants, Companies and Trade: Europe and Asia in the Early Modern Era,* edited by Sushil Chaudhury and Michel Morineau, (Cambridge University Press, UK), pp. 186–188.

158. *"Let people nowhere in this country plant pepper, as is done in Jambi and Palembang . . ."* Quote cited in Anthony Reid, *Southeast Asia in the Age of Commerce,* Volume Two, *Expansion and Crisis* (Yale University Press, 1993) p. 300.

159. *"The Mallayans are such admirers of opium that they would mortgage all they hold most valuable to procure it,"* Charles Lockyer, "An account of the trade in India: containing rules for good government in trade, . . . with descriptions of Fort St. George, . . . Calicut, . . . To which is added, an account of the management of the Dutch and their affairs in India." London 1711. Eighteenth Century Collections Online (ECCO), Gale, New York University.

160. *". . . that opium was the 'chief article' bartered for pepper in Penang . . ."* Constable Pierrepont papers. Manuscripts and Archives Division. The New York Public Library. Astor, Lenox, and Tilden Foundations.

160. *"Nothing is more certain than that opium brings generally 100 percent [profit] when sold to the Malays in Barter . . ."* Constable Pierrepont papers. Manuscripts and Archives Division. The New York Public Library. Astor, Lenox, and Tilden Foundations.

161. *"women and children were decorated with a profusion of silver ornaments . . ."* Lady Raffles, *Memoir of the Life and Public Services of Sir Thomas Stamford Raffles,* (London: F.R.S. &c., 1830) p. 319.

161. *Near the end of the eighteenth century, the English East India Company was importing some fifteen to twenty million pounds of tea from China . . .* Figure cited in Holden Furber, *Rival Empires of Trade in the Orient, 1600–1800,* p. 244.

161. *"The trade in piece goods, which in former times, produced such considerable benefit to the company, is now almost entirely in the hands of the English; . . ."* J. S. Stavorinus, *Voyages to the East Indies,* translated by

S. H. Wilcocke, 1798 (reprinted by Dawsons of Pall Mall, London, 1969) Vol. I, p. 364.

163. *One enterprising employee in Bengal, India, set up his own company in his wife's name to carry on private trade.* Historian Om Prakash has written widely about the many ways that fraud was practiced in the Bengal factory. See his book *The Dutch East India Company and the Economy of Bengal* (Princeton, 1985) and page 85 for the example cited here.

163. *An investigator estimated that fraud and private trading in India had cost the company as much as 3.8 million guilders from 1678 to 1686.* Figure cited in Julia Adams's "Principals and Agents, Colonialists and Company Men: The Decay of Colonial Control in the Dutch East Indies," *American Sociological Review,* 1996, Vol. 61, (February: 12–28), p. 25.

163. *"The seamen [the Dutch] who go to the Spice Islands aren't supposed to bring spice back for themselves, except for a small amount for their own use, a pound or two, . . ."* William Dampier, *A New Voyage Around the World,* Vol. 1, p. 317.

164. *In 1676, a year when the harvest was particularly good, company employees smuggled 152,600 pounds of the drug into Batavia . . .* Om Prakash, *The Dutch East India Company and the Economy of Bengal,* p. 155.

164. *At one time corruption was thought to be the main factor that led to the end of the VOC—the initials VOC were once cynically referred to as* Vergaan Onder Corruptie, *collapsed through corruption.* See C. R. Boxer's *The Dutch Seaborne Empire 1600–1800* (Hutchinson & Co., 1965) p. 205.

164. *"all the extraordinary waste which the fraud and abuse . . ."* Adam Smith as quoted in K. N. Chaudhuri, "The English East India Company in the 17th and 18th Century," in *The Organization of Interoceanic Trade in European Expansion, 1450–1800,* edited by Pieter Emmer and Femme Gaastra (Variorum, Ashgate Publishing Limited, 1996) p. 188.

165. *Desertion was so common among men serving the English and Dutch companies that a standard "form of agreement" for the rendition of desert-*

ers had been drawn by the early eighteenth century. See Furber's *Rival Empires of Trade in the Orient,* pp. 303–304, for more about the miseries of working for the northern European mercantile companies.

165. *"purloining the Company's goods, deceiving private men, insolvent behavior . . . and great wealth they have suddenly gathered together."* Cited in K. N. Chaudhuri's *The English East India Company* (Routledge, 1999) p. 87.

165. *"The man from the 'Westcountry' was 'Friendly and courteously enterteyned by us all in generall.'"* *The Travels of Peter Mundy,* Vol. III, Part II (The Hakluyt Society, 1919; reprinted in 1967 by Karaus Reprint Limited) p. 337.

166. *Englishman Roger Wheatley admitted in 1725 that he had been employed by a lady whose husband had been a member of the Council of Batavia, to smuggle 150 chests, or 21,000 pounds, of opium.* Holden Furber, *Rival Empires of Trade in the Orient, 1600–1800,* p. 277.

166. *"These indulgences were . . . extended to all sorts of commodities, both Indian and European, to the great detriment of our own ships' officers and crews, . . ."* J. S. Stavorinus, *Voyages to the East Indies*, translated by S. H. Wilcocke, 1798 (reprinted by Dawsons of Pall Mall, London, 1969) Vol. I, p. 367–368.

Seven : U.S. Pepper Fortunes

169. *"For the coast of Sumatra now I'm bound, . . ."* James W. Gould, "America's Pepperpot: 1784–1873," Essex Institute Historical Collections, Vol. XCII, April 1956, p. 120.

169. *"If our Government does not send a frigate next season and destroy Soosoo, Tangan Tangan, Muckie and South Tallapow, we must bid adieu to the pepper trade."* George G. Putman's *Salem Vessels and Their Voyages: A History of the Pepper Trade with the Island of Sumatra* (Salem, Mass.: The Essex Institute, 1924) p. 126.

169. *"Another class of commercial interloper, who will require our vigilant attention, is the Americans."* *Memoir of the Life and Public Services of Sir Thomas Stamford Raffles, F.R.S.: & c.* (London: 1830), Lady Raffles, p. 74.

170. The best sources for the U.S. pepper trade are: James W. Gould's

three-part "America's Pepperpot: 1784–1873," Essex Institute Historical Collections, XCII, 1956, pp. 83–153, 203–251, 295–348; George G. Putman, *Salem Vessels and Their Voyages: A History of the Pepper Trade with the Island of Sumatra*, Salem, Mass., 1924; James Duncan Phillips, *Salem and the Indies: The Story of the Great Commercial Era of the City* (Houghton Mifflin, 1947). For a more recent account of the trade, see Charles Corn's *The Scents of Eden: A History of the Spice Trade*, (Kodansha International, 1999).

171. *... more than seventeen million silver dollars flowed into Sumatra from the United States in the late eighteenth and early nineteenth centuries.* Gould, Essex Institute Historical Collections, XCII, p. 332.

174. *"... we must express entire disapprobation of the Sale of pepper to neutral vessels as it must of course materially interfere with our Sales of that article for foreign Markets."* Gould, Essex Institute Historical Collections, XCII, p. 110.

175. *The firm paid duty of more than $37,000, which would be worth roughly $19 million today. The firm's America imported more than 800,000 pounds of pepper in 1802. The duty paid was more than $56,000, or about $28 million in today's dollars.* These comparisons are rough estimates and were made using the datasets at http://www.measuring worth.org/datasets/usgdp/index.php. The conversion into twenty-first century dollars is based on the nominal value of the gross domestic product per capita [GDP/C] in 1800 and in 2009, which produces a conversion ratio of about 511. Thus, $37,000 multiplied by 511 equals about $19 million. No wonder the duties paid from the pepper trade helped shore up the economy of the United States.

175. *"'Blank Journals' for the 'great object of their institution ... was the acquiring of nautical knowledge ...' Each captain would be furnished with a log, which was to be 'a regular diary of the winds, weather, remarkable occurrences, during his voyage ...'"* The logbook of the *Putnam*, Nov. 1802–Dec. 25, 1803, Phillips Library, Peabody Essex Museum, Salem, Massachusetts, reprinted with permission.

176. *"... long passage in which there is such a sameness & the same tedious recurrence to nautical observations that I am, obliged to rally all my little philosophy to drive off the hypochondriac ..."* The logbook of the

William and Henry, Phillips Library, Peabody Essex Museum, reprinted with permission.

176. *". . . a cargo of those (unhappy fellow animals) whose happiness is sacrificed to satisfy the ambition of avarice, men who are proud of living under the light of Christianity and more especially of philosophy. . . ."* Ibid.

176. *"The darken sky how thick it lowers . . ."* The logbook of the *Grand Turk,* Phillips Library, Peabody Essex Museum, reprinted with permission.

177. *"He did not talk but very little for about half of an hour before he died. I was obliged to bury him at sea . . ."* Logbook of the *Eliza,* Phillips Library, Peabody Essex Museum, reprinted with permission.

177. *"rolling heavily and thumping very hard endangering the masts . . ."* Logbook of the *Sooloo,* Phillips Library, Peabody Essex Museum, reprinted with permission.

178. *"Finished taking pepper out of the between decks the water about 1 foot above the between decks. During the night the ship sunk at her anchors carrying one Malay with her."* Ibid.

178. *"Then we went out on the mountain top to gaze at the view and it was one of the most beautiful scenes that I have ever beheld."* The story of Gorham P. Low's life at sea is published in *The Sea Made Men: The Story of a Gloucester Lad,* edited by Elizabeth L. Alling (Fleming H. Revell Company, 1937) p. 196.

179. *". . . Could an American of the north have been conveyed suddenly from his home and placed where we stood as we stepped from the boat, he would have been in ecstasy, if he had any susceptibility to the beauty of nature."* Fitch W. Taylor, *A Voyage Round the World . . . in the United States Frigate* Columbia. . . . New Haven and New York, 1846, p. 302.

181. *"On arrival at any of these ports you contact with the Dattoo for the pepper and fix the price . . ."* Logbook of the *Putnam,* from Nov. 1802 to Dec. 1803, kept by Master Nathaniel Bowditch. Phillips Library, Peabody Essex Museum, reprinted with permission. Bowditch's notes on West Sumatra have been widely published.

182. *When an American captain was outbid for pepper by a rival in 1839, the losing captain sent a letter to the local chief in the village of Bakungan*

threatening to sink his prahus if he gave any pepper to his rival. Gould, Essex Institute Historical Collections, XCII, p. 299.

182. *George Nicols, a Salem seaman and merchant who sailed to the Far East, Sumatra, and Europe, was the master and supercargo of the Active, which set out from Salem to Sumatra in December 1801.* Nicols was eighty years old when he dictated his autobiography. See George G. Putman, *Salem Vessels and Their Voyages*, pp. 17–19.

183. *The Strait of Malacca was, and still is, notoriously dangerous.* Piracy in the Strait has a long history. In 2000 more than seventy-five armed robberies occurred in the Malacca and Singapore Straits. See "Can U.S. Efforts Reduce Piracy in the Malacca and Singapore Straits," by Jeffrey L. Scudder, http:handle.detc.il/100.2/ADA 463868

184. *"They carry on a considerable trade and are generally provided with . . . pepper . . ."* Constable Pierrepont papers. Manuscripts and Archives Division. The New York Public Library. Astor, Lenox, and Tilden Foundations.

184. *Malaysian pirates captured the American ship, stole twenty thousand silver dollars, and sunk her. Twelve officers and crew escaped by boat. The Asiatic Journal,* London, February 01, 1819, p. 217; Issue 38, Empire, from 19th Century UK Periodicals, Gale, Cengage Learning, Gale Document Number CC1903193170.

185. *"Americans carry 'complete sets of false weights thus often times getting five Piculs of pepper by paying but for one . . .'"* Cruise of the U.S. Frigate *Potomac*, commanded by Captain John Downes from Sandy Hook [New Jersey] to Sumatra, by Levi Lincoln, Jr. The son of Gov. Levi Lincoln of Massachusetts, Levi Lincoln was born on August 22, 1810, and he died on September 1, 1845. Levi went to West Point briefly, dropped out, and became a midshipman at seventeen. He resigned nine years later. He provides a rare eyewitness account of the attack on Qualah-Battoo that is sympathetic to the Malays. Manuscripts and Archives Division. The New York Public Library. Astor, Lenox, and Tilden Foundations.

185. *"Who brought to the coast 56 lb. weights with a screw in the bottom which opened for the insertion of from ten to fifteen pounds of lead, after*

their correctness had been tried by the native in comparison with his own weights? . . ." Gould, Essex Institute Historical Collections, XCII, p. 231.

187. *"exulting and hooting . . . 'Who great man now, Malay or American?' 'How many man American dead?' 'How many man Malay dead.'"* George G. Putman, *Salem Vessels and Their Voyages*, pp. 71–89. Quote is from Captain Charles Moses Endicott's lecture to the Essex Institute in Salem, Massachusetts, on January 28, 1858.

188. *"The curiosity of some visitors was so great that they would not be satisfied until they knew . . ."* "The Narrative of Piracy and Plunder of the Ship *Friendship*, of Salem, On the West Coast of Sumatra in February, 1831; and the massacre of part of her crew; also recapture out of the hands of the Malay Pirates," by Charles M. Endicott, Historical Collections of the Essex Institute, 1859.

188. *"every necessary preparation be made . . . to demand immediate redress for the outrage committed."* Gould, Essex Institute Historical Collections, XCII, 1956, p. 233.

188. *John Downes, the commander of the Potomac, was an experienced hand who had served in the War of 1812 . . .* For a summary of Downes's career, see David F. Long's article "Martial Thunder: The First Official American Armed Intervention in Asia," *The Pacific Historical Review*, Vol. 42. No. 2 (May, 1973), pp. 143–162, Published by University of California Press, URL: http://www.jstor.org/stable/3638464.

188. *If he didn't get a response, he was authorized to seize the murderers and send them back to the United States for trial or take harsher measures.* Ibid. p. 150.

189. *". . . seemed to leave no doubt, that neither the character of the people on the coast of Sumatra, particularly at Quallah-Battoo, nor the government under which they nominally lived, . . ."* Jeremiah N. Reynolds, *Voyage of the United State Frigate* Potomac *. . . in 1831, 1832, 1833, and 1834* (New York, 1835), p. 98, and available on Google books at http://books.google.com/books.

190. *". . . such was the desperation with which these fellows resisted us, that [in the northernmost fort] . . ."* Manuscripts and Archives Division. The New York Public Library. Astor, Lenox, and Tilden Foundations.

191. *"spirit of a desperado,"* according to Francis Warriner, the *Potomac's* chaplain. William Meacham Murrell, *Cruise of the U.S. Frigate Potomac Round the World, 1831–1834* (New York and Boston, 1835) p. 89.

191. *The number of native men, women, and children killed ranged from about sixty, according to an account by the people of Qualah Battoo, to at least 150, according to Shubrick's estimate.* See David F. Long's article "Martial Thunder: The First Official American Armed Intervention in Asia," *The Pacific Historical Review,* Vol. 42. No. 2 (May, 1973), p. 152.

192. *"All around us in ambush . . ."*
     Poem published in Putnam's *Salem Vessels,* p. 92.

192. *"The marines entered the second fort at bayonet charge . . ."* Manuscripts and Archives Division. The New York Public Library. Astor, Lenox, and Tilden Foundations.

193. *"If some of the Malays are pirates, we must be allowed to say . . ."* Ibid.

194. The Salem Gazette *opined that "Neither the President of the United States nor the Captain of a Frigate has power to make or proclaim war."* See Long, p. 157.

194. *"The President regrets that you were not able [,] before attacking the Malays at Qualah Battoo, to obtain . . ."* Ibid. p. 158.

196. *"In execution of your order to me for the entire destruction of the town of Muckie, I this day landed on the beach at the head of the harbor, . . ."* Fitch W. Taylor, *A Voyage Round the World . . . in the United States Frigate* Columbia . . . . New Haven and New York, p. 296.

196. *"The town now exhibited one scene of extended and extending ruins . . ."* Ibid., p. 295.

198. *"The establishment of American business houses there eliminated the previous advantages of the private contacts and knowledge which had sustained so much of the old trades. . . ."* For the decline of the pepper trade to Sumatra, see Gould, pp. 295–348.

Eight : An Infinite Number of Seals

199. *"On the third of August the general went in his pinnace, and other boats with him, to kill whales, for all the bay is full of them." The Voyage of Sir Henry Middleton to the Moluccas, 1604–1606,* Sir William Foster, ed., (The Hakluyt Society, 1943) p. 11.

200. ... *birds "similar in size to swans," were found* ... Quote published in Errol Fuller's *Dodo: From Extinction to Icon* (HarperCollins, 2002) p. 59.

200. ... *described killing a hundred birds "with sticks and hands."* Mundy, *The Travels of Peter Mundy*, Vol II., p. 328.

201. *"It (Ascension) is uninhabited, and perfectly sterile, being almost nothing but a bear rock,"* J. S. Stavorinus, *Voyages to the East Indies*, translated by S. H. Wilcocke, 1798, Vol. III, p. 191.

201. *"The beach abounds in turtles, who lay their eggs in the sand, in order to be hatched by the heat of the sun . . ."* Ibid, p. 191.

201. *"are easily taken, not being able to flye nor runne, only bite a little to noe purpose . . ."* Mundy, *The Travels of Peter Mundy*, Vol II., p. 328.

202. *"swarme of lame and weake, diseased cripples," and beholding this "lamentable sight . . ."* The Voyage of Sir Henry Middleton to the Moluccas, 1604–1606, (The Hakluyt Society, 1943) p. 10. The quotes from Middleton's voyage in this chapter are from an anonymous account called "The Last East-Indian Voyage," which was printed for Walter Burre in 1606. It is the only account of an English East India voyage in the early seventeenth century that was published separately from the Hakluyt-Purchas narratives. Walter Burre may have been Middleton's son-in-law.

203. *"where wee found such infinite number of seals that was admirable to behold. . . ."* Ibid., p. 10.

203. *"kill whales; for all the bay is full of them."* Ibid., p. 11.

204. *"we began to see many flying fish* [Exocoetus volitans] *and we frequently made a good breakfast, upon such as had fallen upon the ship, during the night, as they frequently do . . ."* J. S. Stavorinus, *Voyages to the East Indies*, translated by S. H. Wilcocke, 1798, Vol. I, p. 13.

204. *"the more fish we had about the ship, of which we caught large quantities; dorados, albacores, and likewise bonitos, sharks, and others; which afforded a most welcome and agreeable refreshment to the seamen."* Ibid., Vol. I, p. 17.

204. *"the most delicious seafish that is caught. It is long and flat, and covered with very small scales . . ."* Ibid., Volume 1, pp. 17–23.

205. *"These animals were about the size of a spaniel, with long tails, which,*

when they ran, they turned upwards. . . ." J. S. Stavorinus, *Voyages to the East Indies*, translated by S. H. Wilcocke, 1798, Vol. I, pp. 132–133.

205. *". . . for their superstitious belief in the transmigration of souls after death, makes them think that these creatures, in particular, are the receptacles of human souls."* Ibid., p. 133.

206. *"When he walked, he let the whole hang loose, without seeming to be in the least incommoded."* Ibid., p. 134.

206. *"Dodoes, a strange kinde of fowle, twice as bigg as a Goose, that can neither flye nor swymm . . ."* Peter Mundy's quote appears in Fuller, p. 66.

207. *"covered with Downe, having little hanguing wings like short sleeves, altogether unuseffull to Fly withal . . ."* Mundy, *The Travels of Peter Mundy*, (Vol. III, Part II, The Hakluyt Society, 1919), and reprinted in 1967, p. 353.

207. *". . . ships began to call and man came to stay, hogs and dogs, cats and rats, sailors and settlers began . . ."* Alfred North-Coombes, *The Vindication of François Leguat*, Organisation Normale des Entreprises Limitée, Port Louis, Mauritius, p. 8.

208. *"After having been forc'd to leave my Native Country, with so many thousands of my Brethren, to abandon my small Inheritance . . ."* The *Voyage of François Leguat of Bresse to Rodriguez, Mauritius, Java, and the Cape of Good Hope,* Edited and Annotated by Captain Pasfield Oliver (The Hakluyt Society, 1891) p. lxxxvi.

209. *"The Females are wonderfully beautiful, some fair, some brown; I call them fair . . ."* Ibid., p. 78.

210. *A little over one hundred years later, bones were finally discovered on Rodrigues that confirmed Leguat's story, including the existence of a little round bony mass that existed under the feathers of the wings in both male and female solitaires.* See North-Coombes, pp. 60–61.

210. *". . . such a plenty of Land-Turtles in this Isle . . ."* Leguat, p. 71.

210. *"This Flesh is very wholsom, and tastes something like Mutton . . ."* Ibid., p. 71.

211. *"We all unanimously agreed, 'twas better than the best Butter in Europe. . . ."* Ibid., p. 71.

211. *A party landing on Aldabra in 1878 took three days to find one animal.*

See D. R. Stoddart, J. F. Peake, C. Gordon, and R. Burleigh, "Historical Records of Indian Ocean Giant Tortoise Populations," Philosophical Transactions of the Royal Society of London. Series, B, Biological Sciences, Vol. 286, No. 1011, *The Terrestrial Ecology of Aldabra* (Vol. 3, 1979), p. 155.

212. *". . . behold these really wondrous tortoises . . ."* Herman Melville, "The Encantadas," in *Billy Budd, Sailor and Other Stories* (Viking Penguin, 1986) pp. 75–79.

Nine : Medicinal Pepper

214. *"Many physiological effects of black pepper, its extracts or its major active principle, piperine, have been reported in recent decades."* Krishnapura Srinivasan, "Black Pepper and its Pungent Principle—Piperine: A review of Diverse Physiological Effects," *Critical Reviews in Food Science and Nutrition,* Volume 47, Issue 8, November 2007, p. 735–748.

215. *Scientists in the United States, Britain, and Italy are now testing pepper's potency as an anti-inflammatory and antimicrobial agent . . .* There is no way to provide a complete list of the hundreds of scientific articles on pepper's physiological effects, but interested readers may find the following articles of interest. For an evaluation of pepper's ability to stimulate proliferation of melanin-producing cells in the skin, and thereby provide a potential treatment for vitiligo, see Faas L., Venkatasamy R., Hilder R.C., Young A.R., Soumyanath A., "In vivo evaluation of piperine and synthetic analogues as potential treatments for vitiligo using a sparsely pigmented mouse model," *British Journal of Dermatology* 2008, May; 158(5):941–50. For suggestions that pepper might be helpful in alleviating the joint stiffness, pain, and inflammation of arthritis, see J. S. Bang, et al., "Anti-inflammatory and anti-arthritic effects of piperine in human interleukin-1-beta-stimulated fibroblast-like synoviocytes and in rat arthritis models." *Arthritis Research and Therapy* 11 R49 (2009). As an analgesic see McNamara, Fergal N., Randall, Andrew, Gunthorpe, Martin J., "Effects of piperine, the pungent component of black pepper, at the human vanilloid receptor," *British Journal of*

Pharmacology 144 (6): 781–790, March 2005; and Szallasi, Arpad, "Piperine: Researchers discover new flavor in an ancient spice," *Trends in Pharmacological Sciences* 26 (9): 437–439 September 2005.

215. *... inhaling the aroma of black pepper oil ...* Ebihara, Takae, et al. "A randomized trial of olfactory stimulation using black pepper oil in older people with swallowing dysfunction," *Journal of the American Geriatric Society* 54 (9): 1401–1406, Sept. 2006.

215. *... the property that is attracting the most attention is piperine's ability to act as a sort of booster, or biological enabler, of other medicines.* Personal e-mail communication with Krishnapura Srinivasan.

216. *House of Lords issued a report saying that there wasn't evidence to support Ayurvedic medicine's role in diagnosis and treatment of disease.* See Bodeker, Gerard, "Evaluating Ayurveda," in *The Journal of Alternative and Complementary Medicine,* Volume 7, Number 5, 2001, p. 389.

216. *... studies involving some 166 plant species ...* See Sarah Khan and Michael J. Balick, "Therapeutic Plants of Ayurveda: A Review of Selected Clinical and Other Studies for 166 Species," ibid. pp. 405–515.

217. *... some seven hundred drugs derived from pepper, turmeric, ginger, cinnamon, and other spices, were described by a physician named Sashruta the Second in about 500 B.C.* See Susheela Raghavan Uhl, *Handbook of Spices, Seasonings, and Flavorings,* (Lancaster, PA.: Technomic Pub. Co., 2000) p. 154.

217. *In South Asia pepper is also widely employed in a broad array of folk remedies, especially as a treatment for diarrhea.* Krishnapura Srinivasan, "Black Pepper (*Piper nigrum*) and its Bioactive Compound, Piperine," p. 56, in *Molecular Targets and Therapeutic Uses of Spice: Modern Uses for Ancient Medicine,* editors Bharat B. Aggarwal and Ajaikumar B. Kunnumakkara (World Scientific Publishing, 2009).

218. *The ability of piperine to boost the effectiveness of a particular treatment for cancer is the focus of a research project underway at Fox Chase Cancer Center ...* Telephone interview with Vladimir Kolenko. For more information about the Fox Chase project, see the Web site for the American Institute for Cancer Research.

219. *It was this property that led Bharat B. Aggarwal, chief of the Cytokine*

Research Section at MD Anderson . . . to explore the feasibility of using curcumin as an anticancer agent. Karolyn A. Gazella, "Pioneering Biochemist Bharat B. Aggarwal, Ph.D., of the MD Anderson Cancer Center, on Discovering Novel and Effective Cancer Treatments," *Natural Medicine Journal* 1(4), December 2009.

220. *. . . more than eight hundred compounds . . .* See www.nf.kb.org, a Web site devoted to nuclear factor Kappa B and maintained by Boston University biologist Thomas Gilmore.

220. *. . . using piperine to improve the bioavailability of curcumin . . .* See Anand P, Kunnumakkara AB, Newman RA, and Aggarawal BB, "Bioavailability of curcumin: problems and promises," *Mol Pharm.* 2007 Nov–Dec; 4(6): 807–18.

220. *In a small laboratory study published in 2009 by researchers at the University of Michigan, each compound . . ." inhibited the renewal, or generation, of certain stem cells in the breast that may be the source of cancer cells."* Kakarala, Madhuri, et al., "Targeting breast stem cells with the cancer preventive compounds curcumin and piperine," *Breast Cancer Research Treatment,* 07, November 2009.

221. *Rats and mice fed up to one hundred times more black pepper than is normally consumed in the Indian diet did not suffer any ill consequences; their gastrointestinal tracts did just fine.* E-mail with K. Srinivasan. Asked if pepper could be toxic, he responded: "I have absolutely no anxiety about the toxicity of piperine. Even if we were to consume black pepper one hundred times what Indians are normally consuming in their diets, it is absolutely safe."

221. *. . . "limited application" as a preservative, especially in comparison to other spices, such as turmeric and garlic.* E-mail communication with Krishnapura Srinivasan.

221. *. . . pepper may have a less exalted role in natural insect repellents,* see Katrizky, Alan R., "Synthesis and bioassay of improved mosquito repellents predicted from chemical structure," *Proceedings of the National Academy of Sciences,* May 27, 2008, Vol. 105, no. 21, 7359–7364, and press release from the American Chemical Society dated Aug. 16, 2009.

223. *. . . some six hundred million people are estimated to consume betel*

daily. See Pragya Misra, et al. "Pro-apoptotic effect of the landrace Bangla Mahoba of *Piper betle* on *Leishmania donovani* may be due to the high content of eugenol," *Journal of Medical Microbiology* (2009), 58, 1058–1066.

223. *. . . people in the Chinese city of Xiangtan in Hunan Province like to chew only the husk of fresh areca nut, which they call "binglang," the basis for an 1.18 billion-dollar industry.* Dan Levin, "Despite Risks, an Addictive Treat Fuels a Chinese City," *The New York Times,* August, 19, 2010.

223. *. . . extracts from Piper betle and Psidium guajava . . . suppressed the growth of bacteria that contributes to dental plaque.* A. R. Fathilah, et al. "Bacteriostatic Effect of *Piper betle* and *Psidium guajava* Extracts on Dental Plaque Bacteria," *Pakistan Journal of Biological Sciences* 12 (6): 518–521, 2009.

223. *Allopurinol . . . inhibits the enzyme,* Kazyua Murata et al, "Hydroxychavicol: a potent xanthine oxidase inhibitor obtained from the leaves of betel, *Piper betle*," *Journal of Natural Medicine* (2009), 63: 355–359.

224. *Current therapies for the visceral form of the disease aren't very effective and have a variety of side effects.* See Pragya Misra, et al, p. 1058.

Epilogue

225. *Some 640 million pounds are harvested annually in the world.* See Karvy Comtrade Limited Special Reports, http://www.karvycom trade.com.

SELECTED BIBLIOGRAPHY

Abdullah, Bin Abdul Kadir. *The Hikayat Abdullah,* an annotated translation by A. H. Hill. Oxford in Asia Historical Reprints, Oxford University Press, 1970.

Adams, Julia. "Principals and Agents, Colonialists and Company Men: The Decay of Colonial Control in the Dutch East Indies." *American Sociological Review,* Vol. 61, No. 1 (Feb. 1996) pp. 12–28.

Aggarwal, Bharat B., and Kunnumakkara, Ajaikumar B. editors. *Molecular Targets and Therapeutic Uses of Spice: Modern Uses for Ancient Medicine.* Singapore: World Scientific Publishing, 2009.

Alden, Dauril. *The Making of an Enterprise: The Society for Jesus in Portugal, Its Empire and Beyond, 1540–1750.* Stanford University Press, 1996.

Andaya, Barbara Watson, "Adapting to Political and Economic Change: Palembang in the Late Eighteenth and Early Ninteenth Centuries," in *The Last Stand of Asian Autonomies,* edited by Anthony Reid. New York: St. Martin's Press, 1997.

———. *To Live as Brothers: Southeast Sumatra in the Seventeenth and Eighteenth Centuries.* University of Hawaii Press, 1993.

———. "Women and Economic Change: The Pepper Trade in Pre-Modern Southeast Asia." *Journal of Economic and Social History of the*

Orient, Vol. 38, Number 2, Women's History (1995) 165–190 (published by Brill, the Netherlands). http://www.jstor.org/stable/3632514

Andaya, Leonard Y. "The Bugis-Makassar Diasporas." *The Journal of Malaysian Branch of the Royal Asiatic Society,* Vol. 68, Part 1 (1995).

———. *The Heritage of Arung Palakka: A History of South Sulawesi (Celebes) in the seventeenth century.* The Hague: Martinus Nijhoff, 1981.

Andrews, Kenneth R. *Trade, Plunder and Settlement: Maritime Enterprise and the Genesis of the British Empire, 1480–1630.* Cambridge University Press, 1984.

Barley, Nigel. *The Duke of Puddle Dock.* Henry Holt and Company, 1991.

Bassett, D. K. "The 'Amboyna Massacre' of 1623." *Journal of Southeast Asian History,* Vol. 1, No. 2 (Sept. 1960) 1–19. http://www.jstor.org/stable/20067299

———. "European Influence in South-East Asia, c. 1500–1630." *Journal of Southeast Asian History,* Vol. 4, No. 2 (Sept. 1963) 134–165. http://www.jstor.org/stable/20067447

Bastin, John. *The Native Policies of Sir Stamford Raffles in Java and Sumatra; An Economic Interpretation.* Clarendon Press, London, 1957.

———. *Essays on Indonesian and Malayan History.* Singapore, 1961.

———. *The British in West Sumatra (1685–1825): A selection of documents, mainly from the East India Company records preserved in the India Office Library, Commonwealth Relations Office, London,* with an introduction and notes by John Bastin. University of Malaya Press, Kuala Lumpur, 1965.

Bastin, John and Winks, Robin W. *Malaysia Selected Historical Readings.* Oxford University Press, 1966.

Best, Thomas, *The Voyage Of Thomas Best to the East Indies, 1612–1614.* Edited by Sir Willam Foster. London: The Hakluyt Society, 1934.

Blussé, Leonard. "Batavia, 1619–1740: The Rise and Fall of a Chinese Colonial Town." *Journal of Southeast Asian Studies,* Vol. 12, No. 1, Ethnic Chinese in Southeast Asia (March, 1981) 159–178. (Cambridge University Press). http://www.jstor.org./stable/20070419

———. *Strange Company: Chinese Settlers, Mestizo Women and the Dutch in VOC Batavia,* Foris Publications, 1986.

———. "No Boats to China. The Dutch East India Company and the

Changing Pattern of the China Sea Trade, 1635–1690." *Modern Asian Studies,* Vol. 30, No. 1 (Feb. 1996) 51–76 (Cambridge University Press). http://www.jstor.org/stable/312901

Bourn, David, Gibson, Charlie, Augeri, Dave, Wilson, Cathleen J., Church, Julia, Hay, Simon I. "The Rise and Fall of the Aldabran Giant Tortoise Population." *Proceedings: Biological Sciences,* Vol. 266, No. 1424 (June 7, 1999) 1091–1100. http://www.jstor.org/stable/51351

Bown, Stephen R. *Scurvy: How a Surgeon, a Mariner and a Gentleman Solved the Greatest Medical Mystery of the Age of Sail.* New York: Thomas Dunne Books, 2003.

———. *Merchant Kings.* New York: Thomas Dunne Books, 2009.

Boxer, C. R. *The Dutch Seaborne Empire, 1600–1800.* London: Hutchinson & Co., 1965.

———. *The Portuguese Seaborne Empire, 1425–1825.* New York: Alfred A Knopf, 1969.

———. *Women in Iberian Expansion Overseas, 1415–1815.* New York: Oxford University Press, 1975.

———. *Jan Compagnie in War and Peace 1602–1799.* Heinemann Asia, 1979.

———. *Dutch Merchants and Mariners in Asia 1602–1795.* London: Variorum Reprints, 1988.

———. *The Tragic History of the Sea.* Edited and translated by C. R. Boxer, with foreword and additional translation by Josiah Blackmore. University of Minnesota Press, 2001.

Braudel, Fernand. *Capitalism and Material Life, 1400–1800.* New York: Harper & Row, 1973. (Originally published in 1967 by Librairie Armand Colin under the title *Civilisation Materielle et Capitalisme).*

———. *Civilization and Capitalism, 15th–18th Century,* in three volumes. (Originally published in France under the title *Les Temps du Monde* in 1979).

———. *The Structures of Everyday Life,* Vol. 1. London: Phoenix Press, 2002.

———. *The Wheels of Commerce,* Vol. II. London: Phoenix Press, 2002.

———. *The Perspective of the World,* Vol. III. London: Phoenix Press, 2002.

Bruijn, Jaap R., and Gaastra, Femme S. *Ships, Sailors and Spices: East India Companies and Their Shipping in the 16th, 17th and 18th Centuries.* Amsterdam: NEHA, 1993.

Calendar of State Papers, Domestic series, of the reigns of Edward VI, Mary, Elizabeth, 1547–1625, and Volume 1: 1625–1626, Volume 2: 1627–1628, and Volume 3:1628–1629, Great Britain–Public Record Office.

Carpenter, Kenneth, J. *The History of Scurvy and Vitamin C.* U.K.: Cambridge University Press, 1986.

Castro, Filipe. "The Pepper Wreck, an early 17th-century Portuguese Indiaman at the mouth of the Tagus River, Portugal." *The International Journal of Nautical Archaeology* (2003) 32.1:6–23.

Cave, Jonathan. *Naning in Melaka.* Kuala Lumpur: Malaysian Branch of the Royal Asiatic Society, 1989.

Chaudhuri, K. N. *The English East India Company: The study of an early joint-stock company 1600–1640.* Originally published in 1965 and reprinted by Routledge/Thoemmes Press, 1999.

———. *The Trading World of Asia and the English East India Company 1660–1760.* Cambridge University Press, 1978.

Chaudhuri, K. N., and Israel, Jonathan I. "The English and East India Companies and the Glorious Revolution of 1688–9," in *The Anglo-Dutch Moment: Essays on the Glorious Revolution and its world impact,* edited by Jonathan I. Israel, 407–439. U.K.: Cambridge University Press, 1991.

Chaudhury, Sushil, and Morineau, Michael, editors. *Merchants, Companies and Trade: Europe and Asia in the Early Modern Era.* U.K.: Cambridge University Press, 1999.

Corn, Charles. *The Scents of Eden: A History of the Spice Trade.* Kodansha International, 1999.

Dampier, William, *A New Voyage Round the World,* (1685), Rare Books and Manuscripts Division, New York Public Library.

Dampier, William et al. *A collection of voyages: in four volumes: containing I. Captain William Dampier's Voyages around the world . . . : II. The voyages of Lionel . . .* Volume 2. London, 1729 (Sabin Americana. Gale, Gengate Learning. New York University. Gate Document Number cy103299575

Davis, John. *Voyages and Works of.* Hakluyt Society, 1880.

Delano, Amasa. *Narrative of Voyages and Travels in the Northern and Southern Hemispheres.* Upper Saddle River, New Jersey: The Gregg Press, 1970.

Disney, Anthony, and Booth, Emily, editors. *Vasco da Gama and the Linking of Europe and Asia.* Oxford University Press, 2000.

Donkin, R. A. *Between East and West: The Moluccas and the Traffic in Spice.* Philadelphia: American Philosophical Society, 2003.

Emmer, Pieter, and Gaastra, Femme, editors. *The Organization of Interoceanic Trade in European Expansion, 1450–1800.* Variorum, Ashgate Publishing Limited, 1996.

Farrington, Anthony. *Trading Places: the East India Co. and Asia, 1600–1834.* London: British Library, 2002.

———. "Bengkulu: An Anglo-Chinese Partnership." In *The Worlds of the East India Company.* Edited by H. V. Bowen, Margarette Lincoln, and Nigel Rigby. Boydell Press, 2002.

Foster, Sir William. *England's Quest for Eastern Trade.* London: A. & C. Black, Ltd., 1933.

Freedman, Paul. *Out of the East: Spices and the Medieval Imagination.* New Haven: Yale University Press, 2008.

Fuller, Errol. *Dodo: From Extinction to Icon.* New York: HarperCollins, 2002.

Furber, Holden. *Rival Empires of Trade in the Orient, 1600–1800.* University of Minnesota Press, 1976.

Gaastra, Femme S., "War, Competition and Collaboration: Relations between the English and Dutch East India Company in the Seventeenth and Eighteen Centuries." In *The Worlds of the East India Company,* edited by H. V. Bowen, Margarette Lincoln, and Nigel Rigby. Boydell Press, 2002.

———. *The Dutch East India Company: Expansion and Decline,* Walburg Pers, 2003.

Gallagher, Louis J., translator. *China in the Sixteenth Century: The Journals of Matteo Ricci, 1583–1610.* New York: Random House, 1953.

Gazella, Karolyn A. "Pioneering Biochemist Bharat B. Aggarwal, PhD, of the MD Anderson Cancer Center, on Discovering Novel and Effective Cancer Treatments." *Natural Medicine Journal* 1(4) (December 2009).

Gernet, Jacques. *A History of Chinese Civilization.* Cambridge University Press, 1982.

Glamann, Kristoff. *Dutch Asiatic Trade 1620–1740.* The Hague: Nijhoff, 1958.

Gould, James W. *Sumatra—America's Pepperpot 1784–1873.* Essex Institute Historical Collections, XCII (1956) 83–153, 203–251, 295–348.

Grove, Richard H. *Green Imperialism: Colonial Expansion, Tropical Island Edens, and the Origins of Environmentalism, 1600–1960.* Cambridge University Press, 1995.

Grainger, Sally. "The Myth of Apicius." *Gastronomica* (Spring 2007).

Hackel, Heidi Brayman, and Mancall, C. Peter. "Richard Hakluyt the Younger's Notes for the East India Company in 1601: A Transcription of Huntington Library Manuscript EL2360." *The Huntington Library Quarterly,* Vol. 67, No. 3 (2004) 423–436 (University of California Press). http:/www.jstor.org/stable/38180007

Hahn, Emily. *Raffles of Singapore.* New York: Doubleday, 1946.

Harfield, A. G. *Bencoolen: A History of the Honourable East India Company's Garrison on the West Coast of Sumatra, 1685–1825.* Hampshire: Barton-on-Sea, 1995.

Hochstrasser, Julie Berger. *Still Life and Trade in the Dutch Golden Age.* New Haven: Yale University Press, 2007.

Israel, Jonathan, I. *The Anglo-Dutch Moment: Essays on the Glorious Revolution and Its World Impact.* Cambridge University Press, 1991.

s'Jacob, Hugo K. *The Rajas of Cochin 1663–1720: Kings, Chiefs and The Dutch East India Company.* Munshiram Manoharlal Publishers Pvt. Ltd., 2000.

Jenson, John R. *Journal and Letter Book of Nicholas Bukeridge, 1651–1654.* University of Minnesota Press, 1973.

Kakarala, Madhuri, et al. "Targeting breast stem cells with the cancer preventive compounds curcumin and piperine." *Breast Cancer Research Treatment.* Springer Verlag, (November 7, 2009).

Keeling, William. *The East India Company Journals of Captain William Keeling and Master Thomas Bonner, 1615–1617.* Edited by Michael Strachan and Boies Penrose. University of Minnesota Press, 1971.

Keay, John. *The Honourable Company*. New York: Macmillan Publishing Co., 1994.

———. *The Spice Route*. London: John Murray Publishers, 2005.

Lach, Donald F. *Asia in the Making of Europe,* Volume I, Book One & Two, *The Century of Discovery*. The University of Chicago Press, 1965.

Lancaster, Sir James. *The Voyages of.* The Hakluyt Society, 1940.

Lancaster, Sir James. *The Voyages of Sir James Lancaster to the East Indies with Abstracts of Journals of Voyages to the East Indies During the Seventeenth Century*. Preserved in the India Office, edited by Clements R. Markham, The Hakluyt Society, 1877.

Lardicci, Francesca, editor. *A Synoptic Edition of the Log of Columbus's First Voyage*. Brepols, 1999.

Leguat, François. *The Voyage of François Leguat of Bresse to Rodriguez, Mauritius, Java, and the Cape of Good Hope*. Edited and Annotated by Captain Pasfield Oliver. The Hakluyt Society, 1891.

Levathes, Louise. *When China Ruled the Sea: The Treasure Fleet of the Dragon Throne, 1405–1433*. Oxford University Press, 1994.

Lindgren, James M. "That Every Mariner May Possess the History of the World: A Cabinet for the East India Marine Society of Salem." *The New England Quarterly*, Vol. 68, No. 2. (June, 1995) 179–205.

Long, David F. "Martial Thunder: The First Official American Armed Intervention in Asia," *The Pacific Historical Review*, Vol. 42. No. 2 (May, 1973) 143–162 (University of California Press). http://www.jstor/org/stable/3638464

Loth, Vincent C. "Armed Incidents and Unpaid Bills: Anglo-Dutch Rivalry in the Banda Islands in the Seventeenth Century." *Modern Asian Studies,* Vol. 29, No. 4 (Oct., 1995) 705–740. http://www.jstor.org/stable/312802

Low, Gorham, P. *The Sea Made Men: The Story of a Gloucester Lad*. Fleming H. Revell Company, 1937.

Ly-Tio-Fane, Madeleine. *Mauritius and the Spice Trade: The Odyssey of Pierre Poivre*. Port Louis, Mauritius: Esclapon, 1958.

Ma Huan. *The Overall Survey of the Ocean's Shores*. Published for the Hakluyt Society by Cambridge University Press, 1970.

Mancall, Peter C. *Fatal Journey: The Final Expedition of Henry Hudson.* New York: Perseus Books, 2009.

Meilink-Roelofsz, M. A. P., *Asian Trade and European Influence.* The Hague, Netherlands: Martinus Nijhoff, 1962.

Melville, Herman. *Billy Budd and Other Stories,* with an introduction by Frederick Busch. New York: Viking Penguin Inc., 1986.

Menzies, Gavin. *1421, The Year China Discovered America.* New York: HarperCollins Publishers, 2002.

Miller, J. Innes. *The Spice Trade of the Roman Empire.* Oxford University Press, 1969.

Middleton, Sir Henry. *The Voyages of Sir Henry Middleton to Bantam and the Maluco Islands.* Edited by Bolton Corney. London: The Haklyut Society, 1855.

———. *The Voyage of Sir Henry Middleton to the Moluccas, 1604–1606.* Edited by Sir William Foster. London: The Haklyut Society, 1944.

Miller, J. Innes. *The Spice Trade of the Roman Empire.* Oxford University Press, 1969.

Montanari, Massimo. *The Culture of Food.* Cambridge, MA: Blackwell, 1994.

Morton, Timothy. *The Poetics of Spice: Romantic Consumerism and the Exotic.* Cambridge University Press, 2000.

Moseley, C. W. R. D. translator. *The Travels of Sir John Mandeville.* New York: Penguin Books, 2005.

Mulherin, Jennifer. *The Macmillan Treasury of Spices and Natural Flavoring.* New York: Macmillan, 1988.

Mundy, Peter. *The Travels of.* Edited by Sir Richard Carnac Temple. The Hakluyt Society 1919; reprinted by Kraus Reprint Limited, Nendeln/Liechtenstein, 1967.

Mundy, Peter. *The Travels of Peter Mundy, 1597–1667.* Edited by John Keast. Redruth, Cornwall: Dyllansow Truran, 1984.

Nair, K. P. Prabhakaran. "The Agronomy and Economy of Black Pepper (*Piper Nigrum* L.)—'The King of Spices.'" *Advances in Agronomy,* Volume 82 (2004) 271–389.

Nightingale, Pamela. *A Medieval Mercantile Community—The Grocers Company.* New Haven: Yale University Press, 1995.

North-Coombes, Alfred. *The Vindication of François Leguat.* Port Louis, Mauritius: Organisation Normale des Entreprises Limitée, 1979.

Parsell, Diana. "Palm-Nut Problem: Asian chewing habit linked to oral cancer." *Science News* (Jan. 15, 2005) 43–44.

Pearson, M. N. editor. *Spices in the Indian Ocean World.* U.K.: Ashgate Publishing Co., 1996.

Phillips, James Duncan. *Salem and the Indies: The Story of the Great Commercial Era of the City.* Boston: Houghton Mifflin, 1947.

Phillips, William D., Jr., and Phillips, Carla Rahn. *The Worlds of Christopher Columbus.* Cambridge University Press, 1992.

Prakash, Om. *The Dutch East India Company and the Economy of Bengal 1630–1720.* Princeton University Press, 1985.

———. ed. *European Commercial Expansion in Early Modern Asia.* Variorum, 1997.

———. "The Portuguese and the Dutch in Asian Maritime Trade: A Comparative Analysis." *Merchants, Companies and Trade: Europe and Asia in the Early Modern Era.* Edited by Sushil Chaudhury and Michel Morineau. Cambridge University Press, 1999: 175–188.

Prest, John. *The Garden of Eden: The Botanic Garden and the Re-Creation of Paradise.* New Haven: Yale University Press, 1982.

Preston, Diana, and Preston, Michael. *A Pirate of Exquisite Mind: Explorer, Naturalist and Buccaneer: The Life of William Dampier.* New York: Walker & Co, 2004.

Putnam, George G. *Salem Vessels and Their Voyages: A History of the Pepper Trade with the Island of Sumatra.* Salem, MA.: The Essex Institute, 1924.

Pyrard, François. *The Voyage of.* Translated by Albert Gray. The Hakluyt Society, 1887; reprinted in the U.S.A. by Burt Franklin, 1964.

Raffles, Lady Sophia. *Memoir of the Life and Public Service of Sir Thomas Stamford Raffles: F.R.S. &c.* London, 1830.

Ravindran, P. N., editor. *Black Pepper, Piper Nigrum.* Amsterdam: Harwood Academic Publishers, 2000.

Rees, Aubrey Joseph. *The Grocery Trade, Its History and Romance*. London: Duckworth and Co., 1910.

Reid, Anthony. *Heaven's Will and Man's Fault*. Bedford Park: Flinders University of South Australia, 1975.

———. *The Contest for North Sumatra: Atjeh, the Netherlands and Britain 1858–1898*. Oxford University Press, 1969.

———. *Southeast Asia in the Age of Commerce, 1450–1680*; Volume One, *The Lands Below the Winds*. New Haven: Yale University Press, 1988. Volume Two, *Expansion and Crisis*. Yale, 1993.

———. "Economic and Social Change, c. 1500 to c. 1800" in *The Cambridge History of Southeast Asia,* Volume One. Edited by Nicholas Tarling. Cambridge University Press, 1992.

———. "A New Phase of Commercial Expansion in Southeast Asia, 1760–1850." *The Last Stand of Asian Autonomies: Responses to modernity in the Diverse States of Southeast Asia and Korea, 1750–1900*. Edited by Anthony Reid. New York: St. Martin's Press, 1997.

———. "Humans and Forests in Pre-colonial Southeast Asia" in *Nature and the Orient*. Edited by Richard H. Grove, Vinita Damodaran, and Satpal Sangwan. Oxford University Press, 1998.

———. *An Indonesian Frontier: Acehnese and Other Histories of Sumatra*. Oxford University Press, 2005.

Reynolds, N. Jeremiah. *Voyage of the United State Frigate Potomac . . . in 1831, 1832, 1833, and 1834* (New York, 1835).

Rienstra, Howard, M. editor and translator. *Jesuit Letters from China 1583–1584,* University of Minnesota Press, 1986.

Ronan, Charles, E., and Oh, Bonnie, B. C., editors. *East Meets West: The Jesuits in China*. Chicago: Loyola Press, 1988.

Root, Waverley. *Food: An Authoritative and Visual History and Dictionary of the Foods of the World*. New York: Simon and Schuster, 1980.

Rosengarten, Frederic, *The Book of Spices*. New York: Pyramid Books, 1973.

Rowbotham, Arnold H. *Missionary and Mandarin: The Jesuits at the Court of China,* University of California Press, Berkeley, 1942.

Russell-Wood, A. J. R. *The Portuguese Empire, 1415–1808: A World on the Move*. Johns Hopkins University Press, 1998.

Sales, Kirkpatrick. *The Conquest of Paradise.* New York: Knopf, 1990.

Sandhu, Kernial Singh, and Wheatley, Paul, with contributions from Abdul Aziz bin mat Ton . . . et al. *Melaka: The Transformation of a Malay Capital, c. 1400–1980*, Volume 1. Kuala Lumpur; New York: Oxford University Press, 1983.

Sass, Lorna J. *To the King's Taste: Richard II's Book of Feasts and Recipes Adapted for Modern Cooking.* New York: St. Martin's/Marek, 1975.

Scammell, G. V. *Seafaring, Sailors and Trade, 1450–1750.* Burlington, Vermont: Ashgate/Variorum, 2003.

Schivelbusch, Wolfgang. *Tastes of Paradise: A Social History of Spices, Stimulants, and Intoxicants.* New York: Pantheon, 1992.

Shorto, Russell. *The Island at the Center of the World.* New York: Doubleday, 2004.

Stavorinus, J. S., *Voyages to the East Indies,* in three volumes. Translated by S. H. Wilcocke, 1798. Reprinted 1969, Dawsons of Pall Mall, London.

Stoddart, D. R., Peake, J. F., Gordon, C., Burleigh, R. "Historical Records of Indian Ocean Giant Tortoise Populations." Philosophical Transactions of the Royal Society of London. Series B, Biological Sciences, Vol. 286, No. 1011, *The Terrestrial Ecology of Aldabra* (Vol. 3, 1979) 147–161, http://www.jstor.org/stable/2418093

Subrahmanyam, Sanjay. *The Career and Legend of Vasco da Gama.* Cambridge University Press, 1997.

Tarling, Nicholas, editor. *The Cambridge History of Southeast Asia, Volume One, From Early Times to c. 1800,* and *Volume Two, The Nineteenth and Twentieth Centuries.* Cambridge University Press, 1992.

———. "The Establishment of the Colonial Regimes" in *The Cambridge History of Southeast Asia, Volume Two, The Nineteenth and Twentieth Centuries.* Cambridge University Press, 1992.

Taylor, Fitch W. *A Voyage Round the World . . . in the United States Frigate Columbia . . . New Haven and New York 1846.*

Turner, Jack. *Spice: The History of a Temptation.* New York: Knopf, 2004.

Uhl, Susheela Raghavan. *Handbook of Spices, Seasonings, and Flavorings.* Lancaster, PA: Technomic Pub. Co., 2000.

Wake, C. H. H. "The Changing Patterns of Europe's Pepper and Spice